DOG TRICKS

EVEN YOU CAN TEACH YOUR PET

DOG TRICKS
EVEN YOU CAN TEACH YOUR PET

A Step-by-Step Guide to Teaching Your Pet to
Sit, Catch, Fetch, and Impress

CARINA MACDONALD

**Technical Review by Elizabeth Bunting, VMD
Photographs by Stephen Gorman and Eli Burakian**

LP

LYONS
PRESS

Essex, Connecticut

An imprint of Globe Pequot, the trade division of
The Rowman & Littlefield Publishing Group, Inc.
4501 Forbes Blvd., Ste. 200
Lanham, MD 20706
www.rowman.com

Distributed by NATIONAL BOOK NETWORK

Cover photos: (left to right) © shutterstock, © istockphoto, © Joy Brown/shutterstock, © shutterstock; (back cover) Stephen Gorman and Eli Burakian

Interior photos by Stephen Gorman and Eli Burakian with the exception of p. 4 (right): © Ankevanwyk | Dreamstime.com; p. 5 (left): Margo Harrison/shutterstock; p. 5 (right): Eriklam | Dreamstime.com; p. 6 (left): © istockphoto; p. 7 (left): Aaron Whitney/shutterstock; p. 7 (right): Chin Kit Sen/shutterstock; p. 9 (left): Jean Frooms/shutterstock; p. 9 (right): Waldemar Dabrowski/shutterstock; p. 11 (left): Sergey Lavrentev/shutterstock; p. 12 (right): Lasting Moments/shutterstock; p. 19 (left): Stephen Coburn/shutterstock; p. 23 (left): Anke van Wyk/shutterstock; p. 23 (right): shutterstock; p. 26 (right): Courtesy of jogadog.com; p. 30 (left): vera bogaerts/shutterstock; p. 56 (left): Zenotri/shutterstock; p. 56 (right): Andreas Weiss/shutterstock; p. 80 (left): Robert J. Beyers II/shutterstock; p. 84 (left): AnnalA/shutterstock; p. 92 (left): gglers/shutterstock; p. 96 (right): Jim Parkin/shutterstock; p. 111 (right): © istockphoto; p. 133 (left): Annette/shutterstock; p. 133 (right): WilleeCole/shutterstock; p. 135 (right): Dee Hunter/shutterstock; p. 136 (left): Kati Molin/shutterstock; p. 136 (right): Marcel Jancovic/shutterstock; p. 137 (left): glen gaffney/shutterstock; p. 137 (right): Alexander Maksimov/shutterstock; p. 138 (left): Jaimie Duplass/shutterstock; p. 138 (right): © istockphoto; p. 139 (left): © Peanutx32 | Dreamstime.com; p. 140 (left): © shutterstock; p. 140 (right): © shutterstock; p. 142 (left): George Lee/shutterstock; p. 142 (right): George Lee/shutterstock; p. 143 (left): George Lee/shutterstock; p. 144 (left): © Onepony | Dreamstime.com; p. 144 (right): Gorilla/shutterstock; p. 145 (left): kristian sekulic/shutterstock; p. 148 (left): Groomee/shutterstock; p. 150 (right): © Cindyinnc | Dreamstime.com; p. 152 (left): © istockphoto; p. 153 (left): Jim Parkin/shutterstock; p. 153 (right): plastique/shutterstock; p. 154 (left): EcoPrint/shutterstock; p. 154 (right): Melissa Schalke/shutterstock; p. 155 (left): Jason Keith Heydorn/shutterstock; p. 155 (right): © Iofoto | Dreamstime.com; p. 160 (right): Tose | Dreamstime.com; p. 161 (left): © istockphoto; p. 162 (left): © istockphoto; p. 162 (right): MaxPhoto/shutterstock; p. 163 (left): © istockphoto; p. 164 (right): © istockphoto; p. 165 (left): © Albln | Dreamstime.com; p. 166 (left): © istockphoto; p. 166 (right): © istockphoto; p. 167 (left): Fotokate | Dreamstime.com; p. 168 (left): © istockphoto; p. 176 (left): pixshots/shutterstock; p. 176 (right): Tad Denson/shutterstock; p. 177 (left): Jan Erasmus/shutterstock; p. 177 (right): cynoclub/shutterstock; p. 178 (right): © Barsik | Dreamstime.com; p. 179 (left): © Elenathewi... | Dreamstime.com; p. 181 (left): © istockphoto; p. 188 (right): Jacek Chabraszewski/shutterstock; p. 191 (right): Crystal Kirk/shutterstock; p. 205 (left): Margo Harrison/shutterstock; p. 205 (right): Martin Valigursky/shutterstock; p. 211 (right): Joy Brown/shutterstock; p. 214 (right): © istockphoto; p. 215 (left): © istockphoto; p. 226 (left): Iofoto | Dreamstime.com; p. 227 (right): Russ Beinder/shutterstock

British Library Cataloguing in Publication Information available

The Knack edition of this book was cataloged by the Library of Congress as follows:

MacDonald, Carina Beth, 1958-
  Knack dog tricks : a step-by-step guide to teaching your pet to sit, catch, fetch & impress / Carina MacDonald ; technical review by Elizabeth Marion Bunting ; photographs by Stephen Gorman and Eli Burakian.
     p. cm.
  Includes index.
  ISBN 978-1-59921-612-6
  1. Dogs—Training. I. Title. II. Title: Dog tricks.
  SF431.M33 2010
  636.7'0887—dc22
                                                    2009017993

ISBN 9781493069224 (paperback) | ISBN 9781493070831 (ebook)

♾™ The paper used in this publication meets the minimum requirements of American National Standard for Information Sciences—Permanence of Paper for Printed Library Materials, ANSI/NISO Z39.48-1992.

Photographer Acknowledgments

We would like to thank Robin Young and her dog, Rosie; Julia Burakian and her dog, Milton; Charlene Swainamer and her dog, Olivia; Jevan Stubits; Kari Nelson and her dog, Yoda; the staff at the Upper Valley Humane Society (Enfield, NH); and Sharon Partridge and the staff at the Lebanon Pet and Aquarium Center (West Lebanon, NH).

—Stephen Gorman and Eli Burakian

CONTENTS

Introduction. viii

Chapter 1: Trick Training 101
The Case for Trick Training xii
The Right Attitude. 2
Size Matters 4
Breed Matters, Too. 6
Finding Your Dog's Drive. 8
Priming the Puppy. 10

Chapter 2: Tricky Tools
Leashes, Collars, & Halters. 12
Finding the Perfect Treat. 14
Toys for Structured Play. 16
Clicker Training 18
Target Sticks & Squeezy Cheese 20
Group Training Classes. 22

Chapter 3: Tricky Techniques
Keep It Fun 24
Breaking Down & Back-Chaining. 26
Timing Is Everything 28
Know Your Dog. 30
Communicating With Your Dog. 32
Troubleshooting Tricks. 34

Chapter 4: Trickster Clickers
Priming the Clicker 36
Know When to Click 38
Luring, Bribing, & Rewarding. 40
Get What You Train For. 42
Turn Your Head 44
On-Leash Clicking 46

Chapter 5: The Basics
An Enthusiastic Recall. 48
Puppy Push-Ups. 50
Stay & Wait 52
No-Pull Leash Manners 54
Tug Games 56
Long-Distance Learning 58

Chapter 6: Tricks to Build On
Shake Hands 60
Fetch! 62
Roll Over 64
Leap Tall Buildings 66
Spin Around 68
Through the Legs. 70

Chapter 7: Controlled Canine
Control Means Better Manners. 72
Wait & Release. 74
Teaching "Leave It" 76
"Drop It" 78
"Take It Nice". 80
The "Ready, Ready" Game 82

Chapter 8: Advanced Basics
Hello, High Five, Goodbye 84
"Bang, You're Dead". 86
Cookie on the Nose. 88
Controlled Jumping 90
Sit Pretty. 92
Sequencing 94

Chapter 9: Smart Dog Tricks
Types of Canine Intelligence 96
Teach Him to Count 98
The Right Commands 100
Dogs, Too, Have Feelings. 102
The Canine Courier 104
Name That Toy. 106

Chapter 10: Obedience Games
"Watch Me". 108
Make Heeling Fun 110
Front & Finish. 112
Moving Sits & Downs 114
Article Scent Discrimination 116
Retrieve & Jump 118

Chapter 11: The Helpful Hound
Find the Remote....................................120
Find the Cat 122
Retrieve the Newspaper 124
Carry the Groceries 126
Ring a Bell 128
Put Toys Away 130

Chapter 12: Packing & Traveling
Dogwear 132
Doggie Backpacks 134
Carting Basics 136
Skateboarding Dogs..............................138
Bicycling 140
Weight Pulling....................................142

Chapter 13: Get Out & Play
Socialize for Success 144
Exercise Requirements............................146
Off-Leash Games 148
Fetch & Frisbee 150
Tracking 152
Other Activities 154

Chapter 14: Fixing Bad Habits
The Barking Dog...................................156
Greeting Skills 158
Pottying in Place..................................160
Digging for Treasure 162
Inappropriate Chewing...........................164
Kids & Dogs 166

Chapter 15: Multiple Dog Games
Managing the Dog Pack 168
Under & Over......................................170
Speed Sitting Competition........................172
Get Your Treat 174
Big Dog, Little Dog 176
Performing Dogs 178

Chapter 16: Indoor Games
Hide-n-Seek 180
Intelligence Tests 182
Grooming 184
Speed Heeling.....................................186
Family Games 188
Bedtime Games 190

Chapter 17: Agility Tricks
Footwork...192
Rear-Foot Awareness 194
Pause & Table Games 196
Wild Weavers 198
Crate Games.......................................200
Go Around 202

Chapter 18: Dancing Dogs
Canine Freestyle...................................204
The Weave & Walk 206
Walking Sideways & Backward 208
Dancing in Place...................................210
Bowing to the Crowd..............................212
Combining Moves 214

Chapter 19: Get a Drink
Put It Together.....................................216
Get a Drink 218
Go Open the Fridge 220
Get Beer, Close Fridge 222
Troubleshooting the Beer Run 224
Always Thank Your Dog...........................226

Chapter 20: Resources 228

Glossary 238
Index..240

INTRODUCTION

The dictionary defines a trick as a "feat or skill of dexterity" and an "unusual action . . . learned by an animal." Although some trainers dismiss tricks as not serious dog training, I defy anyone to watch dancing dogs in canine freestyle or to go to an agility trial and then claim these dogs weren't seriously trained! If the precise sits and heeling patterns taught by rote learning in formal obedience aren't "unusual acts learned by animals," then I don't know what is.

Certainly, tricks are usually taught primarily for amusement and don't serve a direct purpose. However, tricks can hone obedience skills and overall good behavior. Because trick training is more light-hearted, you'll have a different mind-set and be willing to experiment with motivating, understanding, and communicating with your dog in ways not always taught in formal training classes. In doing so, you'll learn how to be a better trainer. Trick training practically requires you to be creative and experiment. Not only that, but also it requires you to be receptive to your dog and to find activities she excels in. You might never be able to teach your beagle to do fetching tricks, but she'll blow the retrievers away with her tracking and finding skills. Border collies are great Frisbee trick dogs but aren't worth a darn as dock dogs.

Experiment with training tools, like target sticks, different toys, and a clicker. All training should be structured play, and this goes double for trick training. Dogs love to play. Capitalizing on her play drive will make training fun for your dog, and a dog who is having fun will be a more willing, focused worker. Treats can be used liberally, too. Anyone who claims that dogs trained with treats will "work only for treats" doesn't understand that if done right, giving a dog tangible pay for compliance creates a very reliably trained dog who most certainly does not need treats in order to obey. That's like saying that if you train a dog using a collar and leash, the dog will obey only if she's wearing a collar and leash. The underlying premise is the same—over time, you phase out

the treats, just as over time you phase out a collar and leash. In both cases you'll get reliable off-leash compliance.

In a natural state, dogs are hunters. They work cooperatively for food. They expend effort to get their food. Make yours do this by earning whatever food you give her because it satisfies a primal urge and gives her a sense of accomplishment. No animal—and few people—gets everything handed to them without having to work for it in one way or another. Your dog probably doesn't get a chance to hunt for her own food. Chances are she's never had a chance to do the job she was originally bred for, such as traveling miles in a day moving livestock, controlling vermin, or tracking wild boar. Balancing a treat on her nose or playing hide and seek for a stuffed toy might not be as fun as killing rats, but it's certainly better than nothing!

Your dog needs to learn self-control (not a natural canine trait), basic obedience, and good manners. No training, for tricks or otherwise, will be effective with an uncontrolled, unfocused dog. You can rely a lot on restraints, such as crates, head halters, training collars, and leashes for externally imposed control. None of these tools by itself teaches your dog how to restrain herself. Not only that, but also they don't teach her to enjoy using that restraint and to

recognize that by delaying gratification and being calm, she actually has more power over her environment. Put another way, uncontrolled dogs tend to lead limited lives because they're not as fun to live with and often "too wild" to leave the house much, even for walks. In the worst case scenario, untrained (or poorly trained) dogs become dangerous, often with tragic results.

Dog bites to children are unhappily common, and usually it's the family dog who bites children. Although the dynamics and reasons are varied, a common underlying reason is that a child has not been trained how to act responsibly around the family dog, and the dog sees the child as a subordinate being. Involving children in the household with safe interaction and training goes a long

ix

way toward ensuring a more tolerant and respectful dog and a more dog-savvy child who is capable of both empathy and responsible behavior around animals.

Start with simple tricks, some that barely need any training, such as offering a paw or spinning in a circle. There are dozens of tricks and games that even small children can do with your dog. With a little extra work, simple tricks can be built on to create flashier, sometimes sillier, tricks.

Think your dog can't do arithmetic? Think again. If she can bark, she can solve arithmetic problems. After she's learned a few simple tricks, join them together into a short sequence that will impress the heck out of your friends. Teach her some games that she can play with a group of people and show off at parties.

The more your dog learns, the more she is capable of learning because every skill builds on the last. Not only that, but also you will become more adept at figuring out what motivates her and how to communicate better. After you've learned some techniques and learning theory, you won't find the thought of teaching her to fetch a beer from the fridge intimidating. Your initial thought may be "I could never teach my dog that!" Your initial thought is probably selling yourself—and your dog—short. After you have the basics down, you'll be amazed at what you can teach with a little patience.

Go further and try dog sports. For the most part, people who train for fun, and even compete, are just regular folks engaging in a hobby with their dogs. All of them started out not quite knowing what they were doing and muddling through with their dog, having fun along the way. Most sports allow children as junior handlers in competition, and, of course, just about anyone can take classes, so it can become a hobby for the whole family.

Several dog sports require little training but instead rely on the dog's natural abilities, such as herding trials, tracking, and the competitions of dock dogs (water-loving canines leaping off of docks into the water and competing for distance). Others require quite a bit of training for both dog and handler, such as agility and Rally Obedience (Rally-O). Training classes for most sports are friendly, fun, and relatively inexpensive.

If the thought of organized sports doesn't thrill you, but you still like to get out and play, take your dog along so you both get exercise. Go biking with her. Teach her to pull you on a sled or cart. Take her skateboarding.

Make your dog useful. Teach her to ring a bell to go in or out, to potty in place, to find lost items (including the cat), to pick up her own toys, and to fetch the newspaper. Channel problem behaviors such as barking, digging, and jumping up onto people by teaching her alternate behaviors and using up extra energy.

Got more than one dog? It can take some extra skills to manage a multiple-dog household successfully, and—you guessed it—training is the biggest component. It's not so hard to make the pack toe the line, especially if you mix it up with tricks and control games.

Want to go pro? That's probably a whole 'nother book, but every journey starts with a single step. You and your dog will need to go from basic obedience to simple tricks and then string those together into slick routines. The most accomplished dog stars all started out with a simple "sit" and built from there.

THE CASE FOR TRICK TRAINING

Impress your friends and neighbors, turbocharge your dog's skills, and fix behavior problems, too

Think of the brain as a muscle. The more it gets used, the stronger it gets. Trick training helps a dog "learn to learn" by exercising that muscle in easy, fun ways. Improve his attention, self-control, and willingness to work. Most dogs were developed to perform tasks, and unless they live on working farms, have other jobs, or are trained for sport, their considerable potential goes untapped.

If all your dog knows is the daily routine of going in and out, having his mealtimes, and keeping you company, you may never know just how smart he can be unless you do something to challenge his mind. Learning how to do a precise competition heel pattern and learning how to go fetch

Useful Tricks
- Ring a bell to go in or out
- Fetch the newspaper
- Carry groceries
- Find lost items
- Pick up toys

Trick Requirements

- The most important requirement for any trick is simple: First, your dog has to want to work with you. You provide the motivation.

- Second, she has to be able to do the trick. You're responsible for making sure she's working within her capabilities.

- Then she must understand what you want. Never look at her failure to understand something as her fault. Instead, look for a different way to communicate to her.

- Finally, she needs praise and rewards for offering the correct behavior.

the newspaper are both jobs to a dog, and dogs love jobs. Tricks aren't important tasks such as coming when called or walking nicely on leash, so the attitude can be upbeat and creative. If a dog won't easily grasp one trick, it's easy enough to find something else he can do with enthusiasm.

Use trick training to sharpen skills for dog sports or work, to impress your friends, or to train the dog to help clean up around the house or even to fetch you a beer from the fridge. Complex performances such as fetching something from the fridge are merely a series of simple tricks strung together, so don't assume your dog can't learn them with some patience.

Doing simple tricks is also a great way to encourage positive, structured interaction between children and dogs. Teaching a dog to walk on leash is too much responsibility for a seven-year-old, but teaching a dog to roll over and play dead will strengthen the child-dog bond and teach Fido that there are rewards for obeying commands from the littlest master in the house.

Proper Encouragement

- Corrections have their place in dog training. However, they have no place in teaching a dog new skills, training puppies, and certainly not in trick training.

- You don't use coercion devices like prong, choke, or head halters for trick training. A buckle collar and a regular leash and long line are all you need.

- Tools that encourage rather than force a dog to comply are encouraged: treats, toys, a clicker, and, of course, lots of praise!

Impressive Tricks

- Dancing
- Counting and speaking
- Fetching a drink from the fridge
- Balancing a cookie on her nose
- Putting herself to bed

THE RIGHT ATTITUDE

Training is structured play: Do it right and be astounded at what your dog learns

There are no negative consequences if your dog never learns to shake hands, wave bye-bye, or find the TV remote. There are great reasons to potty train him and to teach him basic obedience and manners. In fact, not doing so will make a dog hard, or even impossible to live with, so these are mandatory skills. However, your dog will be a great pet without

ever learning to wave bye-bye. But a trick-savvy dog can be more fun to own and will be more fulfilled and obedient and smarter than you ever realized.

What does this mean? Because trick training isn't necessary, you can relax. If you are relaxed and having fun training, your dog will be, too. Have a blast with it. Be creative. Come up

Structured Play

- Structured play means incorporating games and playful interaction into training sessions.

- Dogs have a powerful play drive, and unlike most wolves and wild canids, retain a play drive into adulthood.

- Playing is a valuable way to strengthen the bond with your dog.

- Dogs naturally use play to hone social skills, and by setting some rules during play, such as not play-biting humans, you teach your dog important lessons about appropriate manners.

Dog Reactions

- Dogs who comply simply to avoid corrections can learn to perform well in the obedience ring and even learn tricks. But they are not as happy, willing, or creative as dogs who learn because it's rewarding for them.

- Some dogs will react to coercion and punishment

- by becoming so stressed they don't learn effectively.

- Dominant and strong-minded dogs may react aggressively or defensively to force or punishment they consider unfair.

with goofy commands. It doesn't have to be time consuming. Practice during commercial breaks or require one successful trick before each meal. If you are doing rigorous training for the obedience ring, alternate serious training with trick training. Even the serious training should be fun for you and your dog. Look at most training as structured play. You can't use toys and treats in the obedience ring, but you can use them to your heart's content teaching Rover to roll over.

Trick training is no place for venting frustration with your dog. If he simply isn't getting something, quit or change your strategy. Figure out his natural abilities and find something easy for him. Experiment with different teaching methods and tools. Food, play, toys, clickers, target sticks, praise—dogs are individuals, and what doesn't work for one dog may be perfect for another. With multiple dogs, you can figure out what makes each one tick.

Not only will your dog be learning new things, but also your training skills will be strengthened.

Dog Personality

- Observe your dog to determine what he finds most rewarding. Some dogs will do back flips for anything they can eat and would work for pieces of cardboard. Others are more discriminating and work best for cooked meat.

- Dogs with a high prey drive can be trained primarily with toys and brief play sessions as rewards.

- Easily distractible dogs can learn particularly effectively with clicker training as long as they're motivated by treats and you keep sessions short.

Why Dogs Play

- To develop hunting behavior: stalking, chasing, catching, and killing
- To improve strength, coordination, and fitness
- To hone social skills
- To establish pack hierarchy
- To engage in sexual play—although quite often mounting behavior is a dominance ploy and has nothing to do with mating

SIZE MATTERS
Use your dog's size to her advantage but make no assumptions based on size

All too often little dogs skate through life on the basis of their adorableness alone, never encouraged to reach their potential. Big dogs, often from working breeds, spend their days chronically unemployed. Dogs of any size can be trained for both manners and tricks. Chances are that your dog is more capable of learning new skills than you ever imagined.

Think outside of the box. There is nothing cuter than a toy dog harnessed up and hauling a little wagon, although one usually associates large dogs with pulling wagons and sleds. Big, bulky dogs might find it physically impossible to sit or stand on their rear legs without help, unlike smaller dogs, but they can do just about everything else, and don't forget that

Physical Considerations

- Take your dog's age and condition into consideration when training anything new.

- Small dogs are usually able to sit and stand on their hindquarters with ease. Larger dogs may not be capable of this.

- If your dog shows any sign of discomfort or unwillingness to perform something, don't force it. Check with your vet to make sure she is structurally healthy. Conditions such as arthritis can show up in very young dogs as well as older dogs.

Big Dogs

- Generally speaking, the larger the dog, the longer it takes for his skeleton to become fully developed.

- It can take as long as eighteen months for giant breeds to complete skeletal development.

- Although natural exercise—and plenty of it—is important for growing dogs, they shouldn't be drilled with repeated jumps, required to pull or carry heavy weights, or forced to overexercise. Doing this can lead to joint injury, putting the dog at risk for early arthritis.

wearing a bandanna makes bruiser-type dogs look unthreatening. If you ever consider doing pet therapy work by taking your well-mannered canine into schools, hospitals, or nursing homes, a simple piece of doggie clothing makes the biggest dog more approachable.

Very large or very small dogs do have some limitations. A Chihuahua can't bring in the daily paper because it might weigh more than he does. You can't train a Great Dane to walk between your legs unless you are 8 feet tall.

Small Dogs

- Smaller dogs can also be prone to joint problems. Luxating patellas (slipped knee caps) are fairly common in toy dogs.

- Very generally speaking, medium-sized dogs have fewer potential limitations for physical activity. Dogs at either end of the size scale—toy breeds such as Pomeranians and Yorkies or giant breeds such as Great Danes and Newfoundlands—tend to have more joint problems.

- Regular exercise and fitness are important because strong muscles can compensate for weaker joints.

Healthy Dogs

- No matter what size, breed, or age your dog, keeping her lean is one of the most important things you can do for her health and longevity.

- Overweight dogs tend to have more chronic health issues, increased likelihood of joint problems and arthritis, and shorter life spans.

- If you use a lot of treats for training your dog, make sure they're somewhat nutritious and reduce the size of her meals to compensate.

BREED MATTERS, TOO
Your dog was bred for a purpose and will show off her abilities with training

All dogs were bred for a purpose, and breeds are categorized by group. Individual quirks may produce retrievers who do not give a hoot about retrieving or herders who would rather hang out and eat sheep poop than herd sheep, but in general breeds and breed mixes have inbred strengths and weaknesses.

Sporting or gundogs work closely with their people, usually excel at retrieving and carrying things, and are willing and easy to train. In fact, they need lots of training and exercise to calm their energy. Working dogs are usually large and used to haul and to be guardians. Most are easy to train, although with the northern breeds such as huskies and malamutes, patience

Terriers

Retrievers

- A typical terrier is not a calm lap dog and needs an owner who is willing to spend time training, exercising, and playing with the dog daily.

- Avoid "small dog syndrome" by establishing clear boundaries and teaching manners right from the start. Many terriers can be willful and bossy, becoming snappy and territorial without training.

- Most breeds bred for killing vermin love toys, enjoy digging, and have a keen sense of smell.

- Most hunting and retrieving dogs are active, highly trainable, and usually gentle family dogs.

- They excel at most dog sports and trick training. Many retrievers get stuck in puppy mode for the first three years of life. Because of their natural exuberance and intelligence, they need ample training to channel their energy.

- Water retrievers, such as Labradors, love to play fetch, especially in water. They have soft mouths because they're bred to carry downed game without damaging it.

and a sense of humor are definitely required! Terriers, bred for varmint control, are excellent learners. They are independent and feisty and test your training skills with their quick minds and questioning of authority. Herding dogs are also extremely trainable and high energy. They are standouts in physical games such as agility, canine freestyle, and Frisbee, learning most tricks very easily. Toy dogs were bred as companions and lap dogs, but this doesn't mean they can't be taught even complex tricks. Most toy dogs love to learn and benefit greatly by showing off skills other than mere cuteness.

Sighthounds, bred to be independent and to chase game, have a reputation for being slow learners, but if you use their prey drive as a motivator, they can definitely learn tricks. The nonsporting group is a grab bag of canine sizes and shapes, with varying abilities from the notoriously hard-to-train chow to all-star performers such as standard poodles.

Understanding a bit about what your dog was bred for will give you an idea of his natural abilities. The bottom line is that each dog, regardless of breed, has talent.

Herding Dogs

- Plenty of vigorous exercise is mandatory for most herding dogs. Quite often problem behaviors cease if the dog gets enough exercise.

- Some herding dogs have very soft temperaments and do best with lots of positive reinforcement training because corrective measures can make them shut down and refuse to learn for fear of punishment.

- Herding dogs are extremely bright and versatile. Some may nip and bark because these are ways to control and move livestock.

Toy Dogs

- What small dogs lack in size, they often make up for in spirit.

- Many toy dogs never realize their full potential because owners tend to spoil them and don't spend much time training.

- Teaching tricks to a little dog is a fun way to work on canine good manners.

- Be careful with table scraps and treats. Tiny amounts of not-so-great food that can be tolerated by a larger dog can make a tiny dog very ill.

FINDING YOUR DOG'S DRIVE
All dogs have instincts and drives that can be directed for both fun and work

Drive is whatever motivates your dog. Food drive is a strong motivator for most dogs, which is why treats work so well as "paychecks." Prey drive—the urge to chase—is also common in our pet carnivores. Any time your dog chases a ball, her prey drive is switched on. Tugging and "killing" a toy are also manifestations of prey drive. Herding is modified prey drive,

with herding dogs stalking and chasing to control flocks but stopping short of bringing down and eating their woolly charges.

Both drives can be channeled and used to motivate and reward your dog. A dog with a ho-hum attitude toward training can be invigorated if she is perked up with anticipation

Predatory Play

- Predatory play is another way puppies develop natural hunting behavior and is a satisfying outlet for dogs who never have to hunt for anything bigger than a piece of kibble.

- Tracking and digging are prey-driven behaviors, using skills that would be used in the wild to locate and unearth a meal.

- Herding and retrieving are also modified forms of prey drive, "softened" so the dog works without harming other animals.

Prey Drive

- Prey drive is a strong instinct in many dogs because acquisition of food is the underpinning of their very survival.

- Having food supplied daily does not diminish this drive because it's instinctive. Some people feel that not having to hunt actually increases prey drive because there is no natural outlet.

- In addition to providing alternative outlets through training and playing, asking a dog to "work" for food, even by having him sit or do tricks, helps satisfy this instinct.

8

of food or toys. A well-timed treat tells her "*Yes! This is just what I want.*" As a general rule, toys work best for encouraging speed and action, such as retrieving and agility games. Food is an excellent marker for correct position when you are teaching your dog to sit, roll over, or raise her paw.

Use special training toys and food. If your dog has access to food in her bowl all the time and is given frequent treats, food may be less valuable to her. Find a treat she absolutely adores and use it only for training. Dogs also have favorite toys. Some love balls, others squeaky toys, others furry toys.

Find one that gets your dog really excited and reserve it for training only.

Dogs also work for praise, and showing her with your voice and affection is important, too. If the dog loves the activity you are teaching her, the joy of a job well done may be its own reward. Figure out what drives your dog to perform and use it to ramp up the fun quotient in training.

Pack Drive

- Pack drive is the dog's instinct to be part of a group. Again, in the wild, this is often necessary for survival because wolves and wild canids hunt together.

- Domestic dogs retain many of the same wolf instincts when they become part of a human family.

- Acceptance by their pack is important, and if dogs "want to please" us, it's in their own self-interest to do what they can to stay a part of their pack. Therefore, they value the praise and reinforcement they get from obeying their owners.

Independent Versus Dependent Dogs

- Dogs bred to work closely with their owners, such as retrievers and most herding dogs, tend to be easy to train because they have a high pack drive and value teamwork.

- Independent breeds, such as sighthounds and guardian dogs, were bred to work without much direction. They may be harder to train because they put a lower value on teamwork.

- Because both the acquisition and eating of food are so important to dogs, treats work for the vast majority as a reward.

PRIMING THE PUPPY
Start young to raise an Einstein puppy who will remain an obedient family member forever

Puppies are little learning sponges. The minute you walk through the door with your puppy, he starts learning. Don't let your puppy do anything now that you don't want him doing as an adult. It's not fair to change the rules. Pulling on your pants leg might be cute when he weighs 8 pounds but won't be cute when he's 80 pounds. Small-breed puppies benefit from the same structure and training as larger dogs. Don't let your toy dog prove the stereotype of a "yappy ankle biter" for lack of basic training.

Be consistent. Use the same words for everything and watch his vocabulary grow. After he connects a word with an action, it can become a command later. "Let's go *outside*"

Bringing Puppy Home

- When you bring a puppy home at eight weeks old, you have to take over the job that his mama and littermates were doing. He needs to be trained, socialized, and taught manners so he grows up polite and confident.

- Introduce him to a variety of friendly people and different environments. Puppies who are isolated can become fearful and reactive adult dogs.

- If you plan on doing any clicker training, you can start right away with little puppies.

Training Puppy

- Most puppies are natural followers and want to be with you. As soon as your dog realizes that coming when called means good things for him, he'll happily comply.

- Even if he tests you during adolescence, you are laying an important foundation now.

- All training cements the dog-owner bond. Untrained dogs are poorly bonded with their families. This inevitably manifests in behavior problems.

- Spend time every day playing and interacting with him.

10

becomes "Go *outside*." He is learning to learn and, most importantly, learning from *you*. This is building a bond and laying the foundation for a well-mannered adult dog. If you don't lay the foundation, your biddable puppy can become very naughty as he hits adolescence, and at that point, establishing manners will be tougher for both of you.

Use his name and call him to you only for good things, never for punishment. Redirect unwanted behavior and reward good behavior. There may be a time and place for punishing him later, but it's unnecessary for baby puppies,

who need guidance rather than harsh corrections. Call him for mealtimes, for playing, grooming, and cuddling. You are both reinforcing the "come" command and teaching him to look to you for the good things in life. As he progresses, expect more from him. Ask for a behavior such as a sit or paw shake for meals and treats. Set him up early to realize that good things come from you, if he behaves, and that obeying you is rewarding.

Acclimating Puppy into the Location

Puppies Need a Lot from You

- Consistent, fair boundaries and rules

- Daily exercise and play

- Just the right amount of good food

- Lots of praise

- Socialization so he grows up brave and confident

- Country settings, even parks, provide a rich, natural environment for a curious pup.

- Getting a puppy to a farm to meet different species and smell different smells will help boost his confidence about other animals in general.

- Let him off leash or use a long line to let him be independent.

- Avoid comforting a scared puppy. This can reinforce anxiety. Be cheerful and distract him instead.

LEASHES, COLLARS, & HALTERS

These are vital tools of the trade, but some have no place in trick training

Ever since dogs were first domesticated, they have worn collars for identification and control. The best collar for the dog is comfortable and looks good. Cheap nylon collars, with their sharp edges, may irritate thin-coated dogs by rubbing the skin. For most dogs, cotton or leather collars are perfect. Some dogs, such as pugs, because of their body and head shape, can easily slip out of a collar and wear harnesses instead. Fluffy dogs may look best in rolled leather collars that don't mess their long fur.

Specialized training chain, prong, or electronic collars have their place in the training toolbox but not in the trick training toolbox. Head halters are useful for teaching exuberant dogs

Harnesses

- Harnesses are necessary for dogs whose necks are the same widths as their heads.

- They're also recommended for dogs inclined to breathing problems or with sensitive tracheas. In some toy breeds, collars cause tracheal spasms ("collapsing trachea") and distress.

- Most harnesses offer less leash control than a regular collar, although this isn't usually as much of a problem with small dogs.

- If your dog wears a harness make sure it's soft and loose enough to allow unrestricted movement.

Leashes

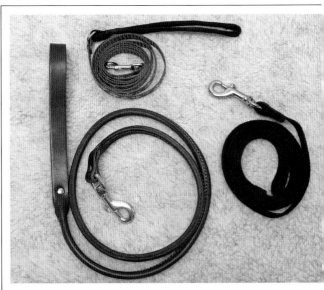

- Choose a leash that feels comfortable in your hands.

- Leather leashes become more pliable and develop more "character" with age. Braided leather leashes are very strong and soft.

- True dog geeks have multiple leashes in different materials and styles and can't walk past a leash booth at a dog show without stopping.

- Tug leashes are popular with performance dog owners. They're made of thick braided felt or fake fur and designed to be used as both a leash and a tug toy.

12

not to pull on leash but also should not be used for fun training. Keep it positive and motivating, not demotivating!

Leashes are used to guide and to keep a dog safe. We teach a dog to walk on leash without pulling because it is more comfortable for us and because an attentive, obedient dog has learned self-control. A 4- to 6-foot leash gives the dog a little freedom of movement and is the standard length for city walks and obedience classes. Choose a leash that is comfortable to hold and won't skin your palms if Fido lunges after a squirrel. Long lines are usually 20- to 40-foot-long cotton webbing and indispensable when teaching your dog distance work or taking him for a rural walk and giving him room to range back and forth. Often a dog who pulls on a shorter leash is less likely to pull on a long line. Retractable leashes can be handy but should be used only when the dog already has basic leash manners. The constant tension teaches a dog that a little pulling is acceptable.

Halters

- A head halter is a great tool for controlling your dog so she walks with you on leash without lunging after other dogs, cars, or squirrels.

- However, it shouldn't be used to direct or force her into any position for tricks or any other purpose.

- Many dogs resist a head halter at first. Put it on and take your dog directly out for a walk. Chances are his excitement about going for a walk will override his concern about the head halter.

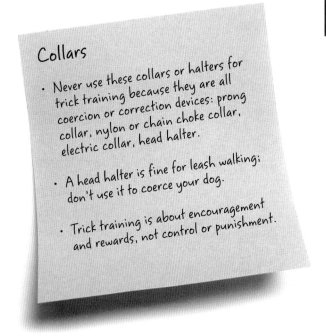

Collars

- Never use these collars or halters for trick training because they are all coercion or correction devices: prong collar, nylon or chain choke collar, electric collar, head halter.

- A head halter is fine for leash walking; don't use it to coerce your dog.

- Trick training is about encouragement and rewards, not control or punishment.

FINDING THE PERFECT TREAT

The size, consistency, and even color of your treats will make a big difference

Food is a powerful motivator for dogs, which is why food works so well for training. To dispel a common myth, using treats for training will not make a dog "work only for treats." This is just as silly as saying that when you put a leash on your dog while training, he'll work only with a leash attached. Treats work to form a positive association in the dog's mind, to let him know when he's done just the right thing, and to keep his attention on the job. After he learns the skill, the treats are used intermittently and are phased out. Some trainers don't believe in treats, and that's fine. They are merely a tool in the toolbox and like any other tool can be abused!

To Treat or Not to Treat

- A bait bag, fanny pack, or something with big pockets will allow you to get to treats quickly for immediate rewarding.

- In most dog sports, such as agility and obedience, you are not allowed to reward or even touch your dog during competition.

- Having treats in your pocket during competition can be the basis for automatic disqualification.

- It's fine to leave a reward for your dog outside of the ring so you can "pay" her after you're done.

Training Treats

- Training treats can be minuscule—a mere crumb works fine.

- Anything that your dog needs to take a moment to chew is too large.

- Reserve slightly larger or whole treats for an especially good performance or for a "jackpot" at the end of a routine. This way your dog will work harder to do well.

- Soft treats should be used for classes, but you don't need to be as particular when training at home.

14

Good training treats should be very small. You are not feeding the dog; you are giving him tiny little rewards. They should be soft, so he doesn't inhale one and then get distracted coughing it up when he's supposed to be doing a perfect heeling pattern. They shouldn't be crumbly, so they don't sprinkle all over the ground and distract him or, worse yet, other dogs in a training class. Finally, if you're doing training such as agility, where treats are often thrown, they should be a different color than the ground so he can get them fast.

Some obedience trainers tuck treats into their mouths and spit them at the dog to keep their hands free and the dog focused. This explains the rapt attention that competition obedience dogs often have on their handlers' faces. Choose special treats your dog really loves and use them only for training. Many training treats are on the market, or use your own. Hot dogs cut into tiny pieces work well, as do cheese and lunchmeat.

Types of Treats

- Soft commercial treats can be pinched into tinier pieces.

- If you're using a lot of treats to train a new behavior, avoid low-quality ones with food coloring and synthetic preservatives, if possible. Some very healthful treats are on the market.

- Some dogs get diarrhea from too many real liver treats, so proceed with caution. Liver-flavored treats probably contain no liver—check ingredients.

- It's fine to vary and mix up treats.

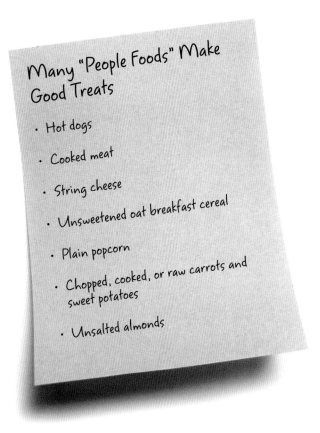

Many "People Foods" Make Good Treats

- Hot dogs

- Cooked meat

- String cheese

- Unsweetened oat breakfast cereal

- Plain popcorn

- Chopped, cooked, or raw carrots and sweet potatoes

- Unsalted almonds

15

TOYS FOR STRUCTURED PLAY

Use toys for drive, motivation, reward, and better bonding with your dog during training

Trainers talk of dogs who have "play drive," which means just a dog's desire to chase, tug, and "kill" toys. It's another great way to motivate and reward a dog during training. Some dogs get more excited about toys than food, which can make for some high-energy training sessions. Because most training should be structured play, it's wonderful if you have a play-driven dog. Terriers are often extremely focused on toys because of their development as vermin-killing dogs.

As with treats, it works best if you have a special toy that your dog adores just for training sessions. Again, you are creating a positive association—obeying is a fun game.

The type of toy depends on what you're teaching and what

Tug

- Playing tug is very satisfying for many dogs. Unconfident dogs may be hesitant to "challenge" their people over a tug, even in play. These dogs will quickly drop it or have a half-hearted grip.

- Encourage a shy dog to take it and tug. Don't pull too hard and give him plenty of praise when he drops it on command.

- Try snaking it along the floor, as you would if playing with a cat. This helps trigger a dog's prey drive.

Fetch/Catch

- When throwing a ball for your dog to catch in midair, make sure it's not so small that he could accidentally gulp it down and choke.

- Most pet stores have a big selection of fetch toys that make noise, bounce in unpredictable directions, and are easy for a dog to catch and pick up. These are more fun than tennis balls!

- If your dog plays "keep away" and runs from you after getting a thrown toy, never chase him!

your dog likes. It could be as low-tech as a length of heavy knotted rope or empty plastic water bottle or an expensive rabbit fur woven tug. If choosing toys for group training classes, avoid squeaker toys, which can completely unravel the other dogs. Toys in class can keep your dog focused on obeying you and having fun while you wait for other dogs to take their turns. Take a toy along on walks and play-train in the park for distraction training. Stop your training sessions before your dog starts to lose interest. Short sessions work better and keep his motivation high.

Real Fur Toys

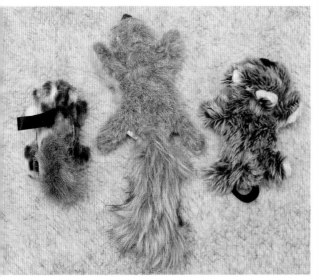

It's OK for you to play tug-of-war with your dog as long as you set the rules. Use tug to teach your dog the "drop" command—his reward is that he gets to play again after he releases. Work on sits, downs and stays and reward him with a brief tug session each time. No matter what you use play-training for, it strengthens your bond with the dog and builds motivation.

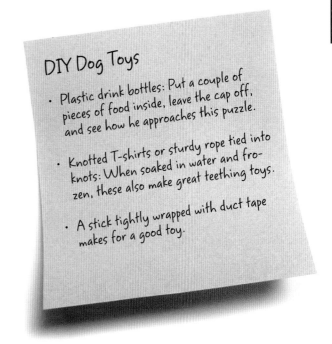

DIY Dog Toys

- Plastic drink bottles: Put a couple of pieces of food inside, leave the cap off, and see how he approaches this puzzle.

- Knotted T-shirts or sturdy rope tied into knots: When soaked in water and frozen, these also make great teething toys.

- A stick tightly wrapped with duct tape makes for a good toy.

- Some dogs are highly motivated by toys made of real instead of faux fur. Try these for a dog who shows little interest in other toys.

- Online training supply stores sell sturdy tugs made from sheepskin or rabbit fur.

- Very high-value toys such as these can start guarding behavior. It's best to reserve such toys for training and play sessions only and not to leave them lying around.

CLICKER TRAINING

Even sheep can be clicker trained for agility—it will work wonders for your dog

Developed initially to train large marine mammals, clicker training has become a useful dog training tool. The operant conditioning theory is that an animal will learn to repeat an action if it has a positive consequence, such as food. A clicker is a small plastic box with a metal strip that, when pressed with your finger, makes a sharp click. The distinctive click is

an unequivocal and consistent signal to a dog that she's performed the desired action when immediately followed by a small treat reward.

Very specific behaviors, such as tail wags and head turns are easily trained with a clicker. Because the click happens at the precise moment the dog performs the behavior, it

Clickers

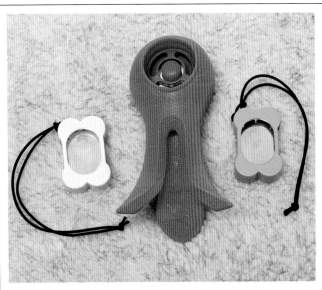

- Clickers are widely available. You can also use a retractable ballpoint pen to make a quieter click. This works for very sound-sensitive dogs.

- Dogs quickly recognize their own clicker sound and aren't distracted by other clickers in a training class.

- If you have multiple dogs, separate them while clicker training because it can confuse the dog who is hearing the clicker but not getting rewarded.

Teaching through Clicking

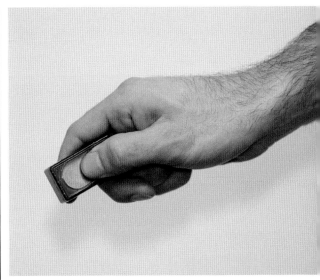

- A clicker can be used as a tool to provide general training, to teach tricks, or just to shape very specific behaviors.

- Even "hard to teach" dogs can grasp concepts quickly through clicker training.

- Teach a beginner dog away from distractions at first. Increase distractions as she gets more proficient.

- Don't do any treat-training right after a meal unless your dog is a real chowhound. A dog who is a little hungry works harder.

bridges the gap between the behavior and the treat. Think of the clicker as a camera, with the click taking an imaginary photo of the correct behavior.

Clicker training makes a dog work to figure out what she has to do in order to get the click-treat, and because it makes her think, she learns fast and retains what she's learned. Clicker training involves only guidance, not corrections. Incorrect actions are simply ignored. As a result, the dog works hard to figure out how to get *you* to perform and give her a treat.

ZOOM

When you use operant conditioning, your dog will repeat behaviors that are rewarded and won't repeat behaviors that are unrewarded. Rewards often cannot be given at precisely the right instant, so the clicker gives an immediate "Yes, that's it!" The treat comes afterward and is faded out as the dog learns the command.

Perfect for Training

You can't put a collar and leash on a dolphin. Clicker training is used to train marine mammals at Sea World and all types of birds and other animals for film and TV.

Most species become fearful or aggressive if corrected. Clicker training uses no corrections. Unwanted behavior is ignored; correct behavior is rewarded.

- Clicker training is ideal for tricks because the dog rarely does anything wrong in trick training. She simply doesn't understand, and this isn't a basis for correction.

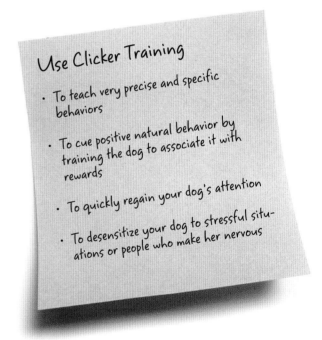

Use Clicker Training

- To teach very precise and specific behaviors

- To cue positive natural behavior by training the dog to associate it with rewards

- To quickly regain your dog's attention

- To desensitize your dog to stressful situations or people who make her nervous

TARGET STICKS & SQUEEZY CHEESE

A stick and cheese out of a tube make an invaluable training tool—who knew?

A target stick is a tool to help teach your dog to work at a distance, be comfortable moving away from you, walk backward, and do a myriad of actions when you can't control or lure her by hand. A target stick can also be used to teach a dog to touch named objects with her nose, which translates to tricks such as ringing a bell to go out or identifying different toys by name. Often used with clickers, some commercially available target sticks have a built-in clicker in the handle.

You don't need to buy a professional telescoping target stick, though. A small fishing pole works, as does a cheap driveway marker, thin PVC pipe, or wooden dowel. They are

Move the Stick

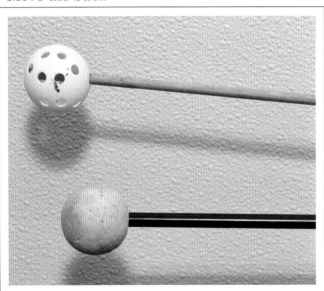

- Move the stick around while getting your dog used to it. Have her follow it up, down, and in different directions with her nose.

- Moving it in quick, jerky motions will catch her interest faster.

- If using a clicker, click-treat for following or touching it with her nose, but don't give any reward for trying to grab or bite the stick. End the game if she does this and try again later when she's calmer.

Target Sticks

- Because it's impractical to keep bending over to give a tiny dog treats, target sticks can be used to teach very small dogs the initial phase of heeling or walking on leash without pulling.

- Target sticks allow you to direct your dog to move around you without bending, stretching, or looming over her.

- Phase out the use of target sticks and lures as soon as your dog understands what you want her to do.

20

usually 3 feet long, sometimes with a small ball or bulb at the end to make it easier for the dog to follow. This ball or bulb can also be fashioned at home by using a table tennis ball or by wrapping the end of the stick with a bulb of duct tape.

Soft cheese makes an excellent lure because it can be dabbed onto the end of a target stick or onto anything you want your dog to go touch. As with clicker training, treats and then the stick are phased out after the dog understands each concept.

MAKE IT EASY

Some dogs will be nervous about a stick at first. Place it on the ground and reward your dog for any interest, from moving toward it to sniffing it. Dab cheese or peanut butter onto the end. Hold it while you are preparing her food. Try a clicker to click-treat interest.

Food Lures

- Use sticky food lures on the stick only until she understands that the point is to follow and touch it.

- Using the same method, teach her to touch your hand on command. This makes a cute trick.

- If she's unwilling to touch the stick or your hand without food, bump it briefly to her nose and immediately give her a treat from your other hand. Also sniff the target, say, "Yummm, treats," then offer it to her to touch.

Transfer the Touch

- After she is following and touching the stick, move it away from you so she's used to turning her back and leaving you to follow it.

- Start transferring the "touch" command to other objects while you stand back. For instance, when teaching her to ring a bell, you'll use the stick to direct her to the bell.

- Dab sticky food onto the object you are transferring to so she understands she now has to touch that instead of the target stick.

21

GROUP TRAINING CLASSES

Sometimes it takes a village: Group classes are informational and loads of fun

People have some misconceptions about dog training classes. Beginner and novice classes aren't just for novice dog owners. They're for beginner and novice dogs, often brought to class by experienced dog owners. The dogs learn to pay attention to their owners in the face of distractions and interact politely with other dogs and people. Another misconception is that basic obedience classes are for puppies and young dogs. Most are held for beginner dogs of any age because old dogs can learn new tricks. Finally, many people think their dog is too wild for classes. Many classes are tailored *exactly* for the unruly dog—how will he learn to behave in public if he's never *in* public?

Group Classes

- The difference between an unruly dog on the first night of class and a controlled dog at the end of the class can be quite dramatic.

- Unless a dog has serious aggression issues, group classes work very well to teach restraint and calm around other dogs.

- Most training facilities will do some private lessons to evaluate and work with a dog before entering group classes. If you're unsure how your dog will do, call and ask first.

Structured Play

- Even serious obedience classes should be structured play. Effective trainers encourage the use of treats, toys, and games for control and attention.

- Classes for puppies and beginners are usually more lax. At higher levels, especially competition-level classes, dogs are expected to be controlled and to ignore other dogs during class or competition.

- A more experienced dog is expected to keep his focus on his owner and the job in class. He can play with his owner but not with other dogs.

Obedience training isn't just an eight-week class. It's a process, and repeating classes is OK. You and your dog will learn from the different participants, and it will strengthen your dog's social graces. Most good dog training facilities teach not only basic skills but also dog sports and advanced obedience, so you can continue to higher learning.

Every bit of learning you do with your dog improves his attention span and learning ability. Basic manners are important, and your dog will need some essential commands in order to do most tricks. It's a rare dog who doesn't enjoy learning and who isn't fulfilled and tired after an hour class.

There are several right ways to train dogs and some wrong ways, and every trainer has her own training philosophy. A good trainer will be flexible in her methods and make the classes fun. Ask people with well-behaved dogs whom they recommend. Perhaps your vet will know someone. Observe a class before you sign up and see if it feels like a good fit, then go play!

What to Look For

- One of the most important skills your dog will learn in class is to focus on you—his leader—in a distracting environment.

- When observing a class, ask yourself if both dogs and owners are enjoying themselves. Avoid classes that use choke collars and jerk the dogs around for compliance.

- Punishment should never be a part of any puppy class. Appropriate corrections may be warranted for dogs who have already learned the rules.

Real World Skills

- In class, pups start to learn "real world" skills, such as ignoring other dogs and ignoring tempting items on the ground.

- The dog who must stay still while other dogs are walking by him is called the "honor dog." His job is to stay politely while serving as a distraction for the others.

- In a good class, you can learn from other participants as well as from the trainer. Even experienced owners of titled dogs bring beginner dogs to basic classes.

23

KEEP IT FUN
Make your dog an enthusiastic partner by making learning positive and rewarding

Teach through positive interaction instead of compulsion and force. Encourage your dog to offer the right behaviors instead of being nervous about making mistakes. Some dogs will be inhibited and unwilling to work if they get corrected too many times. You want your dog to be a willing partner, and this goes double for tricks and games.

All games, even elementary ones such as hide-and-seek, have rules. Using play to teach your dog involves rules. When the play is rewarding, dogs are very quick to learn rules! A retriever will stop retrieving a thrown ball unless it's always thrown again on retrieval. If you teach him to sit or to come to your left before throwing the ball, he'll quickly do that.

Rewards

Benefits of Play during Training

- A tired dog is a good dog. Play-training gives him an outlet for energy.

- He'll look at training not as boring but rather as something fun he looks forward to.

- Playing is an important way for dogs to express natural drives.

- It will strengthen your working bond.

- Clickers and treats are very valuable training tools, especially when teaching new behaviors. But they're bridges between you and your dog. Voice, play, and touch are truly direct forms of communication.

- Avoid making food the only way you reward your dog.

- Some behaviors, such as fetching and finding, are more fun for the dog to do. Others, such as heeling and staying in place, can be boring. Reward the boring activities more often.

Food is also a powerful motivator. A common objection is that when a dog is trained using food, he will "work only for food." Most of the top-ranked show, obedience, and competition sport dogs were trained using treats along with play and other reinforcers, so this argument simply doesn't hold up. It's all in how you do it.

When your dog is with you, he is learning. He's learning to take his cues from you, whether you're engaging in a training session or checking e-mail with him lying at your feet.

YELLOW LIGHT

Unless your dog is about to do something dangerous or destructive in trick training, avoid corrections. A bright dog will often offer alternate behaviors in response to commands. Don't quash his creativity! Don't acknowledge incorrect behavior. Dogs who get corrected too often may become inhibited, afraid to make a mistake.

Have Fun

Rules for Play

- Don't let your dog play with you as he would with another dog.

- Don't allow biting, even in play.

- Never chase him, even in play. He can chase you, but it's not good to let him think he can ever make a game of running from you.

- If he gets too wild and won't "turn off," calmly end the game.

- Don't train if you're stressed out. Sometimes it's OK just to take a walk with your dog or even a nap on the couch with him. He'll always benefit from time with you.

- Have everyone in the family follow the same training rules so that he gets consistent messages.

- Include him in family walks or playtimes. One of the worst things you can do to a dog is to make him feel excluded from his pack.

25

BREAKING DOWN & BACK-CHAINING
Make complex tricks easy for your dog by breaking them into baby steps

Even a simple command is actually a series of steps. You probably think that coming when called is a single action, but it's really a chain of behaviors. First the dog has to turn his attention to you when you call, "Here, Rover!" Then he has to leave whatever he was doing and come toward you. Finally, he needs to get all the way to you, and then he has to stop

instead of turning it into a game of chase.

When you start teaching your dog to come, you probably encourage him at every step, which is absolutely the right thing to so. A complex trick is not so different. It's just a chain of behaviors that you teach separately at first, then string together.

Contact Zones

- In agility, dogs need to step on the painted "contact zones" on some obstacles as a safety measure to prevent them from leaping wildly off the equipment at full speed.

- When the dog is taught to pause at the bottom before being taught to go over

the equipment, he already knows what to expect and how to adjust his pace.

- The contact zone pause is highly reinforced, so the dog learns that this position is very rewarding and enjoys the pause.

Agility

- Agility is a prime example of a complex behavior that is first taught in small steps.

- The dog is taught each obstacle separately at first until he is feeling confident, having fun, and performing consistently.

- Gradually the dog learns to do the obstacles in different sequences until he can run an entire course.

- Depending on the amount of training and the dog's ability, it may take months before the dog can put it all together.

"Back-chaining" means teaching a dog the last step of the sequence first. Take a basic game of fetch. In order for you to throw the ball again, your dog needs to drop the ball at your feet or deposit the slimy thing directly into your hand. If he won't do that, it's a very short game. So, first you teach him to release the ball. When he runs to retrieve it, he already knows the next step of the game. He's confident and willing to give it up because he knows that his reward is another ball toss.

Some Einstein dogs will grasp larger concepts quickly, perhaps because they're smart and easily trainable, perhaps because you're teaching them something that comes naturally to many, such as retrieving, or perhaps because you just did a very good job in making it clear to him. Other dogs will need a bit more help. Don't get frustrated—if a dog isn't understanding something, it's up to us brains to figure out how to get the information across to him!

Commands

- Coming when called is also a short sequence. The dog first has to come to attention when called, then come directly to his owner, finally coming to a halt at the owner's feet.

- Dogs are usually taught to sit in front of their owners for a treat.

- In formal obedience, the dog sits in front of the owner after coming when called. Because he already knows the "sit" command, he comes confidently, understanding that the last step is a sit and reward.

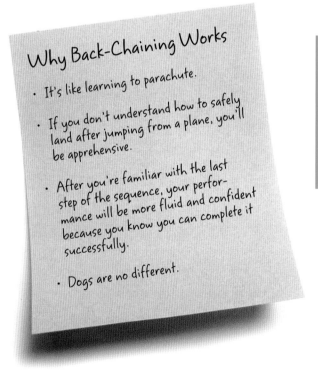

Why Back-Chaining Works

- It's like learning to parachute.

- If you don't understand how to safely land after jumping from a plane, you'll be apprehensive.

- After you're familiar with the last step of the sequence, your performance will be more fluid and confident because you know you can complete it successfully.

- Dogs are no different.

27

TIMING IS EVERYTHING
Be like a professional trainer and time rewards well for fast, effective learning

Timing is one of the most critical skills in communicating effectively with a dog. Because dogs lack language, you can't sit your dog down after the fact and explain what he did wrong. Nor can you teach him by telling him ahead of time what you want him to do. You have to match reward "markers"—clicker, treat, an encouraging word, or physical contact—and corrections precisely with the behavior.

When you want your dog to lie down, giving him a treat before he is settled all the way down on the floor is teaching him to lie partway down, then pop up again. Rewarding him for sitting after you've said "Sit" eight times teaches him to sit after you've repeated yourself for half a minute. If you want

Incorrect Rewards

- Many dog owners inadvertently reinforce undesirable behaviors. For instance, a dog who is threatened by visitors to the home barks incessantly, circles, darts around, and may even nip.

- In response, the owner picks up the dog, cooing, petting, and comforting

him, reassuring him that the visitors are harmless.

- Because the dog is being rewarded for being nervous, barking, and attempting to nip, he naturally assumes that this is what his owner wants him to do!

Correct Rewards

- A better way to deal with a dog threatened by visitors is to reward him only for calm behavior.

- If he can perform an action that is incompatible with rushing and barking, such as fetching or sitting, direct him to that activity and reward for that instead.

- When possible, hand each visitor some treats and ask them to tell your dog to sit, then reward him for sitting.

- Pay attention to reinforcement because it's easy to unwittingly reward the wrong behavior.

him to lie all the way down and settle on command, reward him only when he is down and calm. If you want him to sit the first time you give the cue, don't repeat yourself—reward only for an immediate plopping down of the butt.

The same goes for corrections. If you scold him thirty seconds after he chases the cat, you could well be scolding him for stopping the cat-chasing behavior. Better to correct him in the act. Better still to correct him for preparing to act. When he sees the cat, goes on alert, and tenses up, ready to chase, correcting him for even thinking about it, then praising him

for shifting his attention away, is the optimal strategy.

You get what you train for. If you consistently reward for subpar performance, this is exactly what you will get. If your dog isn't getting feedback on what you really want him to do, you aren't giving him the tools to improve.

Corrections

- Dogs don't understand corrections after the fact. If you come home and find that your dog chewed up a book, don't yell at him. Yell at yourself instead for leaving him access to tempting items!

- If you get mad at your dog for something he did two hours ago, he is going to cringe and "look guilty."

- He's not guilty, and he has no clue about what you are yelling about. He's cringing only because you are mad at him now.

Quick Rewards

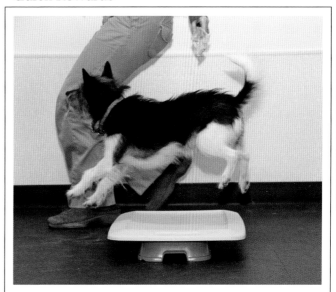

- When teaching finite behaviors such as sitting, reward immediately and only for that behavior performed the way you want.

- It's OK to lure and encourage a puppy when he is still learning what "sit" means.

- After he understands the command and obeys most of the time, he should comply the first time you ask. If he doesn't, it's OK to tell him, "Too bad, no cookies for you" and ignore him. If he wants that treat, he'll sit!

KNOW YOUR DOG

Whether your dog is shy or hyper, use the best training style for her personality

The reason why no single training method works universally is because dogs are individuals. A dog who is uninterested in treats (chows and shar-peis are known for this) isn't going to respond to "cookie training." A soft dog will quickly shut down with even mild disapproval. These dogs need to be reinforced with frequent praise and often taught behaviors in very small increments. A high-drive, dominant dog needs clear direction and a solid foundation in obedience basics. A hyper, easily distracted terrier may need very valuable rewards, shorter sessions, and some control exercises to perform at her best. A working breed can be pragmatic: Unlike a compliant, easily trained retriever who will shake hands fifty

Submissive Dogs

- Submissive (soft) dogs are cautious about new behaviors and react poorly to corrections. Soft dogs need a lot of training and structure to give them confidence.

- Clicker and target stick training works extremely well because it puts a bridge between him and you, allowing for clear signals and lots of positive reinforcement.

- Never comfort your dog for being anxious. It's not fair to reinforce a dog for nervousness. Ignore his concerns and reward frequently for positive behavior.

High-Energy Dogs

- Rambunctious, high-drive dogs need outlets for their energy. Without adequate exercise, it's very difficult to get his attention and gain control.

- Schedule daily exercise and interactive training sessions. Allow him to blow off pent-up energy before expecting him to sit, walk slowly on leash, or spend more than a few minutes at a time training with you.

- Mix in lots of play with frequent, random commands so he has structure and stays attentive.

imes in a row, a rottweiler may simply not see the point after he seventh handshake.

If your dog isn't having fun, isn't understanding, or is simply gnoring you, ask yourself if there could be a bad fit between what you are asking him to do and his personality. Perhaps you were too harsh with a sensitive dog, and he is stressed about making any more mistakes. Have him perform something you know he can do, praise him lavishly, and take a break. Is a bored or distracted dog not on task? Perhaps he needs a better reward, a break for play with you, or a quick game of fetch or tug to rev him up again. Some dogs simply aren't hardwired to retrieve or bark on command, but there is always something they can do well.

No matter what sort of problem you're having, the first strategy is to find something the dog can and will do, have him do it, praise, and then take a break. Always end on a successful note and keep training sessions short, with your dog wanting more.

Focus

- Without your dog's focus, you'll have a hard time teaching him anything! In turn, you have to focus on your dog as well.

- Dogs lose focus if they become bored, stressed, or distracted. It's up to you to determine why your dog isn't paying attention.

- Doing this may take some experimentation. Pay attention to what causes him to stop working and also to what gets and holds his interest. Train in short sessions and use whatever works to motivate him.

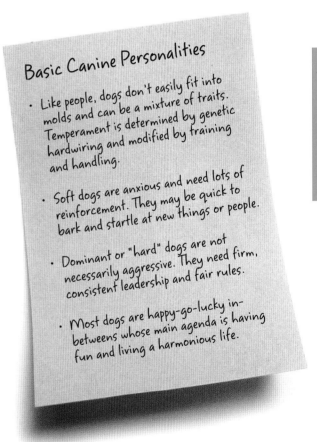

Basic Canine Personalities

- Like people, dogs don't easily fit into molds and can be a mixture of traits. Temperament is determined by genetic hardwiring and modified by training and handling.

- Soft dogs are anxious and need lots of reinforcement. They may be quick to bark and startle at new things or people.

- Dominant or "hard" dogs are not necessarily aggressive. They need firm, consistent leadership and fair rules.

- Most dogs are happy-go-lucky in-betweens whose main agenda is having fun and living a harmonious life.

COMMUNICATING WITH YOUR DOG
Your dog is learning your language; it's only fair to learn his, too

We've established that we want a happy, confident dog who enjoys training. Very often what we see as disobedience is instead an inability to understand, stress, boredom, or even a creative dog asking you if it's OK to try a different method of executing a command. Dogs communicate with body language almost exclusively. Understanding signals helps you be a better trainer.

A happy dog has her tail set high, upright or forward ears and a smile on her face. She is being attentive. If she is the intense type with a strong will to work, she may have a more serious demeanor; she may anticipate your commands or offer extra behavior, such as sitting on command, then offering her paw. This is great initiative, so don't correct it. Simply ignore unwanted behavior and reward what you asked for.

Dog Confidence

- This dog is feeling confident and enjoying herself.

- Pay attention to barking, too. Barking during play or training is usually simple exuberance.

- Avoid correcting a vocal, joyful dog while training because she may think she's being corrected for something else and get confused or inhibited.

- You may notice her barking at you when she gets frustrated. This is often because you've been slow or unclear with your commands. Listen to your dog.

Lost Connections

- If you have a dog who sometimes stops and ignores you during training or even playing, figure out her motivation.

- Some dogs will shut down if corrected or confused. They'll avoid eye contact, may yawn, lift a paw, or walk off sniffing the ground.

- These are stress and avoidance signals.

- Toss a treat or toy, get her focus back, and praise her for paying attention. Then ask yourself if you're overcorrecting her.

A dog who is stressed might act like he's ignoring you, sniffing the ground, placing his tail down, walking away, or averting his eyes. Try lightening up, initiating play, and asking him for something easy. The same goes for a dog who is lagging and responding slowly.

A dog who is being a bully and ignoring you because he doesn't think you're leader enough to tell him what to do may need professional intervention. Exhibiting stiffness, staring, and growling when asked to do something and guarding food, toys, or furniture are behaviors requiring remedial attitude adjustment, sooner rather than later.

One somewhat verbal way that dogs use to communicate is barking. Some dogs bark because they're excited and frequent barkers—you know if yours is one of these! Some dogs bark when frustrated. If your dog frequently barks at you while playing or training, ask yourself if this is normal exuberance or if he's telling you off for being inconsistent or unclear with your commands.

Trainer Confidence

- Project an aura of calm, friendly confidence when working with your dog.

- Getting excited or frustrated can inhibit or confuse her by sending mixed signals. Dogs are much better at reading our body language than hearing our words, and a sensitive dog will quickly pick up our negative emotions.

- Try walking backward with your dog on leash for a change. Your different body position and gait will get her attention.

Communicating Is a Two-Way Street

- Learn to read your dog's body language and use it to tailor training.

- Dogs are honest and tell us just how they're feeling.

- Keep your own body and stance relaxed and confident.

- Modulate your tone of voice, keeping it calm and controlled.

- Babbling or shouting commands is unnecessary and will confuse your dog.

33

TROUBLESHOOTING TRICKS

Fix inevitable training problems with patience, easy tricks, and tweaking

Dogs have to work hard to understand us, and occasional miscommunication is inevitable.

Let's say you want to teach Fido to sit and shake hands. He's got the sit part down pat but is mystified by your "shake" command. You can back-chain this. Because the last step is the action of raising his paw and putting it into your hand,

sit in front of him, reach around, tap the back of his foot to encourage him to put his paw into your hand, immediately tell him, "Yes!" and pop a treat into his mouth. Repeat this over several sessions until he is raising his paw when you extend your hand and say, "Shake." As he becomes more proficient, raise your expectations by requiring him to raise

Fixing Collar Dislikes

- It's not uncommon for dogs to dislike being handled by the collar. Depending on the dog's temperament, such handling can be perceived as either confrontational or threatening.

- Don't grab the collar from the top but rather from the side or below his head. Do

this when having him sit for food so he gets used to it.

- A 6- or 8-inch traffic tab (like a minileash) can help get your dog used to being handled, leashed, or unleashed.

Fixing Troubling Behavior Patterns

- After he is performing a command pretty consistently, start changing your position and distance a little at a time.

- If he learns to obey only when you are standing right in front of him with a treat, he will pattern this behavior.

- Dogs don't generalize easily. To your dog, telling him to sit from 6 feet away instead of from directly in front of him can feel like a totally different command.

his paw on command. You have both back-chained and broken the behavior into small steps. Although some dogs are natural paw-shakers, it's too much to expect every dog to immediately understand the concept of extending a paw on command. Apply these concepts to any new behavior, from complex agility moves to simple tricks. They usually work.

If your dog seems distracted, find a calmer environment for teaching a new skill.

Another "quick fix" might be a better reward. Perhaps he's bored with his regular treats—try cooked chicken or a new toy or try taking a break to play fetch or walk around the block. Try training a chowhound before mealtime. A hungry dog will work extra hard for food. Try filling his bowl and handing him food one piece at a time as reward for learning a new skill. Are you having fun and imparting enthusiasm to your dog? Let your enthusiasm show; get crazy when he does it right. It's OK to be a bit silly with trick training, and your dog likes it.

Fixing Communication Problems

- Don't keep repeating something if he's just not getting it. Take a break, then try it differently. Try a quieter location perhaps, try a different reward, or add a hand signal.

- Break the behavior into smaller pieces. For instance, if you are teaching "stay," and he moves as you step away, first get him solid on staying when you are right next to him.

- Then try shuffling one short step away and rewarding that. Then work on taking a full step away.

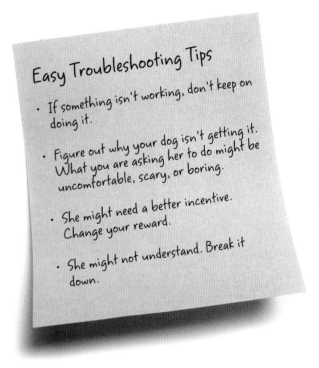

Easy Troubleshooting Tips

- If something isn't working, don't keep on doing it.

- Figure out why your dog isn't getting it. What you are asking her to do might be uncomfortable, scary, or boring.

- She might need a better incentive. Change your reward.

- She might not understand. Break it down.

35

PRIMING THE CLICKER
Before you clicker train, your dog must know what it means to him

Dogs learn quickly with clicker training. Our voices change depending on our mood; we use different words; and we often confuse a dog by giving conflicting body language signals. The clicker is consistent, delivering instant feedback.

"Priming the clicker" means getting the dog to understand that the click is immediately followed by a treat. Do this when your dog is a little hungry so she will be eager for the treats.

Choose a fairly distraction-free environment, arm yourself with ten small, soft treats, and get her attention. Have the clicker in one hand and the treats in the other. You're not going to say anything or expect anything from her. Click and immediately treat. By the time you get to the end of your ten treats, she'll be focusing on the clicker, not on the treats. This means she understands that the click equals a treat.

Clicker Sounds

- Many trainers use the word "Yes!" instead of a click. This works, too, but the clicker sound is more consistent and conveys a very clear meaning to the dog when immediately followed by a reward.

- With very little practice, it's easier to get precise timing by using a clicker than by using a spoken marker word such as "Yes."

- Dogs quickly recognize the sound of "their" clicker and don't get confused if multiple clickers are used in a class situation.

The Reward

- Many people assume that to be effective, the clicker must be followed by a treat. The phrase "click-treat" is used through this book because treats are most commonly used, but there are several possible rewards.

- Other rewards include a ball being thrown, the immediate offer of a tug toy, the opportunity to be released from a position, or even a belly rub.

- A reward is whatever makes your dog happy at a particular point in time.

Now that she knows that the click means a treat, you're both ready to put this to practical use. It's important that the click sound is always followed by a treat. Bear in mind that a clicker is simply a tool to teach your dog new skills or to refine ones she already knows. As training progresses, you phase out the clicker and treats.

Behavior Reinforcement

- Another myth is that clicker-trained dogs won't obey unless they get the click-treat reinforcement.

- This is like saying that after you train a dog using a leash, the dog will never comply unless a leash is attached.

- No matter what method of training one uses, training tools are used for initial training. As the dog becomes proficient with the behavior, the use of the tool is faded out.

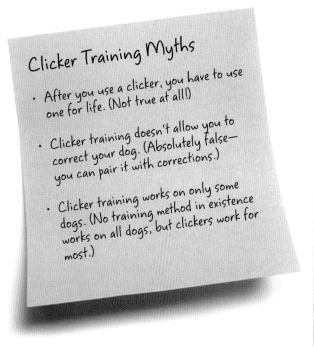

Clicker Training Myths

- After you use a clicker, you have to use one for life. (Not true at all!)

- Clicker training doesn't allow you to correct your dog. (Absolutely false—you can pair it with corrections.)

- Clicker training works on only some dogs. (No training method in existence works on all dogs, but clickers work for most.)

KNOW WHEN TO CLICK
The clicker mantra: Reward for position but click for action

By timing the click to match specific actions, you can teach a dog simple tricks, such as tilting her head just so. By building on a series of simple moves, you can chain together actions for complex tricks. When introducing a new behavior, it's important to remember not to put a voice command or cue to it. This comes later, when your dog is performing the action. Most skills in this book can be taught using a clicker.

For instance, when teaching your dog to shake, the first step is to have him sit, then touch the back of his paw. The very instant he raises his paw off the floor even a little, click-treat. Repeat this until he is reliably lifting his paw, then up the ante. Still saying nothing, wait until he raises his paw higher. Click-treat. Now hold your hand where he can put his paw into it (he may try nosing your hand instead, looking for

Attentiveness

- All training requires attentiveness. Envision exactly what you want your dog to do and be ready to click-treat right when you see that.

- Think of the clicker as a camera. The second you

have the precise behavior or position you want, click as if taking a photo of it.

- Try blinking your eyes at the same time you press the clicker. Some people find that doing this makes it easier to coordinate.

Timing

- Timing is just as important when training without the clicker—it's a crucial element in all animal training. It can take practice to get a feel for correct timing.

- Always give the treat (or other reward) immediately after the click and not at the same time as clicking.

- You will mistime occasionally. This is normal. But because it's your mistake and not your dog's, reward her anyway. You won't destroy a whole training session with a few mistimed clicks.

food; have the treat in your other hand so that he sees it) and click-treat as soon as he touches his paw to your hand. After he is doing this in expectation of his click-treat, you can add your command. Phase out the click-treat after he's got it.

ZOOM

The reason why you do not use a command initially is twofold. First, you are diluting the effectiveness of the clicker by adding words when he doesn't yet understand what you want. Second, he'll understand better when he has to do the work of figuring out and offering the right behavior.

Sounds

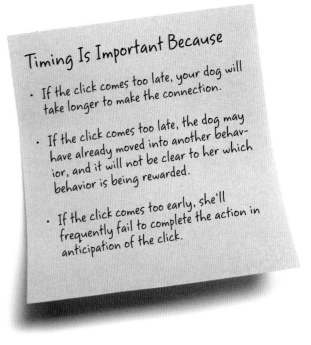

Timing Is Important Because

- If the click comes too late, your dog will take longer to make the connection.

- If the click comes too late, the dog may have already moved into another behavior, and it will not be clear to her which behavior is being rewarded.

- If the click comes too early, she'll frequently fail to complete the action in anticipation of the click.

- The standard clicker is a little rectangular box, but there are many styles, and some might be more comfortable to click with.

- Digital clickers can be programmed to make many different "click" sounds and have volume control. With these, each dog in a

multiple-dog household has his or her own click.

- Some sound-sensitive dogs are nervous about a clicker sound. Look for a softer clicker or use a retractable ballpoint pen as a clicker.

LURING, BRIBING, & REWARDING

There's a difference between luring, bribing, and rewarding a dog: Know which is which

Some people still think that if you use treats to train a dog, he'll "work only for treats." This belief would conceivably be true if your entire relationship were based merely on food and if you used treats alone to motivate a dog with whom you had no other bond. However, most people have a multifaceted relationship with their dogs, and treats are just one

very effective tool in the training toolbox. Dogs don't really want to please us unless doing so also benefits them somehow. They are gloriously selfish beings who do what feels good to them.

Treats are used in three ways. First is a bribe. A bribe is a bargain: "I'll give you this if you do that." You want to bribe a

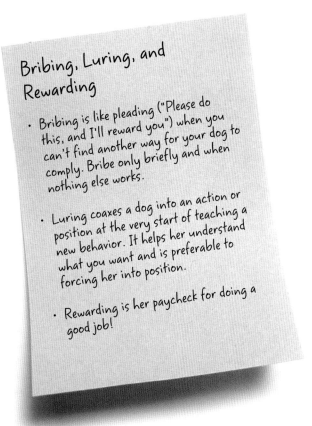

Bribing, Luring, and Rewarding

- Bribing is like pleading ("Please do this, and I'll reward you") when you can't find another way for your dog to comply. Bribe only briefly and when nothing else works.

- Luring coaxes a dog into an action or position at the very start of teaching a new behavior. It helps her understand what you want and is preferable to forcing her into position.

- Rewarding is her paycheck for doing a good job!

Bribing and Luring

- Bribing and luring can help focus a dog who is nervous about performing an unfamiliar or scary skill.

- When she is successful, give tons of praise and make a big deal about how brave and wonderful she is so she is getting approval as well as the promised food.

- Fade bribes and lures as soon as possible so she doesn't become dependent on them. They can be replaced with rewards for successful completion.

dog only infrequently to help him overcome a concern. For instance, a dog who is very nervous about going on the teeter-totter in beginner agility training may be bribed. "If you attempt this scary thing, you'll see it won't hurt you, plus I'll give you a treat."

Second is a lure. A lure is used to direct a dog. When you teach a dog to sit by initially moving a treat over her head until she sits, you are luring her. Both lures and bribes should be quickly extinguished as soon as the dog has overcome a concern or understood the concept.

Rewarding

- When you are paid handsomely for a job, you feel more highly valued and have incentive to perform well in the future to get more pay. Dogs are no different.

- This doesn't mean you get no inherent satisfaction from doing the job well or enjoying it. The promise of a paycheck on completion just makes you work a little harder and a little faster.

- Rewarding a dog for good performance simply gives her greater incentive.

Third is a reward. A reward is given for completion of an action—it's a paycheck. Although a few dogs are happy to work simply for praise, and most will if that is all they get, using treats will make them faster, more willing learners. The combination of click-treat is a powerful tool.

If you have ever watched an agility competition, with dogs racing through the course with incredible intensity and skill, know that every dog was bribed, lured, and rewarded at the beginning of his or her training.

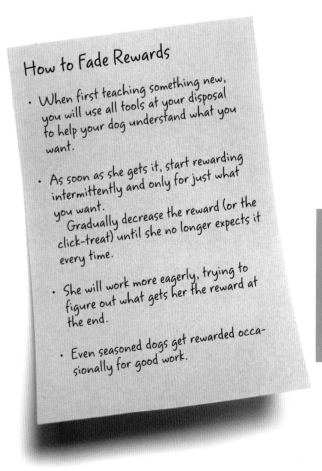

How to Fade Rewards

- When first teaching something new, you will use all tools at your disposal to help your dog understand what you want.

- As soon as she gets it, start rewarding intermittently and only for just what you want.
  Gradually decrease the reward (or the click-treat) until she no longer expects it every time.

- She will work more eagerly, trying to figure out what gets her the reward at the end.

- Even seasoned dogs get rewarded occasionally for good work.

GET WHAT YOU TRAIN FOR

If you don't make instructions perfectly clear, what is your dog really learning?

Good trainers have impeccable timing, and this timing can be learned. It's not simply knowing exactly when to click a specific behavior, although this is important. If you pay attention, you'll learn how to judge how much time your dog needs to comply with your expectation, either unspoken or implied. Puppies or grown dogs learning a new skill will need

time to work out what you want. It's not fair to chastise your dog or to end the training session while she's still trying to figure out the correct action. On the other hand, helping or luring her constantly without giving her the chance to work it out for herself can result in an underconfident dog, too reliant on your direction or food lures. This goes for all types of

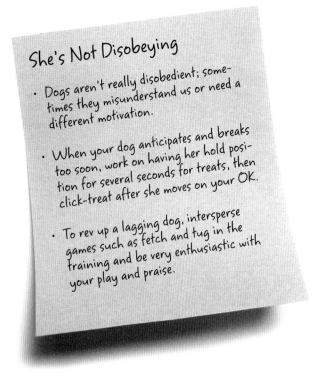

She's Not Disobeying

- Dogs aren't really disobedient; sometimes they misunderstand us or need a different motivation.

- When your dog anticipates and breaks too soon, work on having her hold position for several seconds for treats, then click-treat after she moves on your OK.

- To rev up a lagging dog, intersperse games such as fetch and tug in the training and be very enthusiastic with your play and praise.

Encouragement

- Clicker training works well partly because it encourages a dog to think through her choices to come to the right behavior. She will learn faster and retain new skills better than by rote repetition.

- In trick training, ignore the wrong actions and click-

treat what you want.

- When you do this, your dog won't be inhibited from trying new behaviors. If she's especially innovative, she'll help you come up with brand new tricks.

training, with or without a clicker.

A rule of thumb for a beginner dog might be to allow her about twenty seconds of staring at you blankly after the command "sit" before helping her into position. Even if you help her, click-treat. A dog who is 80 percent reliable on compliance may need about five seconds. An older, accomplished dog should comply within three seconds, or else she gets no reward.

Vary timing on control exercises, too. If you always tell her "stay" and then release and reward her ten seconds later, she will naturally start anticipating your release. If you have a clear release word, such as "OK" or "Break," then no matter what, your dog should stay in position until she hears that word. A smart dog will start anticipating and second guessing you, so beat her to the punch. Don't chastise her for anticipating or for offering a behavior you didn't ask for. As long as she is generally staying attentive to you, ignore the behavior, reposition her if you need to, and start over.

Corrections

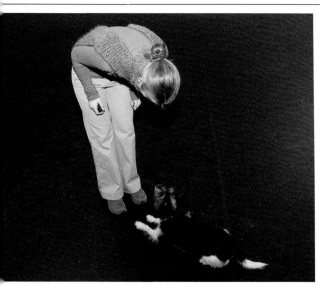

- Compelling and correcting a dog without much praise or reward might make for an obedient dog but also one who is more dependent on her owner for direction.

- Don't physically force your dog to do anything—this is incompatible with clicker training and unnecessary for trick training.

- Soft dogs will lose initiative and be unwilling to try new tricks for fear of correction. This isn't what you want in a dog, especially if you are teaching her tricks!

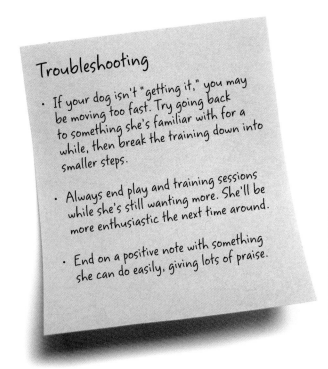

Troubleshooting

- If your dog isn't "getting it," you may be moving too fast. Try going back to something she's familiar with for a while, then break the training down into smaller steps.

- Always end play and training sessions while she's still wanting more. She'll be more enthusiastic the next time around.

- End on a positive note with something she can do easily, giving lots of praise.

TURN YOUR HEAD

A basic clicker exercise can become as cute a trick as you make it

An easy clicker exercise can lead to a really cute trick and takes most dogs very little time to learn. Sit in front of your dog with a handful of treats in one hand and the clicker in the other. At first he will just stare at you, waiting for something to happen. He might try sitting, lying down, or nudging your hand. Say and do nothing. Eventually he will turn his head—click-treat for the smallest of movements. Thereafter,

click and treat only for head movements in that one direction, even tiny ones. This is often achieved in one session—most dogs get this very quickly.

Up the ante. Now don't click unless you get a more exaggerated head turn. Click-treat only for a deliberate turn. After he's doing that reliably, raise your criteria again and wait for a full head turn. Your dog will turn his head just a little, expecting

Concentrate

- If he stares intently at either hand and never turns his head, no matter how long you wait, you have a dog capable of great concentration!

- It's OK at this point to make a move with your shoulders or either hand to make him turn. Remember to click-treat the millisecond you get a head turn.

- Have someone else make a small sound or movement that is enough to make him look around but not enough to make him leave you.

Head Turns

- When you up the ante and require a more deliberate head turn for a treat, your dog will wonder why what was just working—the tiny movement—isn't working now.

- If he were a person trying to get something from a vending machine that had always reliably produced something, he would try different strategies, such as pulling the lever harder.

- He'll do the same thing with head turns, offering you more exaggerated behavior to get you to dispense rewards.

a treat, but suddenly it's not working. He'll then turn his head harder and farther in that direction, trying to get a treat from you. This is exactly what you want to see: a dog who is figuring out what you want and offering the behavior. Click-treat that immediately and now reward only that degree of head turn. At this point you can name the behavior: "Where's your tail?" or "Which way is north?" Be as creative as you want with the command—this can be half the fun.

Easy shaping exercises such as this can be applied to anything your dog might do, such as moving his ears, wagging his tail, sitting, or lying down. It's easy for both of you because you are not forcing him to do anything at all; you are merely shaping a natural behavior and putting it on command.

Associate Cues

Name the behavior when he is turning his head all the way.

When you name the behavior after he is doing the correct behavior, he associates the verbal cue with only the right action, not the ones leading up to it.

- You can build on this. Start asking him to hold the head turn for a few seconds. Then pair the turned-away head with a paw shake or anything else you can think of.

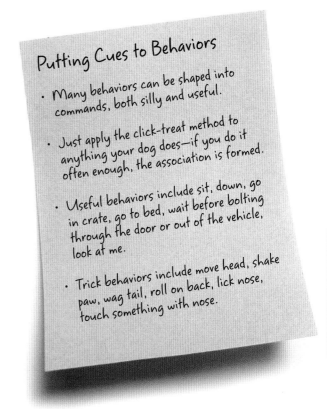

Putting Cues to Behaviors

- Many behaviors can be shaped into commands, both silly and useful.

- Just apply the click-treat method to anything your dog does—if you do it often enough, the association is formed.

- Useful behaviors include sit, down, go in crate, go to bed, wait before bolting through the door or out of the vehicle, look at me.

- Trick behaviors include move head, shake paw, wag tail, roll on back, lick nose, touch something with nose.

ON-LEASH CLICKING
Try a clicker for variety and help your dog with loose leash manners

Clicker training can be used as an occasional strategy for something specific or as an entire system of training. When your dog is having trouble grasping something, it won't hurt to try another tool. Loose leash walking is often frustrating for both owner and dog. Although a clicker might not offer the instant gratification that one sees from a head halter, it is truly a training tool and not a restraint.

Practice somewhere easy and free of distraction, such as your back yard or your home. Arm yourself with a handful of small, soft treats. Put them into a loose pocket or training pouch. Use a 4- or 6-foot leash, never a flexible leash, for teaching this. Hold the leash in one hand and the clicker in the other, prime your dog with a click-treat for attention, and start walking. It takes a little coordination, but it works

Using a Clicker

- You don't have to use a clicker for every stage of leash training. It can be handy as an attention-getting tool and used intermittently to add interest to your walks.

- After your dog realizes that a click means a treat, use it to anticipate situations when he might pull or lunge and get his attention before he focuses on that thing.

- Use a clicker in conjunction with a head halter for a large, strong-willed dog.

Working with the Clicker and Leash

- It can take a little dexterity to hold leash, clicker, and treats. Experiment with what works for you. It's like learning to drive—it gets easier with a little practice.

- Some people have good results looping the leash around their wrist, leaving both hands free. This arrangement can work well with a smaller dog but may be harder to manage with a large dog who pulls.

- Attaching the leash to your belt with a carabiner clip is another option.

well if you can treat him with the leash hand. If he stays with you, reinforce this with a click-treat. If he forges ahead or lags behind, change direction, and as soon as he is within range on a loose leash, click-treat again.

As he gets better at staying with you, reinforce the loose leash walking with random click-treats. Keep his attention by having him sit at curbs. If you walk by something he can safely jump over or up and off, encourage him to do that, too, just for fun. Keep his interest not only with treats but also with interaction and variety.

Formal obedience walking at heel is hard work for a dog and unnecessary for a walk in the park or the neighborhood. For most situations, just walking next to you on a loose leash is an admirable goal. Allow him time to sniff and check "pee mail."

Be Patient

- It might take you several weeks of stopping, turning, clicking, and treating to get past even your own block with a determined dog who has learned to pull. Puppies are much easier!

- Be fair to your dog and don't expect perfect compliance if he's been stuck in the house all day and is raring to go.

- Find a way for an exuberant dog to blow off energy and potty before expecting great attention.

Use Verbal and Physical Cues

- Unless you are training for the show or obedience ring, get your dog used to walking both on your left and right sides. This can be quite practical, especially for city dogs.

- You even can use the words "left" and "right" to teach him the difference. If you do this often enough, there's a pretty impressive trick!

- Vary speed and encourage your dog with verbal cues such as "slow" and "trot." With consistency, he'll learn what these mean as well.

AN ENTHUSIASTIC RECALL

Bet you didn't know that coming when called is actually two different actions

Coming when called is actually two different actions. The dog diverts his attention to you when you call, then he comes to you. The first part—getting his attention—is the most important because that's where the communication often breaks down. Squirrels and smells are just more interesting than you!

Make paying attention to you rewarding. Mealtimes are a good way to do this every day. Wait until your dog is otherwise engaged, then call him to eat. Make a game out of calling him to you for play, for treats, or for praise. When you say his name, and he looks around at you, *immediately* praise him for giving you attention. Then encourage him to come to you

Welcome Stance

- Crouching down and opening your arms in a welcoming stance while calling encourage a dog to come to you quickly.

- Dogs who have ever been reprimanded after being called to you might be hesitant. If your dog understands that coming to you means good things, he'll reliably and willingly obey.

- Training isn't limited to discrete sessions. Day-to-day interaction with your dog determines how attentive and compliant he will be.

Get Excited

- Use his name as well as your "come" command and tell him he's a good boy as he runs toward you.

- Sound happy and excited, as if this is the best possible thing you two could be doing this very minute.

- Don't do too many repetitions of a recall exercise. It's usually counterproductive to bore a dog. Better to quit all sessions with him wanting more play.

- Extra points for having your dog sit immediately after a recall!

so you can give him extra praise.

When calling your dog, adopt a welcoming, relaxed stance. If he doesn't come immediately, turn and run away from him; most dogs will follow.

Never call a dog for something unpleasant such as to reprimand him or clip his toenails—go get him instead. Avoid repeating, "Rover, come; come, Rover, come . . ." until he decides to pay attention. Why? Because you're telling him it's OK to blow you off and come when he decides to. Call your dog only when you're certain he will come (or you can haul him to you on a leash) and always praise him when he gets to you.

As he progresses, a 20–30-foot-long line will be an invaluable tool. Give him the freedom to range to the end of the line on walks and periodically make an enthusiastic game of calling him to you. Use praise, treats, or toys to make coming to you rewarding. Even if you have to tug him to you, praise him all the while. The more often correct behavior is repeated and rewarded, the more it is reinforced.

Ready, Ready

- Having a partner restrain your dog for several seconds while you call the dog builds frustration and drive to get to you quickly.

- Use the phrase "ready, ready" to generate excitement while the dog is being restrained. The "ready, ready" game is useful in many training situations and is perfect for the "come" command.

- For a dog who is ho-hum about coming, make sure he sees that you have food or his favorite toy. Have handy another dog whom he loves? Keep that dog with you while you call Rover.

Mix It Up

- Mix it up. Sometimes offer a treat, other times a game as a reward.

- To teach your dog that coming doesn't always mean the same thing, occasionally wait until he gets to you and stops. Then turn and run away, encouraging him to chase you.

- If you have multiple dogs, have a general "come" command, such as "Puppies!" This can be cute if you have a herd of rottweilers.

PUPPY PUSH-UPS

This fun game quickly teaches your dog "sit," "stand," and "down" from any position

Puppy push-ups is a high-speed game for getting maximum enthusiasm for "sit," "down," and "stand." Use it to teach these commands to a beginner dog or to reinforce what he already knows and get faster compliance.

You're going to start with luring—treats work best for this. If he hasn't learned to sit yet, start slowly by showing him the reward, moving it from his nose along an imaginary line toward his tail and over his head. Say, "Sit!" In a perfect world, his head will follow your hand up, and his butt will hit the floor, at which point he immediately gets the treat. If he backs up, put your hand on his rump so that he sits. Some pups will try jumping for the reward. Make a fist so that the

Sit the Traditional Way

- Most people teach a dog to sit from only two positions: with the dog standing and with the handler either in front of the dog or in the heel position.

- A dog then understands commands such as "Sit" not as positions but rather as actions—in this case lowering his butt into a sitting position.

- The standard way to teach "down" is from a sit. This is inefficient because it inevitably requires two separate commands if he's standing.

Sit with a Clicker

- It is much easier for your dog to understand this if you pair a hand signal with each action.

- A clicker can be used to teach these at first. Remember to click for the right position and fade the clicker use after he understands the commands.

- Start with "sits" and "downs," then add "stand" if you wish. You can also incorporate rollovers, paw shakes, and nose-touches after he's proficient.

50

dog can't get it, keep your hand low enough that he doesn't have to jump for it, and lure him into position.

"Downs" are easy. Show him the treat and quickly move your hand from his nose to the floor. The minute he's completely down, release the treat. If he goes into a bow (you can work on bow later) with his butt in the air, slide the treat along the floor a little until elbows and haunches are all the way down and then reward.

Lure "stand" the same way: by moving the reward in front of his nose until he's standing.

Now put it all together. The more proficient he gets, the faster you can be. Start with sit, down, sit, down. Reward quickly at each position. Add stand and encourage a sit or down from there. Start mixing it up—stand, down, sit, down, sit, stand. Then randomize the treats so he doesn't get one at every position. This increases enthusiasm; he'll work hard for the treat.

Speed and Accuracy

- You are rewarding for speed and accuracy in this game. The better he gets, the stricter your criteria should be. If you always reward for sloppy performance, that's what you'll get.

- Fade treats as your dog becomes good at it and then give them only for the fastest, most accurate actions.

- Don't be too demanding with older or possibly arthritic dogs. Push-ups can be hard for dogs, too. Consider doing this on a soft surface, such as carpet, for senior dogs.

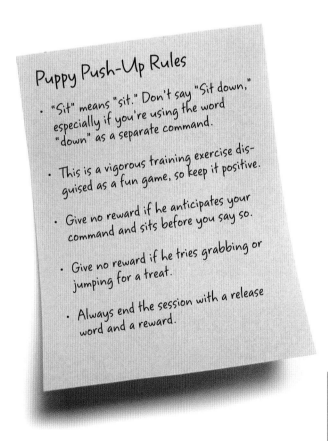

Puppy Push-Up Rules

- "Sit" means "sit." Don't say "Sit down," especially if you're using the word "down" as a separate command.

- This is a vigorous training exercise disguised as a fun game, so keep it positive.

- Give no reward if he anticipates your command and sits before you say so.

- Give no reward if he tries grabbing or jumping for a treat.

- Always end the session with a release word and a reward.

STAY & WAIT
There's a big difference between "stay" and "wait"; teach it for advanced training

After your dog has mastered "sits" and "downs," the "stay" command can be added to help him increase self-control. It's important to remember to always gave a clear release word for him so he knows when to stop staying and to work up to longer stays around distractions very gradually.

Position your dog, put the palm of your hand in front of his face, and tell him to stay. If he is very bouncy, keep your hand in place, wait a second or two, and tell him, "OK!" "Break!" or any release word you choose—just always use the same word. Make your release word very emphatic. Use lots of praise and treats if you wish. Repeat the exercise until he'll stay in position as you lower your hand. If he moves, simply

Start Position

- Start out by using a leash on your dog, so you can give a gentle tug or restrain him if he decides to wander off.

- Be sure to reward him only after you give the release command. Don't reward him for anticipating you and starting to get up

  before you give permission.

- Use a calm voice and demeanor when teaching stay. Flapping around or sounding excited when you want your dog to be still gives him mixed signals.

Next Steps

- After he is steady, start slowly stepping away from or around him.

- Most dogs will start to get up as soon as you take a step. Encourage him to stay in one place and give him lots of praise when he does.

- Work up to being able to walk slowly behind him and to the end of the leash and back and to moving more quickly around him while he stays.

reposition him and repeat the exercise. Always end on a successful execution of a stay.

As with any training exercise, short sessions are most effective. Using TV commercial breaks is a handy strategy. Slowly work on increasing the time until he can stay in place for thirty seconds. Start adding some movement. Step back and forth, walk slowly around him. Work up to moving all the way across the room.

Add distractions slowly. Toss a toy or a treat. Have someone else run past him. As he gets more solid, proof him by saying words other than your emphatic release word—he should stay until he hears that. Take him outside and practice stays. Put him on leash, go to the park, and practice. A long line will come in very handy to work distance safely. If he seems to be having trouble, he is telling you to slow down and keep the difficulty at a level he can handle for a little longer. Set him up to succeed.

Stay

- "Stay" is a useful skill for a controlled canine.

- It's handy for visits to the groomer or vet. Your dog stays while you attach a leash and waits instead of bolting out of the door.

- On longer stays, reinforce the duration by telling him,

"Good stay" and giving him a treat. Rewarding the position as well as the release rewards him for staying in place.

- It's more comfortable for him to lie down for longer stays.

Distractions

- Add distractions such as tossing a toy in front of him or having someone run past. This is called "proofing," and your goal should be for him to stay put in almost any environment.

- Practice short, out-of-sight stays with a helper who can correct your dog if

he breaks his stay in your absence.

- Use play as well as treats—a thrown ball or game of tug—as a reward for a successful stay.

NO-PULL LEASH MANNERS

One of the most common training complaints is a dog who pulls on the leash

It takes practice and patience to teach leash manners. We are asking our dogs to walk unnaturally slowly at our pace, to ignore tantalizing odors and other dogs, and to curb their enthusiasm when they want to run. Pulling on a leash is perfectly natural, and, like people, dogs will resist if pushed or pulled. Often dogs learn to pull because it works—they realize that we follow them when they do.

The plan of action is two-pronged. First, make it unproductive for the dog to pull by stopping and turning each time he pulls. Second, make yourself as interesting as all those other exciting sights and smells. Decide whether you want your dog simply not to pull or to heel with obedience-style

Beginning the Walk

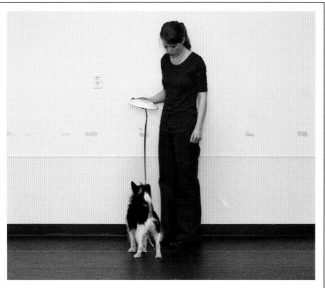

- At the beginning of every walk, make sure he doesn't need to go potty. It will be difficult for him to focus on following you if he really needs to go.

- It's easier if he's had a chance to run a bit and go potty before getting down to work.

- Avoid constant jerking, pulling, and saying, "No!" If this worked, no dog would ever pull! We have to outsmart our dogs with our bigger brains.

Leash Tension

- If you expect him to sit automatically when you stop, be fair and give him warning by slowing down for a few steps first and then stopping.

- Be a tree the moment there's leash tension, then praise and move on when he looks back at you. For some soft dogs, this is enough to dissuade them from pulling.

- If you're consistent he'll come to understand that pulling gets him nowhere but that following you lets him keep moving.

54

precision. For the informal walk, simply not pulling is a realistic goal.

Puppies should be walked on plain collars. Older and more exuberant dogs may benefit from a training collar. Every time the dog puts tension on the leash, stop immediately. The moment the leash slackens, change directions.

Be absolutely consistent. You're teaching the dog that pulling will not get him anywhere and that he has to pay attention to you or else be abruptly turned around. It may take you thirty minutes to get a block from your house, but that's OK! Vary walking speed and praise him when he is not pulling. It's difficult for a dog to learn this. Start in low-distraction environments and work up to busier environments.

Carry treats and make yourself interesting. Keep his attention by practicing sits at curbs and random, enthusiastic recalls. Walking him before mealtime when he's hungry is a useful strategy. If something utterly distracts your dog, don't get frustrated. Simply walk him away from the distraction and praise him when he finally does pay attention. Be consistent and patient, and he'll get it.

Change Directions

- Simply stopping doesn't override the urge to pull for many dogs. This is where doing fast turns every time your dog pulls comes in.

- Don't say anything. Just abruptly change directions and praise when he catches back up to you.

- Timing is everything, so try to anticipate distractions and get his attention before he sees the distraction. After he is in chase or lunge mode, it will be almost impossible to get his attention.

Head Halters

- A head halter is helpful for larger dogs. However, if you rely on it for life, you're not training your dog; you are just controlling him.

- The goal is to use a halter or training collar as a tool to teach him. As he learns, it's faded out, just as you fade out using treats.

- Don't use a leash longer than 6 feet with a head halter and never use a retractable leash with one.

TUG GAMES
Use these simple games to teach a wide variety of commands

Despite what you might have read, tug is an excellent way to teach several commands. As long as you structure and control the game, it won't make your dog "think he's dominant." Quite the opposite, in fact. Many working breeds and terriers in particular love tug games. As long as you're being the leader and setting the rules, oppositional games such as this can really channel obedience.

Use a fast game of tug as reward for stay, wait, or come. For an enthusiastic recall, call your dog and run in the opposite direction holding the tug toy. You want her to race after you and hit the tug at 30 miles an hour. Treats are strong motivators, but sometimes toys and play increase speed, as well as adding another layer of interaction and bonding with your dog.

Why Tug Games Are Important

- Underconfident dogs might find this game stressful, but it's excellent for increasing confidence and bonding. Use lots of encouragement and let her get the toy away from you sometimes.

- Avoid looming over her or staring while pulling because dogs can perceive this posture as threatening.

- Dogs who were isolated as puppies may have to be taught how to play.

- Playing, and training through play, is an excellent way to teach social skills and basic manners.

Dog Behavior

- Some dogs growl fiercely while playing tug. Understand the difference between play-growling and a challenge. Play-growling can sound scary, but she'll also be wiggling her body, jerking the toy, and will release it to you.

- A challenging dog will have a tense, still body and a hard stare and will not release the tug. If you're in doubt, consult a good trainer.

- Tug games can be valuable with a dominant dog but only if you have her respect first.

Teach her to take something on command by saying, "Take it" and offering the tug. Work on "drop" by encouraging her to tug. Then stop tugging, be still, and give the "drop" or "out" command in a low, growly voice. If this doesn't work, pry her jaws away from the tug and praise the moment the toy is free. Her reward? She gets the toy right back. This makes giving something up rewarding and part of the game.

•••••••••••••••••• RED ● LIGHT ••••••••••••••
Don't let young children play tug games, especially with a high-drive or dominant dog. The key to the effectiveness of this game is the owner being the leader and controlling it. Young children won't have the ability to control it, and some dogs see children as equals, not leaders.

Positive Rewards

Tug Rules

• The owner is always the one who initiates and ends the game. The dog must release the toy on command.

• Don't have her release only to end the game. Sometimes her reward is getting the toy back. Use it for a highly motivated dog to build speed in exercises such as coming when called.

• Children, or anyone your dog isn't sure of, should never play tug games because they're too potentially challenging.

• Playing tug is a positive way to teach a dog to release something. Her reward is resumption of play or the occasional treat.

• Stop play before asking her to release something. Doing this gives her a heads-up that you're expecting her to let go.

• Put your hand over her muzzle and squeeze gently near her back teeth. When she opens her mouth, take the toy and immediately reward or praise her.

LONG-DISTANCE LEARNING
Encourage your dog to obey commands when you're nowhere near him

Most training is done within the range of a 6-foot leash. Naturally dogs get good at complying when they are right next to you. Let your dog get 10 feet away, and the compliance rate drops. She is not being disobedient—she is merely doing precisely what you taught her to do! Dogs learn by patterning and repetition. If you've always trained at arm's length,

acting like a treat dispenser, she may simply not understand that "sit" when she is right next to you and about to get a treat is the same command as "sit" when she is out of reach. She may walk over and sit next to you when given a command from a distance because this is what you've trained her to do.

Practice

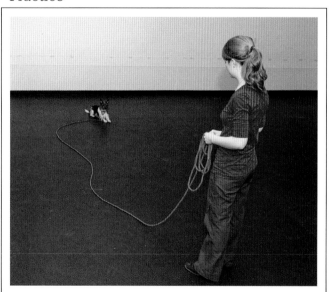

- A learning dog who might think that she doesn't have to sit or lie down when commanded from a distance can be reminded with a quick tug.

- Attach the long line to a harness instead of a collar. This way the dog can differentiate between a collar

tug, which she may assume means to come, and a harness tug as a reminder to comply.

- Practice while you're close to her and gradually build distance.

Leashes

- It's OK to let a dog trail a long leash, but you don't want her racing off and having the leash snag on something and jerking her or tangling around a leg.

- Similarly, don't let her swim while wearing a leash. It can easily catch on something submerged.

- If using a long line for rural walks, consider clipping it to a harness instead of a collar. It's less likely to get tangled between her legs this way.

Build her distance confidence in small steps. If she's sitting reliably right in front of you or in heel position, she's ready. While she's standing, move a few feet away from her and tell her to sit. Good aim helps here because you can toss her a treat when she does. If she plays fetch, have her sit and as a reward toss the toy away from you in random directions. This makes it a game and keeps her attentive. Increase distance over time.

More Leashes

Body Language

- Dogs tend to pull less on a long line, although you have less control. Don't use one until your dog has the basics of leash manners.

- Retractable leashes are handy but not great for training. The constant slight tension and the variable distance at which the dog gets corrected or tugged don't send clear signals.

- A long line is a great way to remind your dog that distance from you is not an impediment to training.

- Your tone of voice and body language are different when your dog is at a distance, and her view of you is also different. Add a consistent hand signal for increased clarity.

- Remember to praise her from a distance, too. Throw treats if you can.

- Enthusiastic praise might make her think she's done and can come over to you. Mute your enthusiasm so she learns to stay put and accept it from a distance.

THE BASICS

SHAKE HANDS
This universal cute dog trick is so easy that some dogs barely need to be trained

Some dogs naturally offer a paw—often submissive and very compliant dogs do this. If so, you're ahead of the game! Put a command and praise to it, and you have a diplomat dog.

Most dogs need a little encouragement. Small and lighter dogs can easily lift a paw while standing up. Large and bulky dogs don't find that so easy. A dog carries the majority of

his weight on his front legs, and bulkier dogs will feel a bit unsteady on one front leg. So this is usually easiest if taught from a sit position.

Have your dog sit, pick up one paw while saying, "Shake," and praise lavishly. Do this a few times, then see if he will raise his paw on command. This is all the encouragement

Raised Paw

- Sometimes a paw raise is offered naturally as a submissive gesture, possibly as a prelude to rolling over.

- A raised paw in another context is in preparation for stalking and getting ready to leap. Cats do this as well. You'll generally see this

while the dog is standing and focusing on something he's thinking about chasing.

- Look at context to see why your dog might naturally raise a paw. If he's the submissive type, training should be gentle and firm with lots of reinforcement.

Encouragement

- Most dogs will lift a paw if you tickle. If your dog firmly plants his feet, raise the paw an inch and praise him just as if he did that of his own volition.

- Another way to encourage him is by moving his whole

leg forward and up from just below the elbow and sliding your hand down to his paw.

- Always try both paws because dogs can be right- or left-"handed" just like people.

many dogs need. (Notice that this method is back-chaining by teaching the end behavior—paw in hand—first.)

He may need more help. Touch the back of his paw. Dogs are ticklish here, and he'll reflexively move his foot up. Quickly reward this. Do between three and ten repetitions per session. Three reps cement behavior; more than ten can get boring. You can also start randomly requesting a paw shake any time he sits for a meal or a treat.

ZOOM

Like people, dogs are naturally right- or left-"handed." If your dog won't offer one paw with touch or encouragement, try the other. If you're teaching this to an older dog, consider that he might be a little stiff in his front legs. Don't force it if you suspect it's uncomfortable.

Body Signs

- Avoid closing your hand around his paw—most dogs dislike this, and it will turn a simple paw shake into an unpleasant exercise.

- Hold your hand flat and give him a treat the moment his paw is in your hand.

- With practice, this can be generalized to the rear paws as well.

- If he's the easygoing sort, raising a paw on command can be useful for nail trimming or paw wiping.

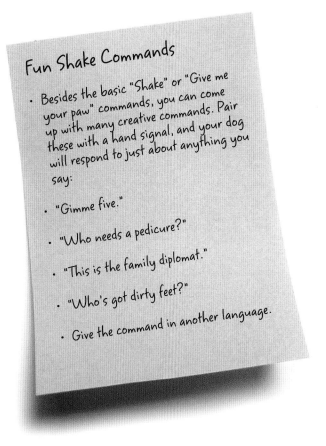

Fun Shake Commands

- Besides the basic "Shake" or "Give me your paw" commands, you can come up with many creative commands. Pair these with a hand signal, and your dog will respond to just about anything you say:

  - "Gimme five."

  - "Who needs a pedicure?"

  - "This is the family diplomat."

  - "Who's got dirty feet?"

  - Give the command in another language.

FETCH!

This is a fun game for high-octane retrievers and the basis for many a cute trick

Retrievers retrieve, but most dogs enjoy chasing and fetching for you. This is a form of prey behavior play. In retrievers, it has been softened through training and selective breeding. A Labrador who shreds the duck instead of bringing it back unshredded isn't helping put roast duck on the table.

Terriers, with their vermin-killing heritage, are often more enthusiastic, biting and shaking a thrown toy. And some dogs simply never see the point in retrieving, figuring that if you threw it away, you must not want it! As with any trick training, if your dog simply doesn't get the point of something, no matter what, find something else for him to do.

Fetching can be a boon on cold days because a dog can

Aids

- Several types of ball-throwing aids are available to make fetching easier for you and allow you to throw the ball farther.

- A tennis racquet, golf club, or baseball bat works well, too, and you can practice your swing at the same time.

- A baseball or tennis ball can be whacked a good distance with a golf club.

- Be careful not to smack your dog in the head when using a club or bat!

Appropriate Items to Throw

- Make sure you are throwing a ball that is big enough that your dog can't choke. He shouldn't be able to completely close his mouth around the ball.

- A golf ball would be too small for all but the tiniest of dogs.

- Frisbees, sticks, plastic drink bottles filled with sand, and even large pieces of knotted rope are good alternatives to the standard tennis ball. Your dog won't care if it's an expensive dog toy or just whatever is handy.

be exercised by chasing something around the house. Some dogs are ball obsessed, others like something furry or squeaky. Because this is prey behavior, a toy that feels and sounds like a hapless prey animal can be very attractive. Some dogs will fetch a rolled-up ball of paper, others will go after only something that has a squeaker or a soft, furry feel. Experiment to find out what really gets your dog excited. When you find that thing, reserve it for special playtime and training.

MAKE IT EASY

Because this is prey behavior, anything you can do to make the toy act like an animal will rev your dog up. Pretend he's a cat and make the toy act in jerky movements. Tie it to a string and drag it. Cat toys can be great fun for tiny dogs.

Rainy Day Activities

- Fetch is a good indoor rainy day activity, and your dog doesn't even need to know any formal tricks yet.

- If she is fit, throw a toy up and down a flight of stairs for her. This isn't a good idea on slippery wooden stairs because a dog at speed can slip too easily.

- Use soft toys for inside throwing.

- Try throwing toys straight up for her to fetch midair. This is great rear leg and glute exercise.

Retrieving

- Some dogs are natural retrievers. Others will love it after they're taught the game, and some will simply never retrieve.

- To teach your dog the game, use a long leash. Throw the toy. When she has it in her mouth, call her and run backward, bringing her to you. Reward and repeat until she's enjoying herself.

- If she absolutely refuses to even chase it, no matter what you do, accept that she's not retriever material and find another game to play!

ROLL OVER
Get creative with commands, and this is another easy, impressive trick

Roll over is easy to teach to a dog who willingly rolls onto her back for belly rubs. First decide if you want your dog to lie on her back or to roll completely over from one side to the other. It's easier for many dogs to just roll onto their backs. Remember that you get what you train for, so reward only the behavior and position you want.

Start with your dog lying on her side. Hold a treat by her ear and move it slowly over her shoulders so she has to turn and roll to get it. Chances are that she'll try to get up. Put your hand on her ribcage to prevent this and make sure you keep the treat right by her nose as she rolls. The moment she's in the position you want, praise and treat.

Calming an Apprehensive Dog

- For a dog who seems apprehensive, spend some time letting her lie there while you stroke her flanks. Encourage her to roll onto her back for a belly rub but don't force this if she seems nervous.

- Treats are a good idea while she is lying quietly. No treats for being up, just for lying down.

- The same strategy is excellent for an insecure dog who doesn't like being in a "submissive" position.

Hand Signals

- Teaching a rollover hand signal allows you to make up all sorts of commands for rolling over—your dog will pay more attention to the hand signal than to your words.

- Drawing a large circle in the air is easy for her to understand because it mimics the signals you made when you were first luring her over.

- With practice, you can have her roll over to the left or right on your hand signal.

Give her several treats in succession while she's in position. This is important. You want her to think that at this moment in time, being on her back is the very best place she can be. It also reinforces the command as both an action (rolling) and a position (or her back or side after having rolled over). Give her your release word and let her up but don't give her a treat after she's up because she'll be tempted to roll over, then immediately get back up for a treat.

A very submissive dog might be nervous being coerced onto her back. Look for a tucked tail, avoidance of eye contact, and flattened ears. This position is stressing her and either should be approached slowly with tons of encouragement or not at all. Some wanna-be dominant dogs will find this a vulnerable position and will resist. It's a good exercise for these dogs. Don't force; again, just use tons of encouragement.

Embellishing the Trick

- Embellish this trick with multiple rollovers. She has to roll all the way over into the down position and then roll over again.

- After she's rolled over once successfully, don't reward her. Ask her to roll over again —if she didn't get rewarded the first time,

she'll try hard to get it the second time.

- Alternately, you can ask her to roll back and forth. Give lots of belly rubs and remember that she can't eat treats while she's upside down!

Kids and Tricks

- Rolling over is a very good trick to introduce your dog to children with, especially if she's large. It's a non-threatening position, and what dog refuses a belly rub?

- A well-mannered, child-friendly dog will roll over for anyone, even a small child.

Kids get a kick out of a dog doing what they tell her.

- Don't forget to warn people that she's likely to snort and sneeze—being upside down can make a dog sneeze rather explosively.

LEAP TALL BUILDINGS

From hopping over a broomstick to leaping through a fiery hoop, trick jumping is fun

Your dog doesn't have to be a ribbon-winning canine athlete to learn some jumping tricks. Whether you have a large house and a small dog or a small apartment and a large dog, there's room for some jumps.

Start with a low jump. Perhaps a rolled-up rug, a broomstick or mop propped on a few books, or shoes lined up in a row.

Unless your dog is a natural jumper, have him on leash and step over with him to start out. Give big praise each time he goes over, even with your help. Toss a treat over the jump. This encourages him to watch where he's going instead of watching you and to arch his body and keep his head down as he goes over.

Encouragement

- If your dog is accustomed to walking with you or walking by your side, he'll tend to want to follow your direction.

- Face the way your dog will jump, say, "Jump," and toss a toy or treat over the object.

Step forward with him to get him going.

- Get him excited about the toy or treat by waggling it around and teasing him with it for a few seconds, then toss it over the jump as you step forward.

Start Small

- Teach easy jumps before you teach your dog to go through a hoop. Dogs can get spooked by jumping through things or over things that move.

- Have a partner hold the hoop or hold it yourself

or wedge it so it won't fall when your dog jumps through it.

- Start by resting the bottom of the hoop on the ground and encourage your dog to step through. Slowly increase height and speed.

66

If he tries running around the jump, set it up in a doorway or hall so he has no choice. Or have a partner hold him while you call him, and the dog gets rewarded only for jumping. Some dogs will be nervous about the concept (please make sure you've ruled out physical limitations first) and need to start really easy. Lay something flat on the ground so all he has to do is step over it and make a big deal when he does.

•••••••••••••••• RED ● LIGHT ••••••••••••••

Safety first. A healthy adult dog should be able to jump to her elbow height, but work up to that unless she's very fit. Keep jumps to ankle or knee height for puppies and overweight dogs and avoid repeated jumping. Jump your dog only on carpet or grass, never on slick flooring.

Jumping Styles

- Dogs have different jumping styles. Some will naturally arc their bodies over the jump and are good at not knocking it with their feet.

- Others will frequently mistime the jump, knocking it with front or rear feet, and not arc their bodies.

- To encourage a good jumping style, throw treats or a toy reasonably close to the other side of the jump so your dog arcs and reward her only when she clears it without touching.

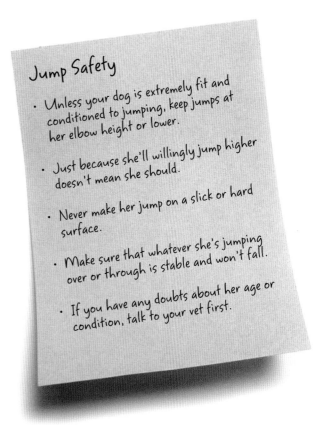

Jump Safety

- Unless your dog is extremely fit and conditioned to jumping, keep jumps at her elbow height or lower.

- Just because she'll willingly jump higher doesn't mean she should.

- Never make her jump on a slick or hard surface.

- Make sure that whatever she's jumping over or through is stable and won't fall.

- If you have any doubts about her age or condition, talk to your vet first.

SPIN AROUND
Teach your dog to spin around, chase his tail, or learn a fancy dance move

Spin is a silly, flashy little trick that can be used to liven up leash walking or refined for canine freestyle dancing. (*Nips* is *spin* spelled backward—bonus points if you can teach your dog to differentiate the two.)

Start by luring your dog into a spin. Hold the treat in front of his nose and have him follow it around in a tight circle while you tell him, "Spin," letting him have the treat on successful completion.

Do this three times and then reverse direction with your "nips" command. Just as dogs have a preference for which paw they'll raise for you, many will more naturally spin in one direction. If you really want to make this a bidirectional trick,

Starting the Trick

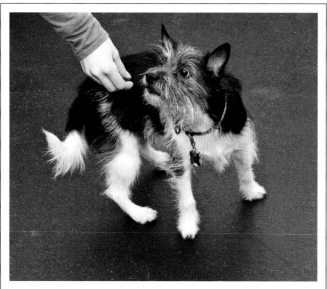

- Lure your dog in as tight a circle as he can manage, so that he is almost pirouetting. Long-bodied dogs will need to turn in a wider circle—experiment to see what's comfortable for him.

- You'll find a target stick invaluable for teaching small dogs to spin.

- There's no need to have him sit first to do this. It's probably easier taught while he's standing in front of or beside you.

Body Signs

- Pointing downward and making a circling motion mimics the luring you did when first teaching this and will be the easiest hand signal for him to understand.

- Start with an exaggerated hand signal, then gradually make the circle smaller. Pair it with a verbal cue, then fade that out.

- Over time, you should be able to make a little movement with one finger and have him spin without anyone knowing you're signaling him.

train and reward his more difficult direction more. He'll gain muscle memory and reinforcement from repeated rewards for this, and it's good physical conditioning, too. Don't do too many fast repetitions because he'll get dizzy.

Fade the lure quickly by drawing a circle in the air with your finger for him to follow around and rewarding every second or third time. Over time, you can fade out the verbal command and just give him the circular hand motion. A dog who can follow silent hand signals really impresses people!

MAKE IT EASY

Keep the treat low enough for him to follow with his head level to the ground or even slightly lowered instead of looking upward. It's easier for him to follow and will lessen the chance that he'll try jumping or stretching up for the treat at the same time as he spins.

Embellishing the Trick

- Then teach your dog to spin around something such as a cane or umbrella.

- Teach it just as you did the original spin. You'll probably need to go back to square one with luring for several sessions until he gets used to the new paradigm.

- Practice with different items for him to spin around so that this becomes a versatile trick.

- Now see if you can teach him to spin around your leg. The possibilities are endless!

Spin Commands

- As with any trick, part of the fun is coming up with cool commands:

- "Spin"

- "Nips"

- "Twirl, twirl back"

- "Pirouette"

- "Whirl, whirlybird"

- "Make yourself dizzy"

THROUGH THE LEGS
Walking between your legs is an easy trick, and most dogs think it is great fun

Walking between your legs is another easy trick that has no practical application, but it adds to your talented dog's repertoire and can be incorporated into many fancier moves. Unless you have a wolfhound or other extremely tall dog, start by teaching her to walk between your legs. The easiest way is to stand in a doorway with her behind you and give a command such as "through" while encouraging her to walk between your legs. As with any trick, never pull or force her.

Build on this trick by having her walk forward and even backward while between your legs. Use treats to keep her in position. Begin by going just a few steps forward and praise her for staying with you. As she gets more comfortable, start

Starting the Trick

- Start by luring her through your legs—use a target stick for little dogs.

- Some dogs find this a little weird at first. Try standing in a doorway with your back to her and her entire food bowl in your hand.

- Make sure she's ready for a meal and has just watched you fill the bowl.

- Have someone else hold her while you call. Play the "ready, ready" game to get her excited to run through your legs for dinner.

Embellishing the Trick

- A variation of this trick is to have her sit stay, walk away from her, and then call her to run through your legs.

- Or walk back and forth, rewarding her for staying with you. Just a few steps in either direction is quite an accomplishment.

- Line up several people and teach her to run through a "tunnel" of legs.

- Get really fancy and teach her to go through so that her head is behind you, then walk backward with her.

varying your speed. Remember to give her ample warning before accelerating or decelerating by adjusting your pace for a couple of steps.

Walking backward is unnatural for a dog. Hold the treat a little below her chin, rewarding for each step at first. Make sure your own path is straight by working along a wall. You will find that your dog's hind end won't be in synch with her front end and that she'll quickly veer to one side. Go slowly and reward only for steps straight back.

MAKE IT EASY

Bending over to reward a little dog can be awkward. Try a target stick with a little squeezy cheese or peanut butter on the end to direct your dog. Keep it level with her head instead of bobbing it around or making her have to reach or jump for it.

More Embellishments

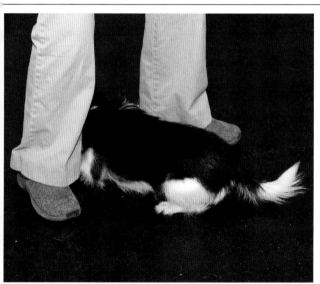

- Another variation: Sit down and bend one leg to make a bridge, then teach her to go under your bent leg. Lure her the same way you did when standing and sit across a doorway if she keeps trying to go around.

- Small dogs can simply trot through, but bigger dogs will need to learn to crawl.

- Paired with rolling over or playing dead, crawling can make for quite an impressive routine.

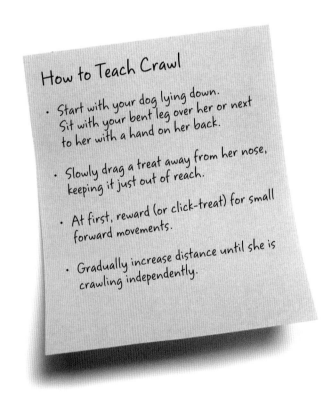

How to Teach Crawl

- Start with your dog lying down. Sit with your bent leg over her or next to her with a hand on her back.

- Slowly drag a treat away from her nose, keeping it just out of reach.

- At first, reward (or click-treat) for small forward movements.

- Gradually increase distance until she is crawling independently.

CONTROL MEANS BETTER MANNERS
Patience is not a natural dog trait, but controlled canines are easier to live with

Self-control does not often come naturally to dogs. They operate from their instinctive brain and have to modify their behavior tremendously in order to live with humans. A dog who has free run of a farm or who travels in a pack of village dogs lives a life with more natural structure and often a more enriched environment than does the city or suburban family dog.

Our dogs are often crated or alone during the day. When the family comes home, they're out and around but often not exercised beyond a trip to the back yard. With few outlets for mental and physical energy, an exuberant young dog can become uncontrollable. If he charges the door when you open it, he isn't "exerting dominance" as some people think.

The Importance of Self-Control

- Your dog doesn't control just himself; he learns to control his environment.

- When he learns to calm down, he gets more of what he wants from you.

- Controlled dogs are easier to live with.

- They get to go to more places because they're not wild and hyper.

Giving Your Dog Attention

- Dogs live in the moment and do what feels good without much regard for anyone else.

- They jump up onto people because doing so gets them attention. Negative attention, such as being yelled at, being smacked, and being pulling away, is still attention. Dogs don't like being ignored.

- By giving your dog attention when he does what you want—keep all four paws on the floor—and ignoring him when he does jump, you are teaching him self-control.

He's just being extremely excited.

When he's overexcited, his brain is simply not receptive to commands. Many people give up and don't take their dog to classes or anywhere beyond the house and yard because he's "too wild." The dog may live his whole life understimulated and underexercised, with nobody realizing his potential. If he is unlucky, he gets relinquished to the pound.

A self-controlled canine actually learns to control not only himself but also his environment. He has more freedom because he's well mannered.

Use mealtimes as a daily exercise to help teach a dog control by having him sit calmly before getting fed. When training an excitable dog, be calm and relaxed. If you're stressed or frustrated with him, he'll pick up on this emotion. Allow him ample physical exercise. Work basic obedience and attention exercises every day. Even a few minutes a day will help. Take him to obedience classes—good classes are a perfect place to get control of a wild pup, and you won't be alone.

Leash Walking

- Leash walking is another hard skill for dogs to learn. What they want is to rush forward or wander back and forth as they walk, investigating smells.

- Because they are so often successful at pulling their owners down the street, they'll keep doing it.

- After they learn that pulling doesn't get them anywhere, they stop. This is easier to say than to put into practice, but every dog in the world will learn with consistency and patience.

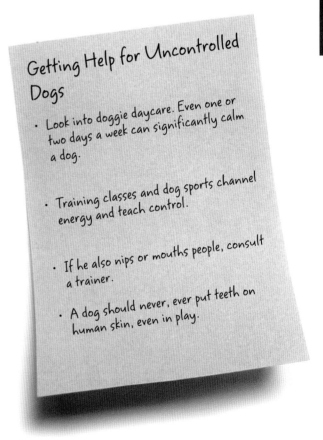

Getting Help for Uncontrolled Dogs

- Look into doggie daycare. Even one or two days a week can significantly calm a dog.

- Training classes and dog sports channel energy and teach control.

- If he also nips or mouths people, consult a trainer.

- A dog should never, ever put teeth on human skin, even in play.

WAIT & RELEASE
Make a daily game of playing wait and release on command with meals, treats, and toys

Keep this in mind: Your dog doesn't own toys, a bed, or food. You own his resources and choose to give them to him. You can and should be a bit of a control freak and ask him to work for everything he gets from you. Dogs like to work because a job well done gives them great satisfaction. By integrating small exercises into your daily interactions, basic manners isn't something you have to make time for.

After your dog has mastered sits and downs, the "stay" command can be added to help him increase self-control. It's important to remember to always give a clear release word for him so that he knows when to stop staying and to work up to longer stays around distractions very gradually.

Mealtimes and Control

- Use mealtimes as a daily opportunity to teach control but work up to it gradually.

- Before requiring your dog to sit briefly until you release him to eat, he has to understand the concept of sitting and staying at least for several seconds.

- It's not fair to ask him to do something he doesn't understand before he's allowed to eat. Make sure you've practiced this exercise with lesser-value rewards first, such as little treats or toys.

Incorporate Play

- Incorporate play. If he likes to fetch or tug, randomly request a brief stay before releasing him to grab or chase. This teaches him that calming down gets him what he wants—resumption of the game.

- Don't expect a twenty second-long stay at first.

Just a couple of seconds of waiting before you release him is a great start.

- Practice with sits, downs, and stand-stays. He might find one position easier than others to hold.

Mealtimes give you two daily opportunities to practice. Make him sit or down-stay for his meal. Increase difficulty until you can put his food down, walk away, and then release him to his food. You don't have to do this for every meal, of course. But training a dog to this level is a good exercise and guarantees polite mealtime manners. If he jumps, lunges, or tries to get food from your hand, don't reprimand him. Simply put the food away and try again later. Being unruly should never be rewarded. For most dogs, meals are a powerful motivator, so use them to teach manners.

Do the same with treats, toys, and even petting. He is learning that being self-controlled and calm gets him what he wants and that unruly behavior doesn't. Additionally, if he is conditioned to sit for petting and treats, he will be easier to control around guests. Have everyone in the family request good behavior for resources so that the dog is secure in his place and mannerly with everyone.

Practice "Stay"

- Work the "stay" command briefly and in random locations. After your dog is solid on short stays in your house, it's time to test his skills out in public.

- It will be a lot harder for him around distractions. Reward for several seconds of staying put, if that's all he's capable of outside.

- Pet stores that allow dogs are excellent places to practice. (It's probably polite to buy something in return for using their space.)

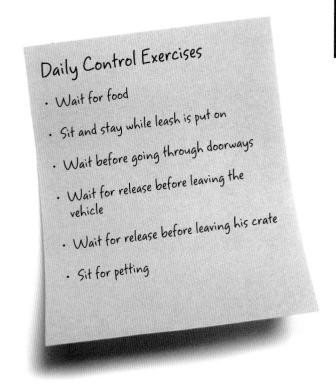

Daily Control Exercises

- Wait for food
- Sit and stay while leash is put on
- Wait before going through doorways
- Wait for release before leaving the vehicle
- Wait for release before leaving his crate
- Sit for petting

TEACHING "LEAVE IT"
Ignoring dropped goodies is a important skill and can even save your dog's life

Many dogs have great focus, but it's not so great when they zero in on leftover barbecue food in the park or something gross on the sidewalk. "Leave it" means "turn your attention away from that icky thing right this minute."

As always, start slowly in a quiet, low-distraction environment such as your living room. Have treats in your hand and

your dog on leash. Throw an object—toy, sock, whatever—ahead of you but out of her reach. She'll be curious, so get her attention and start walking toward the forbidden object. As she starts to veer toward it, tell her to leave it. Praise her the moment she shifts attention back to you. Use a clicker for this, click-treating the second she shifts attention away.

Testing the Dog

- Walk your dog past the forbidden item on leash at first, rewarding or click-treating for any shift of attention to you.

- If you have taught her any other simple behaviors, such as a nose touch or sit, have her do that for a reward as soon as she shifts attention back.

- Sometimes it's easier to tell a dog to do something than to simply not to do something and to offer her an alternate behavior.

Practice Makes Perfect

- If you've perfected the art of spitting treats at your dog, this is an excellent exercise to practice that skill.

- Also try simply dropping the item onto the floor while telling her to leave it.

- If she tries to get it, cover it with your foot, tell her again to leave it, and reward for attention.

- Always start with less-tempting objects, such as a crumpled piece of paper, and work up to more-tempting objects.

Escalate the difficulty level over time by incorporating this exercise on walks and using higher-value objects such as food or multiple objects. If she is persistent about going after food after you've dropped it, cover it with your foot and give her a great treat when she shifts attention to you, even if you have to use the leash to stop her from getting it.

It's important to never let her have the forbidden object as a reward. Otherwise, she will quite naturally think that her reward for ignoring it for a little while is getting to pick it up. You want a shift in attention back to you, not to the forbidden object. Pick it up and put it away after training.

When she understands the concept of "leave it," you can use it for almost anything, including her wanting to rush toward another dog, chase the cat, or jump onto a guest. When the distraction is very enticing, have an alternate behavior or good reward for her.

Focus on the Objective

Things You Want Her to Leave

- Gross things such as discarded hankies
- Chicken bones
- Edible trash on the ground
- Yucky (and possibly dangerous) puddles
- Dropped medications or pill bottles
- Animal poop

- Keep the final objective of this skill in mind: You want her to ignore something on the ground on command, whether on leash or off. It could save her life.

- Carry something with you during on-leash walks and toss it ahead of you. Praise her when she leaves it on command.

- This command is versatile and can be used for dropped items as well as cats, squirrels, and even other dogs.

"DROP IT"

Polite dogs always release items in their mouths on command; here's how to teach it

Dogs don't always know what's good for them. A dropped pill bottle or a cooked chicken bone can be snatched up in a second, and you want your dog to drop dangerous items on command. Use a little sneaky bribery and play to teach your dog to give up whatever is in her mouth instantly.

Encourage your dog to take a toy or chewie into her mouth.

Grab one end and hold a fragrant treat in front of her while giving your "drop it" command. The moment she releases the item to take the treat, praise and reward. Enthusiastically return the item, telling her to take it—this way you're teaching her two commands in the same session.

Gradually escalate to more valuable items, such as jerky

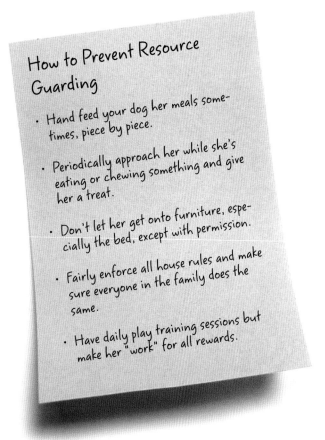

How to Prevent Resource Guarding

- Hand feed your dog her meals sometimes, piece by piece.

- Periodically approach her while she's eating or chewing something and give her a treat.

- Don't let her get onto furniture, especially the bed, except with permission.

- Fairly enforce all house rules and make sure everyone in the family does the same.

- Have daily play training sessions but make her "work" for all rewards.

Trading

- Trading a better thing for a good thing teaches her that giving something up to you is rewarding. If she sees you as a threat to "her" resources, she's more likely to guard them.

- You want her to realize that your proximity often means a reward for her.

- Apart from simple exercises to add treats to her bowl, don't pester her while she is eating. You could make her feel that her food is always threatened, and she'll feel justified in guarding it.

78

sticks. Increase the interval between her release and the reward. Start requiring a sit or down before handing over a treat. If she enjoys tug games or fetch, use the release command during play. Treats are not generally required during play—her reward will be praise and resumption of play. Treats should be phased out after she understands the concept. The goal is for her to drop a Porterhouse steak on request.

She may decide to turn it into a game by running away instead. Don't play; instead ignore her. Lesson learned? If she runs away with the item, you'll stop playing. If she simply

refuses to release the item, place your hand over her muzzle and squeeze until she lets go, then reward.

What is she learning from these exercises? That you control the resources. And that if she doesn't obey, you will either stop being fun or will force her to comply. That interaction with you, on your terms, is rewarding. That is the basis for a deep bond between dog and owner.

Praise

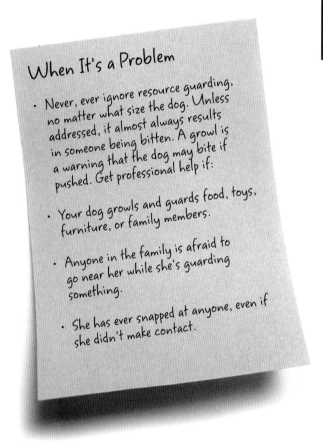

When It's a Problem

- Never, ever ignore resource guarding, no matter what size the dog. Unless addressed, it almost always results in someone being bitten. A growl is a warning that the dog may bite if pushed. Get professional help if:

- Your dog growls and guards food, toys, furniture, or family members.

- Anyone in the family is afraid to go near her while she's guarding something.

- She has ever snapped at anyone, even if she didn't make contact.

- Use the trading game for only as long as you need to. You don't want to get into the habit of bribing her to drop something every time.

- Give tons of praise when she releases the item.

- Sometimes she will give you a really filthy look because she really doesn't want to relinquish something. As long as she gives it up, that's OK. Life isn't a bed of roses every day, even for a dog.

79

"TAKE IT NICE"

Everyone appreciates a dog who takes treats gently from the hand that feeds them

Grabby dogs who snatch treats and other desirable items from people can be scary, especially to children or "nondog people." Some dogs naturally have soft mouths, others have less discretion. A dog with a harder mouth can hurt someone with a toothy grab. You may notice that if you have two dogs, one—usually the subordinate or less-confident dog—will try

quickly snatching treats or food in case the other dog wants to take it away.

A dog being bouncy and grabby doesn't get rewarded. It helps if he will sit first. Curl your hand into a loose fist around the treat and offer it to your dog. Use a calm, quiet voice and tell him, "Take it nice." If he nudges, jumps, or tries to snatch it,

Starting the Trick

- Some dogs naturally take treats gently, others are piranhas. Even if a grabby dog means no harm, such behavior can be startling, and it doesn't take much for a hard tooth to bump skin and hurt.

- First, teach him yourself. Then, when he understands

- "Take it nice," have him take food from other people.

- Avoid holding the treat above his head, where he'll be more likely to jump for it. Hold it below his muzzle.

Practice

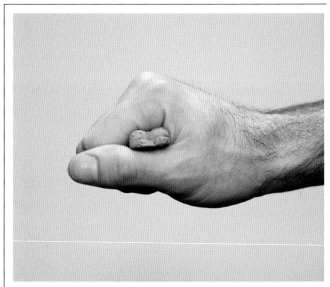

- Practice polite treat-taking after a meal when he's not that hungry.

- If he's especially grabby, don't even use food at first. Start with a crumpled ball of paper, then try a piece of carrot, and feed him real treats only when he's

- starting to get better about grabbing.

- Make a loose fist around the treat, so that you can close your hand around it if he grabs. If his teeth ever make contact, shriek loudly and stop the exercise until later.

move your hand back, get him to settle, and try again.

If he calms for just an instant and is willing to take the treat without grabbing, give it to him. If you have a clicker, click-treat right away for calmness. If, after three tries, he keeps grabbing, stop the exercise for now. You don't want this to go from training to teasing, and he'll see it as teasing if it goes on too long and will get frustrated.

MAKE IT EASY

Practice with low-value treats such as pieces of carrot or something else your dog isn't wild about. Another strategy for a grabby dog is having him lie down and giving the treats between his paws. It's harder for him to bounce when he's lying down, and it's a calm position.

Encouragement

- Make two fists: one with a treat, one without. Don't let your dog see which is which—she can smell it just fine.

- Offer her both fists and tell her to sit. Make like a tree, be still, and say nothing until she stops nudging.

- The minute she's calm, even for a second, offer her the treat.

- You can later encourage a nose touch to indicate the treat hand, giving it to her as a reward.

Multiple Dogs

- If you have another dog, practice this exercise with both dogs separately.

- You might find that if you take group class, your dog will revert to being grabby in the presence of other dogs. If this happens, try to keep a little distance from the others and go back to square one for a bit with the training.

- Always supervise children with your dog, especially when there's food around. Some dogs will take advantage if they think they'll get away with it.

81

THE "READY, READY" GAME
Teach your dog the value of waiting for a release command by making it fun

Use your dog's learned self-control to both increase enthusiasm in a ho-hum dog and to channel it in an eager dog. A common obedience class technique when teaching the "come" command is a restrained recall. The trainer holds the dog while the owner walks away, turns, and calls him. Most dogs, knowing there is a reward waiting when they get to

their owner, get a bit frustrated and eager by being restrained for several seconds. When released, they race to their owner. The underlying theory is that the more the dog is prevented from getting to something he wants, the harder he'll try to get to it.

Use this technique with beginner dogs. For instance, when

Ready, Ready

- The "ready, ready" game can be used to rev up your dog in all sorts of situations. Let's say you want her to go outside to potty. Go toward the door, asking her in an excited tone of voice if she's "ready, ready, to go *outside*?"

- Stand by the door holding the handle and ask her again. Build the suspense . . . and . . .

- Swing open the door while telling her, "Outside," and she'll race out.

Teach Self-Control

- Use this exercise to teach self-control instead of imposed control. Assuming she knows how to stay until you release her, put her in a sit or a down.

- Tell her, "Ready, ready . . . OK!" If she breaks the stay

before you get to "OK," say nothing. Just take her by the collar, reposition her, and try again.

- Make sure she gets an excellent treat when she stays put until released.

teaching your dog to jump over something, hold his collar and toss a treat or toy over the jump. Restrain him gently while asking him, "You ready? Wanna jump? Ready, ready—jump!" Let go and watch him fly! This is also a wonderful ploy for crate training. Put a treat or his meal into the crate and restrain him for a bit until he is pulling to get to it. Anytime you are sending your dog away to do something, play the restraint and "ready, ready" game.

More experienced dogs who have already mastered a "stay" or "wait" command can be proofed this way as long as they understand a release word. Put your dog on a stay. Let's say you want him to come to you. Say to him, "Ready, ready . . . ready . . . OK!" If he breaks before you say "OK," don't correct him. Take him by the collar, reposition him, and try again, making it a little easier the second time so that he succeeds.

Dogs get a great feeling of accomplishment when they learn self-control like this and are more enthusiastic workers.

Ready, Ready

- The "ready, ready" game is a great way to proof stays as well as to build enthusiasm.

- Make it even more challenging. Tell her to stay. Say, "Ready, ready . . ." then give her a small treat if she stays put to reinforce her self-control.

- Make sure you don't always say, "Ready . . ." before releasing her, or else she'll start anticipating you by breaking the stay.

- Don't overdo this game because it can demotivate her. Practice it intermittently just to keep her tuned up.

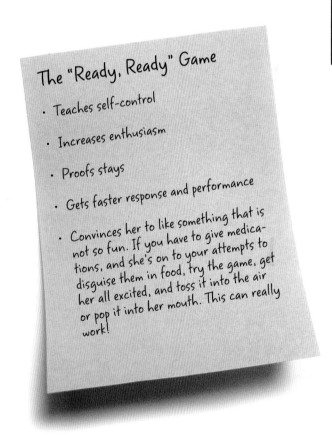

The "Ready, Ready" Game

- Teaches self-control

- Increases enthusiasm

- Proofs stays

- Gets faster response and performance

- Convinces her to like something that is not so fun. If you have to give medications, and she's on to your attempts to disguise them in food, try the game, get her all excited, and toss it into the air or pop it into her mouth. This can really work!

83

HELLO, HIGH FIVE, GOODBYE
The basic shake can quickly morph into waving, high fiving, and even saluting

A high five is just a higher version of a shake. Gradually request a higher paw raise, with your dog touching her paw to your raised hand. Start at shake height and work up to her lifting her paw straight up to meet your hand. Always pair this action with a distinct voice command and a raised hand, so that she differentiates it from a shake. If using a clicker for

this trick, click-treat only for high paw raises.

Waving goodbye is a variation of this, the difference being that there is no touch involved and it is cute and effective when you can have her perform at a distance. Start with the high five but keep your hand just out of reach. Make it clear that this is a completely different trick by using a dissimilar

Starting the Trick

- If she's very adept at offering her paw with little encouragement, try holding your hand, palm facing her, without saying anything first. If she raises her paw, praise or click-treat.

- After she's raising her paw to meet your hand, add the "high five" command.

- For variation, ask for "high five" and "other five" or "left" and "right."

- Make sure she touches your hand each time to differentiate "high five" from a wave.

Practice

- Don't hold your hand so high that she has to jump up to touch it. Most dogs can't reach much higher than their heads, and, of course, this depends on the length of their legs. A dachshund will have a shorter reach than a doberman.

- If she's really good, try getting her to sit up on her haunches and give you "both fives" at once.

- As with most exercises, repeat between three and ten times per session.

hand signal and very different voice command. Because the commands "high five" and "bye bye" can sound similar, say "goodbye" instead or create your own commands. The effectiveness of a good trick is increased by a creative command.

A patriotic salute is a variation of a high five and can be the same motion, with just a different voice cue. It's more like a salute, though, if you can train your dog to hold her paw up close to her head. Again using different cues, encourage her to bring her paw up to your hand but keep your hand close to her head so that her paw brushes her cheek or ear.

Rewards

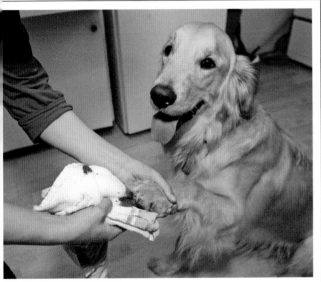

- Like "shake," this can be a useful command for teaching her to raise muddy paws for wiping off or even for clipping toenails.

- Make sure that you reward when his paw is high in the air, not back on the ground, so that it's clear to him

exactly what part of this action is the one you want: paw up, not paw going back down.

- To get some oomph into his high five, play the "ready, ready" game first.

Gradually work back in distance so that she isn't required to touch your hand. Praise and reward lavishly. She will probably revert to merely raising her paw straight up as you step away from her, so help her out and ignore those, rewarding only for a proper "salute." With a clicker, click-treat only for saluting, not for just raising a paw.

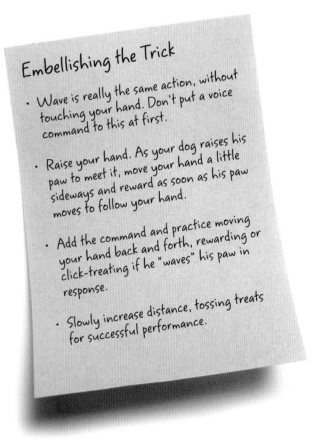

Embellishing the Trick

- Wave is really the same action, without touching your hand. Don't put a voice command to this at first.

- Raise your hand. As your dog raises his paw to meet it, move your hand a little sideways and reward as soon as his paw moves to follow your hand.

- Add the command and practice moving your hand back and forth, rewarding or click-treating if he "waves" his paw in response.

- Slowly increase distance, tossing treats for successful performance.

"BANG, YOU'RE DEAD"
Teach your dog to roll over and play dead

You've taught your dog to down and to roll over from a lying-down position. The "play dead" trick needs just to be refined a bit so that Fido can play dead on your command. If you find "play dead" a bit of a downer, come up with another command—"bedtime" or "are you sleepy?" or "show us your tummy."

Knowing a hand signal for down and roll over will make this much easier for your dog. If you've practiced puppy push-ups, she'll understand down and rolling over as positions as well as actions. For this trick to be effective, she should drop and roll over from any position. For her to understand that the end effect is her lying either on her back or flat on her side (determine which you want before starting), you are going to back-chain this. Have her get into position, say, "Bang!" or

Starting the Trick

- She'll need a "stay" command for this trick. Whatever you call it, a successful performance requires her to hold the position for at least several seconds.

- Practice to see if she finds it easier to stay while lying on her side or flat on her back.

- If you want her on her back, rub her tummy while saying, "Stay, good Fido, goooood stay."

- To help her stay on her side, use treats (she can't eat treats upside down!).

Body Signs

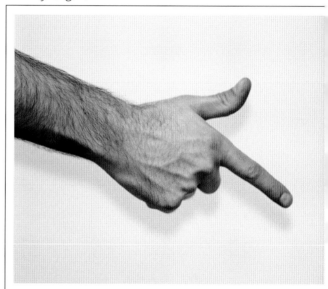

- Start using whatever hand signal you choose while she's in her prone position.

- At first you'll probably need to be sitting next to her, so that you can encourage her to stay in position.

- Gradually work up to having her stay while you're up

on your knees, then standing up, then from a few feet away.

- Use treats or tummy rubs (use your foot when standing) to encourage her to stay down.

KNACK DOG TRICKS

whatever word you're using, and treat profusely for several seconds. Repeat until she's willingly down on the ground.

Now start getting her down from a sit or a stand or rolling over from a down position. At first you'll need to break it into steps: sit, down, roll over, "Bang." If you can use hand signals for any of these and pair the "Bang" with another hand signal, quickly followed by a treat (or click-treat), this will make it easier for her. It can take a little practice. Break it down first, then start increasing the speed until it is a single action, with her flopping down right away on your "Bang."

For teaching any new trick to great reliability, first the dog has to want to work for you. Then she has to understand what to do. After she understands, require speedier compliance. Finally, add distractions and vary the location so she'll perform anywhere.

Rewards

- Remember to use a release word to let her know when she can get up. Because this trick has an element of the "stay" command, she'll need to know when she's done with playing "dead."

- As always, start with small time increments and slowly increase duration. Just a few seconds at first is great.

- It will probably be easier for her to hold the position on her side, rather than on her back, for more than about twenty seconds.

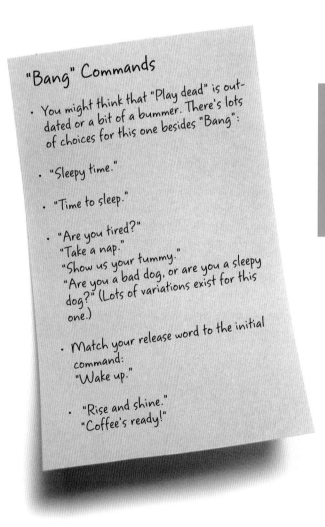

"Bang" Commands

- You might think that "Play dead" is out-dated or a bit of a bummer. There's lots of choices for this one besides "Bang":

  - "Sleepy time."

  - "Time to sleep."

  - "Are you tired?"
    "Take a nap."
    "Show us your tummy."
    "Are you a bad dog, or are you a sleepy dog?" (Lots of variations exist for this one.)

  - Match your release word to the initial command:
    "Wake up."

  - "Rise and shine."
    "Coffee's ready!"

COOKIE ON THE NOSE
Balance a cookie on his nose and flip it into the air? Sure, he can

Put your controlled canine's skills to the test. As a prerequisite, your dog will need to understand how to stay still for several seconds. He'll also need to have a nose, so squishy-faced dogs such as pugs might find this challenging, although you can modify the trick by placing the treat on top of his head.

Before putting a great treat on his nose and expecting him to stay still, practice with something lightweight and nonedible. A little ball of crumpled paper works well. Show it to him first, so that he knows what you're balancing on his nose. Have him sit and place the paper on his snout. You'll probably have to gently hold his muzzle from underneath. Tell him to wait, then take it off and give him a treat.

When he's sitting still with the paper balanced on his nose, move to food. If he gets wild about really great treats, use

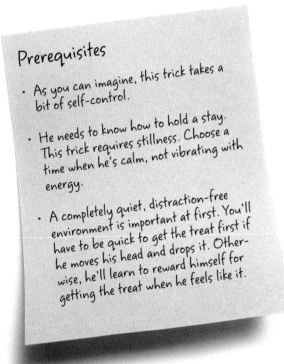

Prerequisites

- As you can imagine, this trick takes a bit of self-control.

- He needs to know how to hold a stay. This trick requires stillness. Choose a time when he's calm, not vibrating with energy.

- A completely quiet, distraction-free environment is important at first. You'll have to be quick to get the treat first if he moves his head and drops it. Otherwise, he'll learn to reward himself for getting the treat when he feels like it.

Starting the Trick

- This will be easier if your dog can already catch treats in midair. This is a learned skill, and puppies in particular need some practice.

- Have him sit; it's easier for him to keep his head level. Hold his chin gently and balance a little nonedible item, such as crumpled paper, near the tip of his nose.

- The first step is merely to have him hold position for a few seconds.

something less interesting, such as a slice of carrot or sweet potato. After he can balance it for several seconds, tell him, "OK, get it!" Chances are he'll jerk his head forward so the treat bounces across the room. Help him flip his head and give him an extra reward each time he catches it in the air.

Next Steps

- After he's able to hold still with the thing on his nose, start using food. Use something square or flat so that it stays put.

- If it's too close to his eyes, he'll practically go cross-eyed looking at it. He'll also be more likely to move his head down trying to focus.

- When he can hold that for a couple of seconds, tell him, "Catch!" while flipping the treat from his nose into his mouth.

More Next Steps

- The next part is easy for him, and the tricky part is catching the treat. This takes just practice, but because he's getting rewarded, he'll enjoy it.

- Some dogs will dip their heads and swipe their muzzles with a paw. To prevent this, keep your hand below his chin but not touching.

- Even if he never gets coordinated enough to catch the treat in midair, merely balancing it on his nose is really impressive.

CONTROLLED JUMPING
After your dog can jump on command, you can work on some very flashy tricks

Now that Fido is jumping reliably over objects, it's not hard to teach her to jump over or through other things. Remember that to a dog, jumping over a bar on the ground looks quite different from jumping through a hoop or over your outstretched arm. Some dogs will take to new jumps quickly; others will be concerned and need plenty of encouragement.

Always start easy. If you want her to jump through a hoop, start with a Hula Hoop, which will look a lot less intimidating than a tire. Hold it on the ground at first, so that she goes through it, and gradually raise it to her jump height. You can then add streamers or tissue paper for added effect.

For portable jump tricks, make a jump out of your bent leg

Starting the Trick

- Your dog might find learning to jump over you or over parts of your body a bit strange. After all, you have probably worked hard to teach her not to jump up onto people! It may feel like a transgression to her.

- Warm her up first with some easy jumps over familiar objects.

- Then have her jump over your outstretched legs while you sit upright on the floor.

Embellishing the Trick

- After she's comfortable, there are lots of variations. Kneel on the floor, make a hoop of your arms, and encourage her to jump through.

- Link hands with someone else to make a wide jump.

- If you have a small dog and children, challenge them to come up with gymnastic postures for her to jump through and over.

- If you have two really accomplished dogs, have one jump over the other!

or outstretched arm. Kneel down and make a hoop out of your arms or grasp your ankle with one hand behind your back to make an opening for your dog to jump through. You will probably need a partner to help you and your dog with some of these moves.

Jazz up regular jumping by teaching your dog to do tight figure-8s around the jump, jump from a distance, or do multiple jumps or broad jumps.

············ YELLOW ●LIGHT ············

In the sport of agility, jumping guidelines and styles can be quite specific. If you plan to take agility classes, delay fancy jumping moves until you can talk to your instructor about proper jump exercises. You want to avoid training some bad habits that will need to be untrained later.

- If you are taking an agility class, your instructor will give you jump exercises to practice at home with a regular jump.

- Teaching your dog to jump in a tight figure-8 pattern over the jump is a valuable exercise for controlled jumping and turning. This teaches her to choose which leg she lands on for controlled turns.

- Try doing this without verbal or hand commands, using just your shoulders and posture to indicate how you want her to jump.

Target Sticks

- Teach her to jump over a stick, or even two sticks in succession, held parallel to the ground. To make this flashier, the sticks can be embellished with streamers.

- If she tries running around the stick, practice with it held against a wall or across a doorway.

- When teaching her to jump over your arm or leg, do the same thing.

- A target stick can be very useful for teaching some jumps; just don't let her get too dependent on it.

SIT PRETTY
This is not only a cute trick but also a workout for doggie glutes and thighs

Many small dogs naturally sit up on their haunches when asking for a treat or attention. Always capitalize on natural behaviors by putting a command or cue to them—only you and your dog will know you didn't actually train her to do it! Some larger, bulkier dogs will have a difficult time doing this trick because they are not designed for it, and tailless dogs

are at a disadvantage with no tail for balance. Modify the trick for these dogs by asking them to put their paws into your hands or onto a bent leg.

Start with Fido sitting and lure him up by passing a treat in front of his nose, up and toward the back of his head. If he jumps, hold the treat lower. Praise him as he's raising up

Quick Tips

- Little dogs often not only can sit pretty with ease but also can learn to walk on their hind legs.

- A dog needs to be fairly fit to do this. Always start with several repetitions and don't ask him to hold the position for long at first.

- You might find that it helps to use a leash attached to a harness to help him balance. Don't attach the leash to his collar; this is uncomfortable and sends him mixed signals.

Modifying the Trick

- Large or bulky dogs may find this simply impossible. Unless your dog seems to catch on quickly, assume that your English bulldog or Newfoundland can't manage it.

- Modify sitting pretty by having your dog sit on his haunches and rest his front paws in your hands or on suitably high furniture.

- As long as his butt is on the ground, reward him for sitting pretty. "May I have this next dance?" is a cute command for this.

and reward him when he's sitting on his haunches. After he's done this a few times, give him several tiny treats in a row while he's up. Don't lift them too high over or behind his head because that's likely to make him lose his balance.

If Fido is a natural, reward (or click-treat) only when he's sitting up. If he's not, reward for every sincere effort that keeps his haunches on the ground and his front feet up.

Luring the Dog

- Luring is the only way you'll convince your dog to sit or stand on his hind legs unless he does it naturally.

- Work up to having him hold the position for about thirty seconds but don't force it any longer than that. Of course, if he is able to walk effortlessly across the room, don't stop him!

- Give him treats only when his front feet are off the ground; otherwise, he'll confuse this with a regular sit.

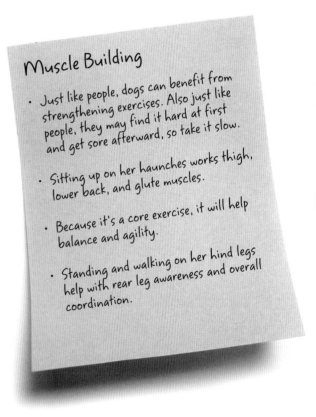

Muscle Building

- Just like people, dogs can benefit from strengthening exercises. Also just like people, they may find it hard at first and get sore afterward, so take it slow.

- Sitting up on her haunches works thigh, lower back, and glute muscles.

- Because it's a core exercise, it will help balance and agility.

- Standing and walking on her hind legs help with rear leg awareness and overall coordination.

ADVANCED BASICS

SEQUENCING
Start putting some of these basic tricks together for a really impressive trick routine

Now that your dog knows a few tricks, and you know about back-chaining, breaking down complex tricks and using clever tools such as clickers, you can put moves together. It's OK to experiment. Try sitting pretty and saluting or pair fetch with a jump. Some of the motion tricks, such as walking between your legs, spinning, and jumping, can be joined up to make some pretty flashy dance moves.

One technique that makes it easier is to use hand and body signals instead of long strings of command words. Dogs understand our actions and postures much more readily than the words we use. An agility dog-and-handler team can often do a whole, complex course at high speed without a single

Purpose of Sequencing

- Your dog needs to perform two or more tricks with reasonable consistency before putting them together.

- Remember that for the purposes of sequencing, basic skills such as sit, down, and stay will be part of the routine. For control, it's often a good idea to start

off a sequence with a basic sit or down.

- Also remember that you and your dog already understand sequencing. If you back-chained or broke down tricks in simple steps and then joined them back together with a single command, you are experienced pros.

Fade Out Lures and Rewards

- One of several reasons for fading out lures and rewards is to stop your dog from expecting a treat after each segment of a sequence.

- If she expects a reward consistently for each action,

she'll keep pausing and waiting for her pay.

- An easy fix for this is to go back to doing a single trick several times in a row. Reward her only every second or third time.

word. Sometimes it's easier for the dog if his handler gives clear physical cues because the dog will be very attuned to his partner. Babbling at a dog and repeating commands can be counterproductive by distracting and confusing him.

Agility is a perfect example of chaining many actions together into a complex performance. Initially, each obstacle is taught separately, with lots of treats, play, and praise. As the dog becomes proficient, the treats are faded out. The dog learns how to move from one obstacle to the next correctly and quickly. The handler learns to cue her dog to the next

obstacle (every course in a trial is different, so the dog has no clue how the obstacles are lined up beforehand) at just the right time, using words and signals. When the timing is right, the whole performance flows at very high speed.

Trick training is just like that. Even putting two simple moves together impresses people, and you can see how complex performance can be built from basic tricks.

Combining Tricks

- Now try combining two different easy tricks, such as a spin followed by a sit. "Pay" her only after she's done both correctly in a row.

- Play the "ready, ready" game in between tricks for a while to keep her enthusiasm level up.

- Try alternating stationary tricks, such as a sit and a paw shake, with tricks in motion, such as jumps and spins. This not only looks good but also helps her stay focused instead of getting too wild or bored.

Learn Together

- You can fit a lot of tricks into one or two minutes. Both of you can get confused or ahead of yourselves by trying to fit too much together too quickly.

- Pick things that she understands hand signals for and work on a silent routine.

This will help you work on giving her clear signals.

- Never forget that you are learning together! You and your dog are working as a team, and you need to be clear and consistent for her.

95

TYPES OF CANINE INTELLIGENCE
There are different types of canine intelligence: It's not only how trainable a dog is

We take an egocentric view of canine intelligence: A smart dog learns quickly from us, and dogs who don't are not so smart. What we mean when we say a dog is "smart" is that she's compliant and obedient. This says nothing about her problem-solving abilities, her emotional or social skills, or her innate abilities, such as herding, tracking, or hunting.

Northern breeds are notoriously difficult to train but renowned for their ability to escape from yards by figuring out gate latches and learning how to open doors. Most retrievers are highly trainable, learning new skills in just a few sessions, but don't tend to be independent thinkers. Guardian breeds may not see the point of learning to shake but

Innate Abilities

- "Hardwired" or innate abilities, such as pack and communication skills, guarding, scenting, hunting, and endurance, can hearken back to wolf ancestry.

- These abilities are all related to the drives, such as pack drive and prey drive. They are what motivate every dog, from the coiffed toy poodle to the rugged old English mastiff.

- Innate abilities are also modified through select breeding for useful skills such as herding, pointing, and retrieving.

Pack Dogs

- Dogs used for working in packs, such as malamutes and foxhounds, are not always the easiest to train because working directly with a human isn't what they were bred for.

- However, such dogs tend to have very high "emotional"

- intelligence and are skilled in maintaining a peaceful pack hierarchy.

- Those bred as guardians to literally keep the wolf from the door can be aggressive toward other dogs but highly trainable and cooperative with their family.

need virtually no training to caretake several hundred head of sheep. Bloodhounds may not be the best obedience competitors, but give them a scenting problem to figure out, and they'll leave other "smarter" dogs in the dust.

An insanely high-energy dog can make her owner crazy, and, unfortunately, an untrained high-drive dog often ends up in a shelter. If she is lucky, someone who wants a performance dog spots her potential, bails her out, and goes on to make a brilliant, ribbon-winning canine athlete out of a dog somebody didn't want.

Hunting and Herd Dogs

- When looking for a trainable and easygoing dog, consider hunting and herding breeds, bred to take direction from their owners.

- These dogs need a formidable amount of physical exercise and may stay mentally puppy-like for many years.

- Although it's very important to consider hardwired tendencies when choosing a breed (or mix), remember that dogs are individuals and that there are hard-to-train border collies, aggressive golden retrievers, and unfailingly sweet-natured pit bulls.

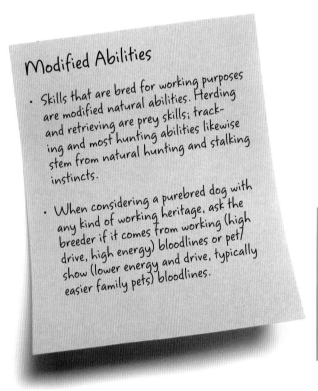

Modified Abilities

- Skills that are bred for working purposes are modified natural abilities. Herding and retrieving are prey skills; tracking and most hunting abilities likewise stem from natural hunting and stalking instincts.

- When considering a purebred dog with any kind of working heritage, ask the breeder if it comes from working (high drive, high energy) bloodlines or pet/show (lower energy and drive, typically easier family pets) bloodlines.

TEACH HIM TO COUNT

Teach your dog to do math with easy tricks using his innate abilities

Do you want to teach your dog to add, subtract, or even calculate square roots? If your dog knows how to say "woof," it is easy to teach him to count. You have to know when he barks. Will he bark when he wants to go outside? When he's playing? When someone rings the doorbell? At squirrels? Use the times he naturally barks to teach him to count.

Have treats at the ready. When you know he's about to bark, raise your finger and say, "Fido, what's *one*?" The very instant he barks, give him a treat and tell him he is wonderful. Repeat this as often as possible. What you are doing is training him to woof at both your raised finger and the word "*one*."

Start varying your wording, always ending with the word

Barking Dogs

- Some dogs were bred for shrill barking. Shetland sheepdogs (Shelties) bark a lot because in their native Scotland, an important job was barking to keep birds of prey away from the flock.

- Some hunting dogs are prized for their "voice,"

which allowed the hunter to follow the quarry.

- Barking can't always be eliminated, but sometimes training a dog to bark means you can then more easily tell it to stop barking.

Hand Signals

- Pairing a hand signal with the command makes this a much more versatile trick.

- If your dog is not a frequent barker, set him up. Most dogs bark at the doorbell, especially at night. Have someone sneak out, then

ring the bell. Other dogs will howl if you howl first and get just the right pitch.

- You also want a hand signal and cue to tell him to stop barking. Try putting your finger to your lips or "patting" the air.

"one" and a raised finger. "What's two minus *one*?" "What's one divided by *one*?" "What is the square root of *one*?" Always reward for a properly placed woof. Don't reward if he barks incessantly. The trick is to reward directly after the first bark. He can't bark a second time if his mouth is full. If using a clicker, click-treat directly after a single woof.

If you are consistent with your command and reward, your dog will start barking once when you say anything that ends with the word "*one*?" and raise your finger.

The finger is important because eventually he will be able to woof when you raise your finger. This means that you can go to advanced mathematics with your dog and teach him to bark twice or even three times by flicking your finger. If you are sneaky about it, nobody else will know that he is responding to a small, surreptitious movement at his eye level.

Rewards

- With a secret hand signal, you can pretend to show him a written arithmetic problem or have someone else present the question and cue him to bark.

- Some dogs will obligingly bark once on your cue; others will get carried away.

- You'll have to experiment to see what works naturally with your dog.

- A click-treat after a single woof lets him know that's a desired action. Be quick to reward the one woof and ignore multiple barks.

Stop Barking

- Work on the "stop barking" cue by calling his name and then your command and following it right away with a treat for quiet.

- Over time, he can learn to woof once, then come "tell you all about it" for a treat. Fade the treats when he starts quieting down.

- What if he's simply not a barker? Teach him to raise his paw on your hand signal, using the "shake" and "wave" commands.

THE RIGHT COMMANDS

Sometimes it's just a matter of pairing a creative command to something he does naturally

All the command suggestions in this book are just that: suggestions. Personalize commands, be creative, or put a command to something your dog is about to do anyway. When Fido is outside and about to pee, announce that your dog pees on command and say, "Fido, squat!" at just the right moment. Instead of teaching your dog to "play dead," ask her if she would rather be a (choose your political party) or dead. If she responds to a single word—such as "dead"—or a hand signal, you can tailor commands to match the occasion or even the people present. If your dog does therapy work or goes to work with you, she can be a real crowd pleaser with tricks and personalized commands.

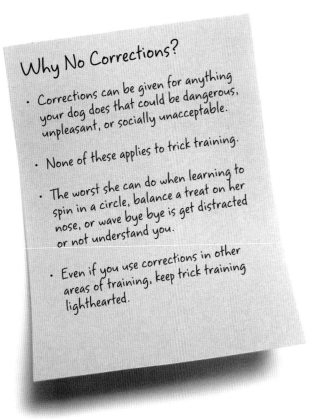

Why No Corrections?

- Corrections can be given for anything your dog does that could be dangerous, unpleasant, or socially unacceptable.

- None of these applies to trick training.

- The worst she can do when learning to spin in a circle, balance a treat on her nose, or wave bye bye is get distracted or not understand you.

- Even if you use corrections in other areas of training, keep trick training lighthearted.

Building a Dog's Vocabulary

- Build your dog's vocabulary by pairing words with everyday actions, such as "Wanna eat?" or "Outside," "In the house," "In the car," "Go pee," or "Walkies."

- If you use the same words consistently, she'll come to associate them with the actions in a neutral, no-stress way.

- After she's done that, you have taught her some useful commands without even trying. Now you can tell her, "Go outside" or "In the car," and she'll know just what you mean.

Entertainers learn to think on their feet. When your dog doesn't comply or complies in an unexpected way, use the moment. If she lets out a volley of barks when you ask her what one times one is, say she slept through multiplication class and move on (don't reward that mistake, though!). If she does an enthusiastic spin instead of rolling over on command, simply give the roll over cue again, and she's just done an even more impressive trick by spinning around before rolling over.

Avoid demotivating your dog by correcting her for doing something "wrong" or for doing it differently. You don't want to quash her spirit or creativity. Sometimes when a dog does something differently, she is asking if you maybe like this version better. This is something that smart, innovative dogs often do.

Practice Makes Perfect

- Your bond with your dog is based on respect and is built through day-to-day interactions and structure.

- Trick training allows you to be a bit unstructured and even silly. Although you don't want to be sloppy with training, it's OK to be flexible and creative.

- Trick training allows you to experiment with different methods and tools without worrying that you'll somehow mess up training more important life skills!

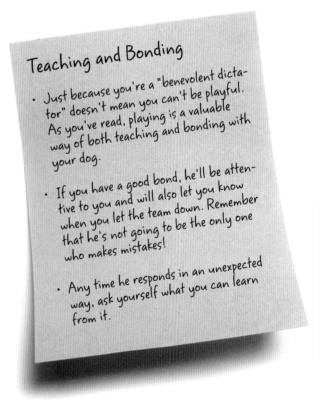

Teaching and Bonding

- Just because you're a "benevolent dictator" doesn't mean you can't be playful. As you've read, playing is a valuable way of both teaching and bonding with your dog.

- If you have a good bond, he'll be attentive to you and will also let you know when you let the team down. Remember that he's not going to be the only one who makes mistakes!

- Any time he responds in an unexpected way, ask yourself what you can learn from it.

SMART DOG TRICKS

DOGS, TOO, HAVE FEELINGS

Ask your dog to display a wide range of emotions on command using a clicker

A clicker is going to come in very handy for some of these tricks. As with the head turn, you can use a clicker to shape some subtle movements.

Some emotions come naturally. You hardly need to encourage a happy dog to wag his tail or give kisses, but you can put them on command. If your dog isn't a natural "kisser," use a

dab of peanut butter or a smear of soft cheese to encourage him to kiss your cheek or gallantly kiss your hand. Wag your butt and tell him to wag his tail, using an excited, happy voice. Head positions can convey a range of emotions. With your dog lying down, lure his head to the ground and click-treat that position. Any time you want him to hold a position, use

Observing Behaviors

- Spend a day or two closely watching your dog. Look for behaviors he does naturally and often enough that you can catch them with a click-treat.

- These behaviors could be lying down with his head between his paws looking up at you, staring up at birds or planes in the sky, and, of course, wagging his tail and "smiling."

- Pick one or two and keep your clicker handy. Every time you catch him doing that behavior, click-treat.

Family Games

- Make it a family game: Arm everyone with a clicker and treats and see how many times everyone can catch him in the act.

- At first he'll just be happy he's randomly getting treats. Over the course of several days, you'll see the light bulb go on.

- Start asking for the action, using a lure to make it easy at first. Let's say you picked looking upward. Say, "Where's the birdie?" Lure his head up and click-treat.

several tiny treats and calm praise to encourage stillness. A dog with his head between his paws looking dolefully upward looks sad, tired, or bored.

Use luring and click-treating to have him lower his head to say his prayers, turn his head away in rebuff, or look up to the sky, wondering if it's going to rain. With a little work, you can encourage him to turn his head both to the left and right, as if shaking his head "no" or looking for someone.

Some dogs will playfully bare their teeth if you get them really excited and move your hands toward their faces in a fluttering, jerky motion. Pair this action with a command to "make an ugly face" but assure onlookers that it's all in fun!

Teach him to stick his tongue out by dabbing tiny bits of peanut butter on his nose and click-treating every lick. Commercial breaks during a television show offer a perfect time frame to practice some emotional moves.

Natural Behaviors

Using a Clicker

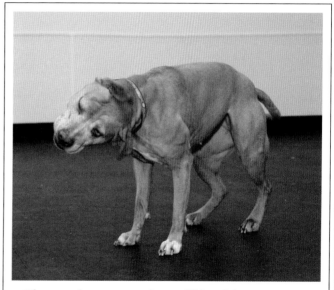

- Use the technique to teach the head turn with a clicker in Chapter 4 for any of these moves because the basic concept is the same.

- The more natural a behavior, the faster he'll learn it.

- Behaviors that have to be taught, such as making an "ugly face," will take a little longer because he depends more strongly on your prompting.

- Of course, these commands can be taught without a clicker by luring and positioning him and then rewarding when he does it the way you want.

- However, it will take a lot longer to teach the actions and shape them into tricks.

- With a clicker, you can capture much more precise movements.

- If more than one person is training him, make sure that everyone uses the same method, commands, and hand signals so he doesn't get confused.

THE CANINE COURIER

Your delivery dog can learn everyone in the house by name and go to work

If you would like a little relief from the household chores, spend a little time turning Fido into your own personal assistant. Break it down into simple steps, and he can learn to identify family members by name and deliver items all over the house—so you don't have to. Start out standing next to the person and using their name, saying "Go to Bob." Have

your assistant try to get the dog's attention by repeating their name with a come command: "Come to Bob."

Award the treat at first when the dog just shifts his attention to Bob, then gradually increase the space between you to a short distance and reward for movement in Bob's direction. Step it up to carrying a toy. While standing a few feet

Encouragement

- Give him something familiar and easy to carry at first, such as a favorite toy.

- Encourage him to take the toy and then hold it by gently holding his muzzle closed while calmly praising him.

- Don't let him see a treat because he'll be tempted to drop the toy in readiness for the treat. If he's very food motivated, you may need to teach him to do this with verbal praise instead of a treat.

Starting the Trick

- Start by having the people just a few feet apart, almost like a relay. Gradually increase distance.

- If he gets excited and drops the toy, encourage him to pick it up. Try nudging it with your foot, shaking it, or tossing it a foot or two.

- If he absolutely won't pick it up by himself, pick it up for him and have him take it but don't reward or praise him until he at least makes it over to the recipient.

apart, give the dog a tug toy. Say "Go find Bob" and have Bob call him at the same time.

If he is less than enthusiastic, using the "ready, ready" game can help prime him to make it successfully to Bob. When he goes to Bob, the dog can have a game of tug as a reward, a treat, or just praise for the behavior. Gradually increase your distance from Bob, rewarding for successful carries the entire distance until the dog will "carry" a favorite toy across the room. Bob can also move out of sight, into other rooms, although still using the "Come to Bob" to encourage the behavior.

Move on to carrying other objects that are less desirable, always giving plenty of praise at the receiving end. Before you know it, you will have your own in home delivery service.

Go Find Bob

- After he has the toy in his mouth, the sender tells him, "Go find Bob!"

- Bob calls him over at the same time, then praises him.

- The praise can be just verbal, a treat, or a quick game of tug or fetch.

- If the reward is tug or fetch, Bob should have another toy on hand. Otherwise, Fido will always expect to chase or bite the item he's delivering.

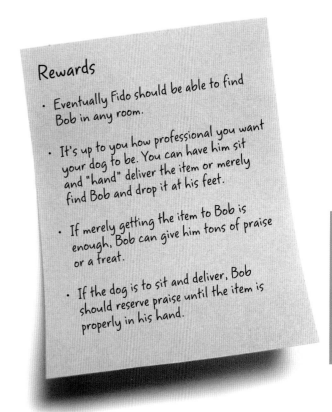

Rewards

- Eventually Fido should be able to find Bob in any room.

- It's up to you how professional you want your dog to be. You can have him sit and "hand" deliver the item or merely find Bob and drop it at his feet.

- If merely getting the item to Bob is enough, Bob can give him tons of praise or a treat.

- If the dog is to sit and deliver, Bob should reserve praise until the item is properly in his hand.

NAME THAT TOY

Teach him different names for his toys and have him go get the right one

Your dog also realizes that there's a difference between his toys. Most likely he has favorites: toys he chases, toys he chews on, toys he likes because they squeak. Giving a name to each toy is just naming something he already knows.

Put a name to his favorite toy first, such as a sheepskin teddy. Spend as many days as it takes (some dogs will get this in a few sessions) throwing and playing with the teddy. Use its name frequently while you play: "Where's your teddy?" and "Get that teddy" and "Catch teddy" until he strongly associates the name with the toy. Bear in mind that to him, "teddy" might simply mean "let's play." So the next step will require a paradigm shift for him. Don't worry, he'll get it.

Favorite Toys

- If there's a particular type of toy that he's not that interested in, don't use it as one of the first toys to teach him with.

- Similarly, if he gets obsessed with a certain toy to the exclusion of every-thing else, avoid using that toy. Otherwise, it will be an unfair contest when he has to choose between the two.

- Concentrate on playing fetch and finding games with each toy because you want the end result to be his bringing the toy to you.

Practice

- When it comes time to choose, make it easy for him at first by putting the two toys close to him at an equal distance.

- Tell him to get the teddy. If he makes a move toward the teddy, say, "Yes, teddy!" Click-treat for any interest in the teddy.

- Now switch the toys around and try again with the teddy.

- Then show him the bone, put the toys down, and repeat the exercise, encouraging him to get the bone instead.

Now put the teddy away and find another, somewhat dissimilar toy, for example, a rubber bone, and repeat the preceding association game using the word *bone* instead. As soon as he's got it, get both toys out at the same time and ask him to take the teddy. If he gets the bone instead, don't say anything; just repeat your request. Make a huge show of praise when he chooses the teddy. Repeat, interchanging both toys until he's reliably choosing the correct one.

Switch It Up

- Vary the order in which you ask him to get the toys. At this point, help him out either by click-treating for the correct one or touching it with your hand.

- Because there is no hand signal associated with this trick, repeat the toy name cheerfully and often to reinforce the association.

- Avoid patterning by keeping it very random because he'll be trying to anticipate your strategy. Toss a coin if that will help.

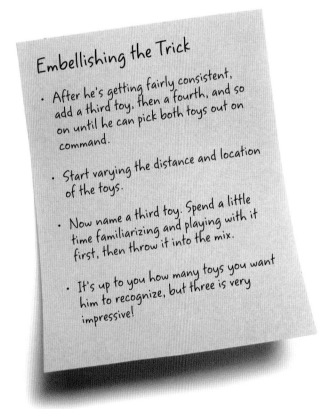

Embellishing the Trick

- After he's getting fairly consistent, add a third toy, then a fourth, and so on until he can pick both toys out on command.

- Start varying the distance and location of the toys.

- Now name a third toy. Spend a little time familiarizing and playing with it first, then throw it into the mix.

- It's up to you how many toys you want him to recognize, but three is very impressive!

SMART DOG TRICKS

"WATCH ME"

Get attention and focus on command with this basic obedience attention exercise

If you've ever watched obedience competition and noticed the dogs heeling with their eyes fixed on their handlers' faces, you can be sure the handlers have spent a lot of time teaching "watch me." Some have become adept at spitting treats from their mouths to keep their dogs attentive.

In the real world, there is no earthly reason for a dog to be walking by your side and staring raptly into your eyes at the same time. However, it's a handy tool to get your dog's attention when he is being distracted or thinking about lunging on leash to get to another dog or a squirrel. With some practice, you can have him whip around and stare at you on command. Of course, there's a little bribery involved.

Attention

- The first step in any command is one that we often don't think about: attention. Without your dog's attention in the first place, you won't get much accomplished.

- This is a very easy exercise. If you get into the habit of getting his attention, he'll get used to snapping to attention when you say, "Watch me."

- Practice initially in a distraction-free environment to make it easy for him.

"Watch Me"

- The reason why you want a separate command and not his name is because he hears his name frequently, and that dilutes its effectiveness.

- "Watch me" is very specific—you are demanding your dog's full attention and eye contact and rewarding him for it.

- It's OK to bring a treat up to your face and hold it for a few seconds, then reward for maintaining eye contact.

With your dog sitting in front of you and some treats handy, say, "Watch me," and the very instant he makes eye contact, pop a treat into his mouth. If he stares at your treat hand instead, make a sharp little sound so that he looks up at you and pop in the treat. If you're doing this with a clicker, say nothing at first; just wait for him to glance at you and click-treat. When using a clicker, don't add a command until he is looking up at you for his reward.

Up the ante by slowly stretching your hands out. His eyes will follow your hands. Again, wait until he looks back at your face and reward. Over time, you can practice this everywhere—on walks, at a stop light, and at random times. Do this only when there's no strong distraction—saying "Watch me" when he's barking furiously at a squirrel is useless until he is extremely proficient at this. The trick is to anticipate and get attention before the distraction.

Body Signs

- Make it more demanding by moving your arms out from your side. He'll watch the hand containing the treat at first. Reward consistently for eye contact.

- Move back and forth and to his side—again rewarding for his full attention.

- Treats are the easiest way to reward instantly, especially at first. When you start phasing them out, verbal praise or physically loving on her is a great substitute.

Practice

- Practice "watch me" while walking, during training class, or any time you're out and about with your dog. It's a no-brainer exercise and done routinely will become an almost conditioned reflex.

- Initially, demand his attention only when you know you'll get it.

- Don't overdo this, though—no more than five repetitions at a time and not too often. You want it to be meaningful and rewarding; otherwise, he'll think you're crying wolf.

109

MAKE HEELING FUN
Leashwork doesn't have to be boring: Spice it up and keep your dog's attention

Five minutes of formal heeling in obedience class takes concentration by a dog. He has to keep his nose aligned just so with your knee, match his speed precisely to yours, make inside and outside turns without losing stride, and sit perfectly straight every time you stop. Although we don't expect our dogs to heel beautifully on daily walks, it's a handy skill, and, of course, necessary for obedience competition.

The more interactive you make it, the more willing Fido wil be to stay attentive and stay with you. If practicing forma heeling on your daily walks, it helps to have separate commands, such as "heel" for heeling and "OK, loose leash" for resuming the regular walk.

Be Compelling

- What most people really want their dogs to do is simply not pull. This means whether he's on a 4-foot leash or a 20-foot-long line, he backs off the moment he feels tension.

- Obedience heeling, when the dog and owner are walking as a team, takes skill and attention from both dog and handler to become fluid and synchronized.

- The bottom line: To get on-leash attention, you have to be more compelling than everything else.

Use the Leash

- Don't expect your dog to be able to heel for an entire 2- mile walk unless he's already very proficient. On walks, allow for him to run ahead on a long line, sniffing and peeing.

- You can use a long line for heeling, too, if you're adept at bundling up the excess when it's time to get down to business.

- Alternately, carry a shorter leash. Switching leashes on the go makes it easy for Fido to differentiate between "loose leash" and heeling.

Engage Fido. Treats are great, but use touch, voice, praise, and toys, too. Mix it up by varying your speed from an amble to a run. Make fast turns if your dog tends to forge ahead by giving him a two-second warning and big praise if he swiftly turns and stays with you. Expect perfection by rewarding only his best turns—if you reward sloppy ones, that's what you'll get. Stop at curbs to practice fast, straight sits. Use toys and encouragement if he tends to lag behind. For speedier turns, have a toy or treat, and as you turn, toss it into his path and release him forward to get it. Play tug while you walk.

Heel for half a block, release him for a minute of play, then resume heeling. While walking past a park bench or retaining wall, release him to jump up and off on the fly, then bring him back to heel position.

Not ever planning on doing obedience competition? Then by all means teach him to heel equally well on both your left and right.

Give Commands

- Cue Fido to do turns, changes in pace, starts, and stops. No fair if he gets corrected for being surprised by an abrupt change in pace!

- When starting, give a verbal command and start out with your left foot (or your right, if he's on that side).

- Because he's getting used to watching your leg to keep pace, it's an easy cue.

- Give him a few steps' notice by slowing or altering your pace when turning or stopping.

Vary Steps

- If he lunges ahead, run backward for several steps, catching him by surprise. Reel him in to a sit in front of you and give him big praise.

- Now turn and heel in the opposite direction. Play "ready, ready . . . heel!"

- Vary this with abrupt turns when he forges, so that he never knows quite what you're going to do when he pulls forward but does know that pulling forward never works.

FRONT & FINISH
This easy-to-teach, flashy obedience move impresses the heck out of people

People who aren't familiar with competitive obedience are really impressed with a dog who can front and finish. To "front" means to sit perfectly straight in front of you after being called. On the "finish" command, the dog whips around behind you to come to rest in heel position on your left.

Teaching front is easy. With hands at your sides, call your dog. If you need to lure him into coming straight toward you and sitting straight at your feet with a tidbit, do that and reward only when he's in perfect position. To help him come in straight, it's OK to take a step backward as he reaches you, encouraging him to sit.

You can use the treat-spitting method, which keeps your

Treats

- With your dog sitting in front of you, show him a treat in your right hand.

- Now take one short step back with your right foot. Show him the treat and say, "Finish!"

- Lure him around behind you with the treat. You'll

need to smoothly transfer it behind your back to your left hand and bring him around to a sit in heel position on your left.

- Try practicing this a few times without your dog to get a feel for it.

Flip Finish

- The flip finish isn't as easy for large dogs and is a bit harder for the handler to learn, too!

- With dog in front, this time the treat is in your left hand. Take a short step back with your left foot.

- As you step back, say, "Flip!" while luring Fido into a semicircle on your left back into the heel-sit position.

- In both versions, the short step is an aid for your dog. When he gets it, eliminate the step.

dog focused on your face. This takes practice, both for you to spit straight (and it helps to like the taste of hot dogs, dried liver, or string cheese) and for your dog to catch accurately instead of missing and scrambling after his reward.

It helps to use a lure at first to teach finish after the front. A target stick works well, with or without a clicker. For your dog to come around behind, target him into a tight circle behind you into a sit on your left.

ZOOM

A flashier version of the finish is a flip finish. The dog swiftly twirls backward into perfect heel position in a single fluid motion. This is quite tricky for the handler to teach and the dog to learn. Find a good obedience class to learn how to execute this move.

Reward

- There is no practical use for the "finish" command unless you plan on competing in obedience. It does make quite an impressive little trick, though, and dogs enjoy it.

- Because you're luring him, do your best to help him

into a straight, perfectly aligned sit on your left as he finishes.

- Give him the treat only after he's sitting properly or after he's adjusted his butt to get into the right position.

Puppy Push-Ups

- Teaching him down while at your side doesn't have a practical use either, but it helps break patterning on his part. The more variety he has in executing commands, the better he learns to generalize.

- He's probably used to you telling him "down" while

standing in front of him and will be hesitant at first, so help him out with treats and encouragement.

- Try a fast game of puppy push-ups with him on either your right or left.

OBEDIENCE GAMES

113

MOVING SITS & DOWNS
Another way to jazz up heeling and leashwork and work on Rally-O skills

Even if you never enter the Rally Obedience ring (Rally-O) or train for schutzhund titles, teaching your dog to sit or down while you keep moving is an impressive skill. The more your dog learns, the more he can learn—skills without any apparent practical purpose are still valuable.

The end result of this move is that while heeling, your dog

sits or downs on command while you keep walking without breaking stride. If your dog also knows how to stand still on cue, add this to the repertoire. Your dog needs to understand heel and sit and down or stand for this.

First, introduce a parallel cue to your dog. This can be a touch of the nose for stand, a head touch for down, or a

Provide Cues

- Get your dog used to the different cue first; otherwise, you'll confuse him. With him on your left, give him your verbal command, such as "sit," at the same time as the shoulder touch or sounds you've chosen.

- Tell him, "OK!" and give him a reward.

- If using a clicker, click-treat the release but not the sit. He already knows how to sit; what you are rewarding now is his staying put until you say, "OK."

Next Steps

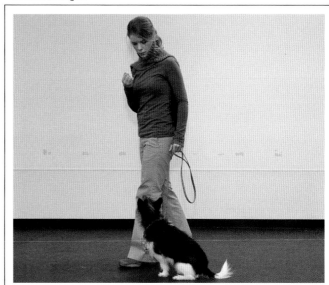

- Now have him sit, take one step forward, say, "OK!" and click-treat or reward.

- He will probably start to follow you when you move forward. Don't correct this in any way; simply reposition him and try again.

- Step forward with your right foot instead of your left so that he doesn't get conflicting signals.

- If he's having trouble, just move your body forward but don't actually take a step, then work up to stepping out.

shoulder touch for sit. For smaller dogs, an auditory cue, such as a tongue click, hiss, or short whistle, works. When he is heeling, cue your dog with the extra cue before asking for the action. At this point you are just getting him used to the added cue.

When he obeys the cue, start conditioning him to stay while you move slightly ahead. If he's had plenty of obedience training, he'll be used to staying at your side automatically as you move forward. The extra cue helps him understand that this is now a different exercise. Heel, cue, and, as he sits smoothly,

take one step in front of him so he can't move forward. If he holds position for a couple of seconds, give big praise.

Gradually increase the distance you move away from him and always praise for his staying in place. It helps to keep your back to him because successful execution of this involves your walking away. You may enlist the help of a partner at first to keep him in place as you move away.

Put It in Sequence

- Now put it in sequence: Sit at heel position, a few steps forward, cue him to sit, and take one step. Release and give big praise for doing this!

- After he's staying when you step forward once, add another step, then another.

After a while, you can increase your speed.

- The end result is that you can walk with him at heel, have him stop, and continue without breaking stride. It will take patience, but it's a real accomplishment for both of you!

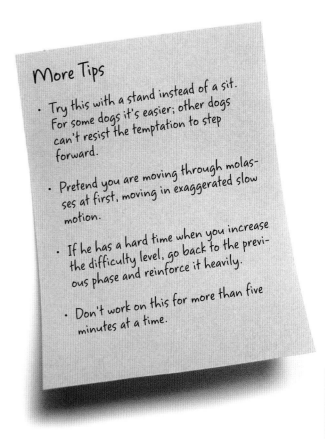

More Tips

- Try this with a stand instead of a sit. For some dogs it's easier; other dogs can't resist the temptation to step forward.

- Pretend you are moving through molasses at first, moving in exaggerated slow motion.

- If he has a hard time when you increase the difficulty level, go back to the previous phase and reinforce it heavily.

- Don't work on this for more than five minutes at a time.

ARTICLE SCENT DISCRIMINATION
Teach your dog advanced obedience skills in your living room with nose games

Your dog has superior olfactory skills and knows how to tell things apart by smell. The trick in teaching scent discrimination is having her choose a particular object—usually one that smells most like you—and having her bring it to you.

In obedience competition, she will choose from a pile of dumbbells, but you can use a group of any similar objects to train the concept. Socks work very well. Get three or four clean socks and one unwashed sock. Tuck a treat into the toe of the unwashed sock. Use tongs or a plastic bag wrapped around your hand to handle the clean socks and arrange them in a group on the floor.

Toss the unwashed sock into the pile and encourage Fido

Use a Variety of Items

Encourage Play

- Over time, you can use a variety of different items, ranging in texture and weight from metal to leather and cloth.

- To start with, make it easy for your dog by using identical items, such as socks, cotton gardening gloves, or even six identical dog toys.

- Although she's certainly able to identify the scented article without food aid, putting a treat in the article makes it really enticing when she's starting out.

- Make it even easier by encouraging her to play with the sock for a few minutes before starting the exercise. This will make it even more recognizable and attractive.

- Throw it several times and give her a treat in

reward for retrieving it. This will help back-chain the behavior.

- If you're using a sock from the dirty laundry hamper, make sure it's one that you, instead of another family member, have been wearing.

to get it. She'll probably check each sock and identify the one with the treat. Immediately call her and give her a treat. Don't give her the treat from the sock. If using a clicker, click-treat as soon as she noses the correct sock at first, then click-treat when she brings it to you.

Over time, reduce the size of the treat in the smelly sock until you don't have to use a treat at all, and she's choosing the scented article.

Next Steps

- After you've grouped all the socks, put Fido on a sit. If you plan to enter competition (this is an advanced obedience competition exercise), a heel-sit will be your starting position.

- Unless she's already raring to go, play the "ready, ready" game before telling her to go get it.

- You may not even need a verbal command. For scenting games, it's best to stay quiet and let your dog work, just giving praise when she identifies the right article.

Praise

- As soon as she's identified the article, encourage her to bring it to you with lots of praise.

- The reason why you don't give her the treat from the sock is so she doesn't figure out that she can self-reinforce by getting it herself.

- You want her final reward to come from you after she has brought the sock back to you. It's OK if she lays it at your feet it; doesn't have to be delivered to your hand.

117

RETRIEVE & JUMP
Put these together for a fast-paced game

Retrieving over a jump is an advanced competition exercise. The sport of flyball also has a variation of jump retrieving in which the dog races over a line of hurdles, grabs a ball, and races back over the hurdles.

Prerequisites are a willingness to both retrieve and jump. This makes a good indoor exercise as well. Start by just seeing if your dog will retrieve over a jump without help. Set up

the jump, throw the ball over it, and see if your dog comes back over the jump. Keep the jump really low at first. If he jumps, retrieves, and jumps back, you have a natural!

Most dogs will go around the jump. Why? First, because it's an obstacle slowing them down. Dogs are pragmatic. Why jump when you don't have to? Second, because on the way out, they're focused on the thrown article. On the way back,

Starting the Trick

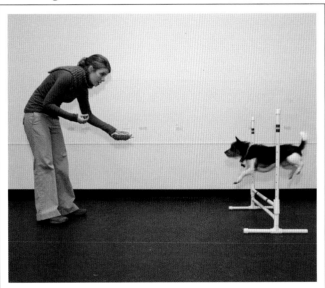

- This will be easier if he has done some basic jumping exercises first and understands that he doesn't get rewarded for going around the jump. You can always set up in a door or hallway so that he has no choice.

- Start with a very low jump. You can even start with a board laid flat on the ground.

- As well as making this an easier exercise, it allows him to see the objective—the ball.

Problem Solving

- It's OK to use a leash at first if you need to. Reward only for the return jump.

- It's common for dogs to forget to jump as they return to you, so give lots of encouragement for this.

- Increase the height as he gets more proficient. You may find that he drops the ball while jumping. To fix this, choose a softer object, such as a stuffed toy. That's easier for him to hold.

they're focused on the handler. Again, they'll take the most efficient way to reach the goal. In order to teach your dog to take the jump, he has to be rewarded for the jump.

Work on jumping by itself at first, using treats, then begin throwing a ball over and reinforcing the behavior. Start intermittently throwing the ball when he is taking the jump at least 80 percent of the time.

.... YELLOW ● LIGHT ....

Use a leash to help him back and forth over the jump at first if this seems to help him. However, never let him jump while trailing the leash if there is anything it can get caught on. Being jerked or knocking over part of the jump will spook him.

Switch It Up

- After he's got the routine down, change the way the jump looks so that he doesn't get patterned to the same jump each time. He'll encounter different-looking jumps in competition.

- Make a broad jump out of 2-by-4 boards for variety.

- The maximum width he'll see in competition is twice his height at the withers (shoulders). Don't make him jump farther than that, even if he can. As with regular jumps, start narrow and work up to full width.

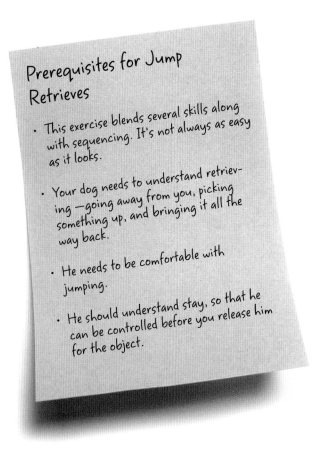

Prerequisites for Jump Retrieves

- This exercise blends several skills along with sequencing. It's not always as easy as it looks.

- Your dog needs to understand retrieving —going away from you, picking something up, and bringing it all the way back.

- He needs to be comfortable with jumping.

- He should understand stay, so that he can be controlled before you release him for the object.

FIND THE REMOTE

Teach your dog search and rescue to find important items such as TV remotes and keys

Finding lost items can be a truly useful trick. This trick blends your dog's scent discrimination and toy-naming skills. Think of something that is often misplaced in your household: keys, the remote, glasses, even his leash. If you have a scatter-brained household and a long list of items, pick just one to start with and make it easy for him! This works well with retrieving and sniffing dogs.

Start by tossing the remote (or whatever you choose) and making it a toy. If he's hesitant about an item that doesn't feel like one of his normal toys, try dabbing a little peanut butter on the end. Use the "ready, ready" game concept and tease him a bit with it first. Hold it and run around the room,

Prep the Remote

- Make sure Fido can and will pick up the remote or whatever you're using without damaging it.

- Most dogs won't want to pick up a bunch of metal keys. Attach a soft tab or knotted piece of rope to them so that he can comfortably pick them up.

- A remote can have duct tape wrapped around the outer edges or ends. If he tends to be rough, practice with an old, dummy remote first.

Starting the Trick

- Use the first steps in "Name That Toy." The remote has to become a valued object, and he needs to know it by name.

- Spend some time tossing it for him. Click-treat for both showing interest in it and then for bringing it to you.

- He might try bringing you similar-looking or similar-feeling objects or even decide that you'll appreciate his toys, too. Thank him but give no reward!

keeping it just out of his reach. This capitalizes on one of the basic rules of dog play: If you aren't letting me have it, it must be really valuable. Use a clicker and click-treat any show of interest in the remote.

Play hide-and-seek with it. First, let him watch you slide it under a couch cushion and tell him to find that remote. Reward him for interest, and if he brings it to you, give him a jackpot reward.

ZOOM

Drug- and cadaver-sniffing dogs learn to alert their handlers by sitting when they find their quarry, sometimes also barking. Obviously they don't retrieve drugs and bodies. If your dog isn't a natural retriever, look for other signs that he is telling you he found the remote and reward that.

Reward

- Dogs with initiative might also bring you the remote when you didn't ask for it. Again, that's great—but give no reward.

- When he's good at carrying the remote and bringing it to you, add this to his courier skills.

- Reward Fido for finding it, then send him off to give it to Bob.

- Don't teach him to find items you normally don't want him to pick up, such as pill bottles.

Switch It Up

- When you start hiding it from him, put it in places where you think it might legitimately be misplaced.

- For instance, if there's never an occasion for the remote to be left in the guest bedroom, don't send him there looking for it.

- Watch for signs that he's found it but can't reach it, such as way under the couch. He'll give a signal—barking perhaps or coming to get you. Definitely reward him for this!

FIND THE CAT
Need to find the cat to give medications? Teach your dog to find that cat

It's seven in the morning, and your cat is due to be at the vet to be neutered in an hour. However, he has gone into deep hiding because somehow cats know these things. If you have a patient cat and a friendly dog, teach your dog to track down the cat.

Begin by asking, "Where's *Elvis*?" (or whatever your cat's name is) and making a display of petting the cat in front of your dog. Call him over, encouraging and rewarding for any interest or movement toward Elvis. If you're using a clicker, click-treat and don't name Elvis until Fido is showing directed interest in him.

Over the course of several days or weeks, randomly call Fido

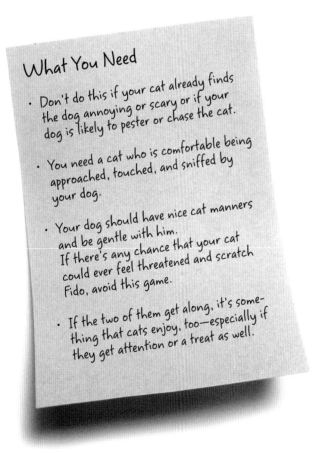

What You Need

- Don't do this if your cat already finds the dog annoying or scary or if your dog is likely to pester or chase the cat.

- You need a cat who is comfortable being approached, touched, and sniffed by your dog.

- Your dog should have nice cat manners and be gentle with him. If there's any chance that your cat could ever feel threatened and scratch Fido, avoid this game.

- If the two of them get along, it's something that cats enjoy, too—especially if they get attention or a treat as well.

Prepping for the Trick

- This is somewhat similar to the "Name the Toy" game, except you obviously aren't going to throw the cat for Fido to fetch.

- Make this rewarding for your cat as well. Pet him nicely or give him a dab of canned food for complying.

- If you have more than one cat, teach Fido to differentiate them by name. If he can do it with toys and family members, he can do it with your cats.

to "show" him Elvis and reward exuberantly for interest. Try filling his food bowl at mealtimes, walking over to the cat, and putting his food down only when he's directed interest away from his food and toward Elvis.

Start training this trick from a short distance away. If the cat doesn't mind the added intrusion, use a target stick to direct your dog to the cat. Make looking for Elvis a game. Walk through the house with your dog, asking him to find Elvis. When you find him, make a big show of excitement and praise for Fido, as if he found the cat all by himself.

He will eventually be able to "find *Elvis*" when the cat is not only right in the same room but also anywhere in the house by using his nose. At some point your dog might start looking at you as if you're an imbecile when the cat is 10 feet away in plain sight, but if you reward him only for going over and "showing" you, he'll realize that this is an integral part of the game.

Starting the Trick

- When training this trick, make sure you know where Elvis is before sending Fido off on a cat hunt. It's OK to help Fido succeed by directing him at first.

- He will learn by succeeding. If he's unsuccessful in finding the cat, he can get frustrated or discouraged or offer you an alternate object to see if that will suffice.

- If he gets discouraged in the early training, it will take him a lot longer to learn because he'll doubt you.

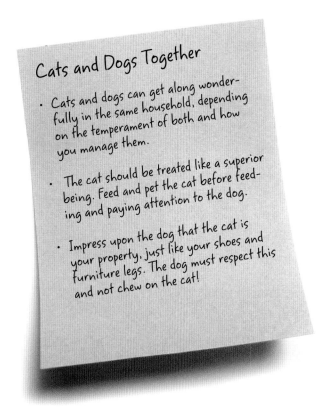

Cats and Dogs Together

- Cats and dogs can get along wonderfully in the same household, depending on the temperament of both and how you manage them.

- The cat should be treated like a superior being. Feed and pet the cat before feeding and paying attention to the dog.

- Impress upon the dog that the cat is your property, just like your shoes and furniture legs. The dog must respect this and not chew on the cat!

RETRIEVE THE NEWSPAPER
A perennial favorite: Send your dog out in the rain to fetch the paper

A 4-pound Chihuahua might struggle a little while bringing in the big Sunday paper, but most dogs can master this trick. For safety's sake, request that your paper be thrown into the back yard instead of the driveway. The convenience of having the the the dog bring the paper inside will be worth the extra tip to the paper boy.

If you have a dog who simply won't retrieve, don't get frustrated trying to force her to get the paper. As long as she shows interest in chasing and retrieving, it's worth a try. Roll up a newspaper and tape it securely. Until she gets the hang of this, she may shred it. Throw it to its usual delivery spot and encourage her to fetch it. Big reward if she brings it in for you! Repeat this several times a day.

Now show her the paper. Take it outside, leaving her inside.

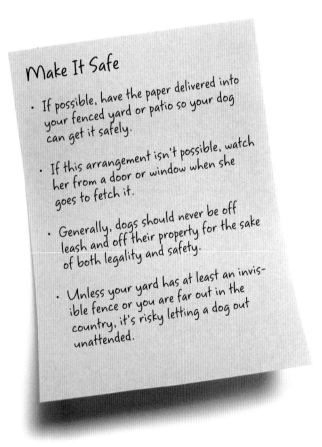

Make It Safe

- If possible, have the paper delivered into your fenced yard or patio so your dog can get it safely.

- If this arrangement isn't possible, watch her from a door or window when she goes to fetch it.

- Generally, dogs should never be off leash and off their property for the sake of both legality and safety.

- Unless your yard has at least an invisible fence or you are far out in the country, it's risky letting a dog out unattended.

Starting the Trick

- Back-chain if she's not a natural retriever. Have her take the paper, then release it to you. Repeat this three to five times per session until she's getting pretty good at it.

- Now start playing fetch with it. If your paper comes early in the morning, have her do one successful paper retrieve before she gets breakfast.

- At first, reward consistently—this is one trick you want her to pattern.

124

Put it in the spot, open the door, and restrain her. Get her perked up, asking if she is "ready, ready?" Let her go! If she has a single retrieving bone in her body, she'll retrieve it.

When she's going out for it reliably, she's ready to start her new job. Practice a few times with plastic-bagged newspapers so that she gets used to those, too.

Next Steps

- She may get carried away and start bringing all sorts of things from the back yard. It's cute, but if you didn't ask her to go get a chewed-up old stick, don't reward her for it.

- On the other hand, never correct her for bringing you something you don't want, even if it's really yucky. This gives her mixed signals.

- While you're teaching her this new skill, have her practice at the time she'd normally bring in the paper.

Multiple Dogs

- If you have multiple dogs, send them out one at a time or alternate their fetching days.

- If you're lucky, one dog will learn from the other. If you're not, they'll play tug-of-war with your paper.

- Some dogs never get the whole fetch-and-retrieve thing. It doesn't mean there's anything wrong with your dog—some of the best working and performance dogs in the world don't retrieve either!

CARRY THE GROCERIES
Have your helpful hound lend a hand by helping with the groceries

Tug games help prepare a dog to take something in his mouth and later drop it on command. Teach him to carry something from the garage into the kitchen.

If possible, begin with anything he might carry around on his own. This might be a favorite stuffie toy, a rawhide, or a tennis ball. Tell him to take it in his mouth and hold still for several seconds, praising him calmly. If you have to gently

hold his muzzle closed for a few seconds, that's OK. Then have him release it and reward him. Work up to about twenty seconds of holding, then step back and have him come to you. Give big praise when he releases it! You are back-chaining this by teaching hold and release first.

Start patterning the behavior. Call him out to your car when you come home, handing him something he'll hold and

Patterned Behaviors

- This is a patterned behavior. If you always bring the groceries in from the car in the garage, start having your dog accompany you to the garage when you get back, even if he's not yet carrying anything.

- At first, you might need to reward him just for coming out to the garage with you.

- Dogs both enjoy and learn from consistent and repeated behaviors, especially if the behaviors are fun and rewarding.

Find the Right Item

- Plastic bags will be hard for him to carry, and paper grocery sacks will be pretty much impossible. Buy at least one cloth grocery bag—go green and make it easier for your dog at the same time.

- Unless he's a total brute, start him off with the bag

with one little item in it. That way he gets used to a little weight but isn't overwhelmed.

- Give low-key praise for taking and holding it, big praise for releasing it on command.

encouraging him to bring it toward the house. Every step might be a small victory. If he drops the item, ignore him. If he releases it to you at any point in the process, reward him. Take it one step at a time—if he'll carry something for two steps, he'll carry it for thirty if you're patient.

MAKE IT EASY

Try giving your dog something edible but fairly uninteresting to carry, such as a carrot (unless he loves carrots). Doing this will increase his willingness to carry a somewhat high-value object without being tempted to eat it on the way. Then give him a much tastier reward for carrying and releasing it.

Make It a Routine

- If he's got a strong work ethic, he'll start expecting to carry groceries inside for you every time you come home.

- Even if you didn't stop at the store, don't disappoint him. Give him your wallet or purse or something else instead.

- After he's eagerly offering to work, you don't need to reward him all the time. The job itself is his reward.

- Of course, that doesn't mean there's anything wrong with the occasional bonus!

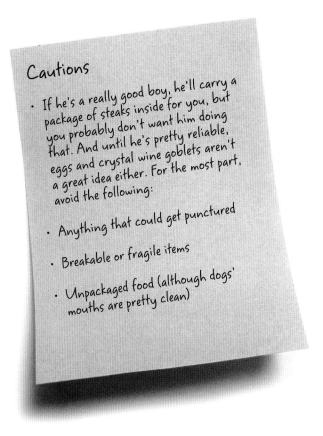

Cautions

- If he's a really good boy, he'll carry a package of steaks inside for you, but you probably don't want him doing that. And until he's pretty reliable, eggs and crystal wine goblets aren't a great idea either. For the most part, avoid the following:

- Anything that could get punctured

- Breakable or fragile items

- Unpackaged food (although dogs' mouths are pretty clean)

RING A BELL

Stop your dog from scratching the door to go out by teaching him to ring a bell

You have to know your dog to figure out how to teach this trick. Some dogs, such as boxers, naturally use their paws for a lot of things. Other dogs don't, but just about any dog can be taught to nose-bump a bell.

Rig up a bell at the right height for your dog. Some pet stores sell leather strips with bells attached for this very

purpose. Craft stores sell bells, or you can even use a wind chime. Depending on whether you put the bell indoors or out, make sure it's melodious enough to be used indoors and loud enough that you can hear it.

Teach your dog to nose-bump the bell by dabbing a little peanut butter or cheese on it. Do this each time she goes in

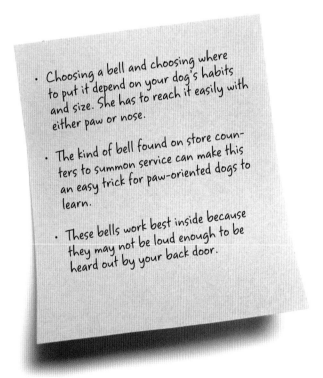

- Choosing a bell and choosing where to put it depend on your dog's habits and size. She has to reach it easily with either paw or nose.

- The kind of bell found on store counters to summon service can make this an easy trick for paw-oriented dogs to learn.

- These bells work best inside because they may not be loud enough to be heard out by your back door.

Starting the Trick

- This is an easy trick because there's really not much training to do as long as you can figure out how to teach her to bump it with a nose or paw every time she goes in and out.

- For nose-bumping a bell, a little dab of food on the bell works. Tap the bell first,

then when you start fading out the food, she'll still sniff when you tap.

- Use a target stick to train little dogs or just to avoid bending over Fido.

128

or out to make the association. Pairing this with a command is unnecessary and may make it harder for her to learn. It's an independent behavior and needs to be associated with the action of going through the door, not with a directional cue. It's important to make an immediate and happy show of opening the door the instant she rings it. Make sure you have it positioned so that she doesn't need to back up as you open the door.

ZOOM

After she has the basic concept, use a target stick to direct her to the bell so that she gets used to bumping it without you being by her side. If she rings the bell—even by mistake—when you're not in the room, run immediately to the door and open it.

Next Steps

- For a paw-inclined dog, rig the bell so that she can touch it with her paw when you tell her, "Shake."

- Pay attention to how high she raises her paw on command and hang the bell so that she'll touch it easily.

- Use the target stick or sticky food and the "ready, ready" game to teach her to go ahead of you to ring the bell. When she does, quickly go open the door.

When You Create a Monster

- Some dogs find it fun when they can train you to do something such as open the door!

- Try practicing this when you're reasonably sure that your dog really needs to go potty.

- Don't go out with her.

- This trick is only for going out to the bathroom, not for going out to play, bark at the mailman, or terrorize squirrels.

PUT TOYS AWAY
House a mess? Your dog can clean up after himself by putting his toys away

Back-chain this impressive and useful trick with a target and basic retrieving skills. This trick can be used to pick up the kids' toys, laundry, and downed twigs on the lawn, too. If you can teach your dog to pick up dog poop, get an agent (and some mouthwash).

Start by teaching him to drop toys into a hamper. First, put a target, such as a small plate with a treat on it, inside the hamper. Tell him to take his toy and, with your hand, lure his head over the hamper, saying, "Clean up!" He'll see the treat and drop the toy for it. Bingo: One toy down, and he's already figured out that this is rewarding. You can click just as he releases the toy into the hamper. If he moves and misses the

Praise

- The best treat to use for inside the hamper is small and soft, something that he'll gobble up in a second.

- He'll want to nose all around the hamper, looking for more food, and he might try picking the toy up again. Try not to let him.

- As soon as he's dropped the toy and eaten the treat, tell him what a good boy he is and repeat the exercise with another treat. Do this three to five times.

Ready, Ready

- Play the "ready, ready" game. Have him sit by you at the hamper and let him see you put a treat into the hamper.

- Hold his collar (or tell him to stay, if he will), toss the toy, and tell him "ready, ready . . . go pick up your toys!" No reward until he puts it back into the hamper.

- Do this several feet away from the hamper and gradually increase the distance until he's not bringing the toy to you but instead is putting it away.

hamper, say, "Oops," block him from diving for the treat, and then try again.

Work on distance and his autonomy by tossing the toy while standing next to the hamper. Call him over, give your command, and let him get the treat. Gradually move away from the hamper so that he's working independently. After he's mastered the skill, encourage him to pick up multiple toys. Start fading out the treats until they're intermittent.

Game Over

- When you're done, game over. Pick up the hamper or distract him with something else.

- If your dog enjoys fetch, pair this with throwing a toy out of sight and quickly tossing a treat into the hamper before he returns.

- If he drops the toy and heads straight for the hamper for his treat, block him. Have him take the toy and go back to luring him over to the hamper again.

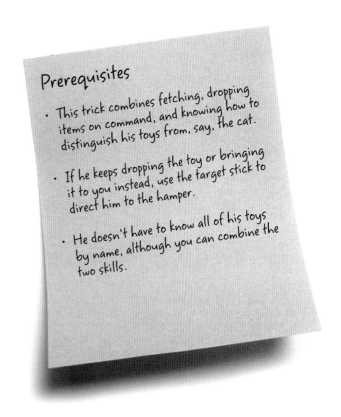

Prerequisites
- This trick combines fetching, dropping items on command, and knowing how to distinguish his toys from, say, the cat.

- If he keeps dropping the toy or bringing it to you instead, use the target stick to direct him to the hamper.

- He doesn't have to know all of his toys by name, although you can combine the two skills.

131

DOGWEAR

Fashionable and functional doggie gear helps your dog look the part when performing

Is it demeaning to dress up your dog? No more demeaning than to put a collar or harness on him. A harness can be decorated with silk flowers or fairy wings, and a pearl necklace looks stunning on a rottweiler. An intimidating-looking dog's appearance is magically softened with even a simple bandanna. As long as it doesn't impede movement or distress the dog, most dogs readily accept a little dressing up. Even a small touch jazzes up a trick routine. Take into consideration what your dog is going to be doing and the temperature.

Dog coats and sweaters aren't about just fashion; they're also functional. Dog coats with reflective stripes are great for walking or jogging in the dark. Dressing a thin-skinned

Dogwear Design

- Some dogs resist wearing a coat, especially a complex one with a hood and multiple straps. Try a loosely fitting sweater or simple lightweight coat to get her used to the idea.

- Check the design, especially if you have a male dog who lifts his leg to pee. Some coats that extend down the dog's belly can be easily soiled.

- If the weather is extremely hot or brutally cold, postpone long walks and exercise your dog inside for the day.

Reflective Coats

- Dark-colored dogs become practically invisible to drivers at night. Reflective stripes on a dog coat are an important safety feature when walking your dog in the dark or when the weather is rainy or foggy.

- Reflective tape is available at hardware stores if you want to decorate your dog's existing coat and make it more visible.

- Hunting dog coats are often sold in bright safety orange or yellow to increase hunting dogs' visibility in the field.

greyhound or Chihuahua for cold weather is simply the kind thing to do. Dog boots protect paws from salt and deicing chemicals. Even hunting dogs are often outfitted in camo or hunting orange coats to keep them warm and dry—a dog won't work efficiently if she's too cold.

Dogs can be dressed for hot weather, too, if they absolutely must be in the heat. Cooling coats may be made of reflective silver mesh to deflect the sun's rays, or nylon capes can be soaked in water to keep the dog's skin cool.

If your dog might need to potty while costumed, make sure he can comfortably do so without peeing on his outfit. Let him get used to the clothing before putting him through his trick paces. If the costume is elaborate, take him for a short walk while wearing it first.

Everyday Dogwear

- Check pet stores or online sites for hats and goggles made to fit dogs.

- Don't put your sunglasses on Fido inside and expect him to be able to see. You can't see well inside, and neither can he.

- Prepare to take your dog for a walk. When he's all excited, put on his gear and immediately go out the door.

- Walkies, excitement, and treats can override the annoyance at wearing headgear.

Costumes

- Costumes can be elaborate, but simple outfits are easier for your dog to move in.

- Put a frilly pink tutu on Fido and take pictures of him hiking his leg to pee.

- A T-shirt knotted around his belly, a biblike tuxedo, a tie or bowtie, gym shorts, necklaces, or a decorated harness: All are simple, cheap costumery.

- Some dogs don't care and enjoy the attention; others dislike it. If your dog seems distressed even after a few tries, don't force him.

DOGGIE BACKPACKS

Whether on country hikes or urban walks, even the tiniest dog can pack her stuff

Dogs love jobs. Several breeds were used to pull carts and sleds or to be pack animals. Today doggie backpacks for recreation are widely available. When a dog associates his own backpack with walkies, he'll really look forward to the job. Plus, he can carry his own poop bags.

Most doggie backpacks are like saddle bags, with straps wrapping around the dog's forechest and ribcage. They range from lightweight "city packs" to complex constructions with multiple compartments. Because there's no "average" shape for a dog, you might have to try several types to find a comfortable one. When buying online, take all his measurements and contact the company to find the best fit.

Backpacks

- A range of packs is available: complex packs for serious hiking or working dogs or day trippers. And some models have removable extra packs to change them from an excursion pack to a basic walk-around-the-park pack.

- A dog walking with a pack acts differently because she has a job and a purpose.

- Be prepared to receive a lot of comments when out with your pack-wearing dog. Many people will assume that she's a service dog.

Backpacks for Every Activity

- Make sure that your dog has unrestricted range of motion with the backpack both empty and weighted.

- There are many styles to choose from. Look for quick-release clasps and soft fabric or padded straps.

- If you plan on doing some serious hiking, look for weather-resistant packs with rainproof zippers and closures to keep gear dry.

- Some packs have grab handles on top so you can assist your dog over rough terrain.

A healthy dog can carry up to 20 percent of his weight in a properly distributed backpack. If you have a long-bodied breed prone to back problems or a dog with joint issues, check first with your vet. A young dog shouldn't carry much weight because doing so can stress growing joints. However, even an empty pack will get him used to the idea. You'll want to start with minimal weight and shorter walks.

Think of how heavy a 30-pound pack will feel to you at the end of a 5-mile hike! Watch your dog for signs of discomfort or fatigue and remember that the extra work could make him thirstier. The point is to efficiently exercise your dog, not exhaust him.

High-energy dogs will get more of a workout when walking with a backpack. Working breeds especially will love wearing a pack because they'll feel a sense of accomplishment and duty. Even tiny dogs enjoy a pack and look darned cute wearing one. Avoid cargo that might poke him and keep the weight evenly distributed. Water or pop bottles work well to start out with.

Special Occasion Backpacks

- For hotter days, try putting ice packs in the pack to keep your dog cooler.

- Wrap hard objects or ones with sharp edges in a towel. Your dog can't tell you if something is uncomfortably poking her.

- To add weight for exercise, try dry beans.

- Carry water and collapsible water bowls, your keys, rain gear, sun block, and even dog treats. Keep the weight equal on both sides of the pack.

Variety of Sizes

- Backpacks are available for any size of dog. Although most pet stores carry them, your best bet for a really wide range of styles and sizes is online.

- Be careful with long-haired dogs when tightening the straps to avoid pinching or tangling the fur.

- Don't put things with sharp corners or edges into the pack without wrapping them first; otherwise, your dog may be getting unnecessarily poked or chafed.

CARTING BASICS

From trips down the block to parade favorites, cart-pulling dogs have a long history

Carting dogs have been "poor man's horses" for centuries. Sled dogs can go where no horse can, and some dogs have been bred specifically to pull carts or sleds. You don't need a big dog to pull a cart. Toy dogs can pull little wagons or sleds. A physically sound dog of any size can pull a cart as long as the weight is proportionate to her size. Generally speaking,

an adult dog can pull her own weight safely, although you must condition her, starting with an empty cart and gradually increasing weight. Depending on the distance, terrain, and type of cart, she may be able to pull twice her own weight. After your dog is used to the cart, she should be able to move effortlessly without straining. If she has to strain or

Harnesses

- A good harness will have a padded breastplate to take the weight and not be so high that it cuts across your dog's neck.

- Many harnesses also have handles on the back so that you can steady the dog without giving leash

corrections. When a leash is used for carting, it's usually attached to a D-ring on the top of the harness.

- All the buckles should be riveted. Good harnesses are adjustable at many points around the dog's body for a snug, comfy fit.

Carts and Sleds

- Avoid the temptation to jerry-rig a sled with pieces of rope for your dog to pull. Such a sled can run into her from behind with very little momentum.

- Carts and sleds use rigid traces, preventing them

from swinging to the side or ramming into the dog from behind.

- It can take a long time, if ever, to get a dog's trust back after being run over by the cart she's pulling.

work hard, decrease the weight.

Many online outlets sell harnesses and carting supplies. A regular harness can be used for pulling very light weights but won't distribute weight comfortably or safely for heavier loads or much distance.

After you have your harness and carting set up, start gently so that your dog isn't spooked by getting bumped from behind or by the pressure of the traces on her sides. Start by walking her just with harness and traces, so that she gets used to the feel. After several sessions, attach something to the traces, such as a couple of milk jugs or small lengths of chain. Doing this gets her used to both a little weight and the sound of something dragging and bouncing behind her. Use treats or toys and encouragement to keep her moving forward but avoid rewarding her for being anxious.

Attach the cart or sled. Spend some time walking her with an empty cart on different surfaces and over bumps and sidewalks before adding weight.

Pulling Cars and Sleds

- Dogs pulling carts can work solo or as a team. Carting is typically done with one or two dogs.

- Sledding in snow usually employs teams of two to twelve dogs. Alaskan huskies and other native or northern breeds have greater stamina than most other dogs and usually love to pull.

- A single, fit dog can pull an adult on snow for several miles, depending on the snow condition. She can certainly pull kids around the block!

Alternatives

- For a safe alternative, try hooking your dog up with a sturdy harness and heavy tarpaulin to pull kids on snow or slick grass.

- Start her off slowly, with lots of encouragement, and have someone leading her while pulling. There is nothing about a canvas tarp that will injure her if it slides into her legs.

- Even though a dog may joyfully want to pull for miles at high speed, don't let her.

SKATEBOARDING DOGS
It's not hard to teach your dog to skateboard or even push a stroller

Look online to find thousands of videos of skateboarding dogs. The sport is particularly popular with bulldog people, perhaps because on a board, these lumbering dogs can go faster than they ever could on four paws!

This is easier for dogs who have done rear leg-awareness exercises and who are used to the idea of something moving underfoot. Get a board that's a comfortable size for Fido and

get him used to the new toy. See if he'll chase if you push it across the floor. Put treats on top of it. Make him realize this is a Really Fun Thing.

Now chock it with 2-by-4s or books so that it's stationary and teach him to put first two, then three, then all four paws on it. You can click-treat for each paw placement. Next, teach him to jump off safely. You are back-chaining this final action

Starting on a Skateboard

- Spend plenty of time with the first two steps, especially if your dog is a little soft and likely to spook easily. If the board flips up and bonks him in the face, you might never get him to go near it again.

- You want absolute familiarity with the board: how it smells, moves, and sounds.

- If you think it might help, glue a carpet strip or non-skid stair treads to it so that it feels more stable.

Encouragement

- He might be the fearless sort who jumps on and off with aplomb just because he can. Most dogs need at least some encouragement.

- Small- to medium-sized dogs are the ideal size—try to find a board that's not so

big that he can't push it and not so small that he has a hard time balancing on it.

- After he's unhesitating about jumping on, off, and even over it, it's time to get moving.

first so that he understands the final step in the process and second so that he is confident and not panicked about jumping off. Spend lots off time rewarding him for stepping on and jumping off.

Now put the board on heavy carpet so that it doesn't roll easily. Encourage two paws on and treat quickly! He'll be surprised when it moves, so distract him. Don't spend too long on this phase—as soon as he's over the surprise, get him moving with all four paws on board. Push the skateboard or pull it with a rope. Treat him frequently as long as he stays on.

You need to teach him how to push off unless he figures it out himself. Encourage him to work up maximum speed while he has two or three paws on the board and let him take it from there.

Have Patience

- Chances are that he'll leap off in horror the first time it moves under his feet. He's not necessarily being fearful. He just doesn't understand it, and you might have let it move too far or too fast.

- Try waiting until he has all four feet on the board and move one of them to the floor.

- As he pushes away with his foot to get back on, the board will move forward. Click-treat, praise, do cartwheels! He's skateboarding!

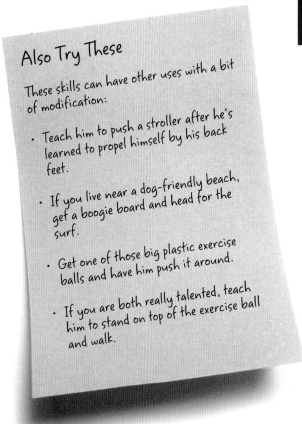

Also Try These

These skills can have other uses with a bit of modification:

- Teach him to push a stroller after he's learned to propel himself by his back feet.

- If you live near a dog-friendly beach, get a boogie board and head for the surf.

- Get one of those big plastic exercise balls and have him push it around.

- If you are both really talented, teach him to stand on top of the exercise ball and walk.

BICYCLING

One of the best ways to exercise a dog efficiently is by biking with her

Biking with a dog is an efficient way to wear her out fast and give her the flat-out running she needs. Most dogs are quickly trained to run safely next to a bicycle. Several bike attachments on the market require virtually no training, and even large, rambunctious dogs are held safely next to the bike. Mountain bike enthusiasts often ride with high-endurance dogs, but a more sedentary dog relishes the change of pace, too.

Dogs should be biked only on trails or quiet suburban areas, not in traffic. Let your dog set the pace and have her run on grass or dirt as much as possible because extended running on hard surfaces can crack paw pads. An exuberant

Bicycling

- Having your dog running next to you might not be an impressive "trick," but it will let her expend extra energy so that she'll have an easier time behaving overall.

- Don't confuse her by using a "heel" command. To her this is nothing like heeling.

- You can use directional commands such as "gee" (right) and "haw" (left) to alert her to upcoming turns.

- Two bike attachments will fit on a single bike so that you can run a dog on each side.

Bike Attachments

- Because bike attachments are secured to the frame right under the seat, your weight keeps you and the bike centered, and you'll barely feel it even if your large dog lunges.

- Walk with your dog on the attachment alongside the bike before starting with a short, slow ride.

- For the first several minutes, give him treats and encouragement. Most dogs get comfortable in about fifteen minutes and love the chance to trot with you at their natural speed.

dog may want to race at full speed until she is exhausted. Slow her down if you think she's overdoing it and carry water if you'll be going more than a few miles, especially on warmer days. Avoid biking with a dog until he is about a year old because that pavement pounding can be damaging to young joints.

Follow packaging instructions if you get an attachment. Most of these can be put to use right away. Teaching a dog to run on leash next to a bike does require a dog with basic leash manners, and it's not a bad idea to use a training collar

and halter at first. Start by walking your dog alongside the bicycle and don't let her cross in front of the wheel. Some dogs will have to be trained not to nip or "herd" the bicycle wheels at first, and some might be nervous about the whole experience. Start slowly in a safe area. If you have good balance, ride one-handed while holding the leash in the other for better control.

Safety Vests

- Remember that drivers can probably see you but may not see your dog.

- A brightly colored safety vest with or without reflective stripes is also a good idea if you bike with her, day or night. Both you and your dog should be highly visible.

- Both hot asphalt and salted winter roads can lead to painful paws. Consider some well-made dog boots to protect her feet. Most pet and sporting supply outlets carry them.

Safety Considerations

- Your dog should be at least a year old before running with the bicycle. Ask your vet. Some larger and giant breeds take up to eighteen months to complete bone development.

- Dogs can overheat quickly, especially running on blacktop. If the weather is very hot or very cold, don't make her run.

- She's working harder than you are. Don't overdo it!

141

WEIGHT PULLING

From little terriers to hulking mastiffs, dogs can pull their own weight and more

Like carting, weight pulling uses a skill that many dogs long have been bred and used for. A well-conditioned weight-pull dog is a canine strongman, even if he's a 15-pound terrier. It is a strength sport that complements faster and more agile pursuits, and many organizations welcome both purebreds and mixed-breed dogs of all sizes.

Dogs compete in pulling the most weight on a wheeled cart or snow sled for 15–20 feet. As with any sport, the dog's safety is paramount, and no good handler forces her dog to pull more than she is safely capable of. Dogs clearly love pulling—whether it's playing tug-of-war or pulling on a leash—and weight pulling provides a structured outlet.

Weight Pulling

- As anyone who's tried to walk an exuberant, untrained dog on leash can tell you, dogs love to pull! Weight pulling is a sport that encourages and rewards this love.

- Weight pulling is to a dog as strength training is to a person. It is an almost unparalleled conditioning exercise, especially combined with running and jumping.

- Conditioning a dog to weight pull will not make him any more likely to pull on leash and may even improve his overall obedience.

Strength

- Terriers, even small ones, excel at this trick because it satisfies their tenacious nature. In fact, terriers can pull many more times their own body weight than can larger dogs.

- With a good harness and a wheeled cart or weight sled, most dogs can very easily pull ten times their own weight without much practice.

- The two basic requirements are strength and a willingness to throw his heart into pulling the sled to you.

142

Although a dog can be started with just a loose harness and very light weights to get him used to it, a proper padded or sheepskin pulling harness is mandatory for a loaded sled. This harness has a broad breastplate and distributes the load evenly. Keep your dog on leash at first until he's used to the empty sled and looks forward to work when he gets his harness put on. Then you can work on his form and start adding weight a little at a time.

Motivation

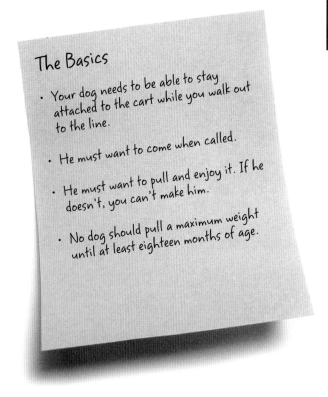

The Basics

- Your dog needs to be able to stay attached to the cart while you walk out to the line.

- He must want to come when called.

- He must want to pull and enjoy it. If he doesn't, you can't make him.

- No dog should pull a maximum weight until at least eighteen months of age.

- Training is minimal as long as your dog can stay for a few minutes and then come when called.

- Use a lot of whatever will motivate the dog. All training is very positive.

- There are no corrections or punishments in weight-pull training. If the dog won't pull toward you, no correction will make that happen.

- If the dog can't pull the weight, he's helped with a push. That way he always feels as if he succeeded.

143

SOCIALIZE FOR SUCCESS

The well-socialized dog can be taken anywhere and handle most any situation

Many dogs who are isolated in puppyhood remain fearful and suspicious their entire lives. The developmental period between one and five months is extremely important for puppies. Providing them with a stimulating, varied environment virtually ensures confident, cheerful adult dogs.

You want your puppy to grow up thinking that all people are friendly. Don't worry that he will be any less of a watchdog as he grows up. A well-adjusted dog knows the difference between friend and foe. A dog who is suspicious and fearful is a liability.

Invite people to your home to visit the puppy. Make sure that all interactions are pleasant and fun. Don't allow anyone,

Treats

- Carry treats in your pocket, so that if he is nervous about some people (men in hats, people of different ethnicities, children) you can hand them a treat to give him.

- It's fine if people you meet ignore him. You want him to accept strangers in a calm, neutral way rather than assume that every person he meets ought to make him the center of attention.

- He doesn't have to greet everyone he meets. Not all breeds are social butterflies.

Introduce Him to the Neighborhood

- Taking him on short walks gets him used to the distractions of different vehicles, weather, noises, and smells.

- Dogs who rarely leave the property may bark excessively and be apprehensive about the world outside.

- Being outside of the house reassures a dog that it's not a threatening place.

- Don't put a puppy into a situation where he will get scared by another dog or a person. Puppies can retain vestiges of that fear for life.

especially children, to roughhouse, tease, or play chase games. Ask your visitors to gently enforce any obedience rules you have established, such as not jumping up or play-biting. Let friends run a brush through your puppy's coat and handle his feet gently. Doing this will get the puppy used to being groomed and going to the vet. Don't force anything at this point. Keep it pleasant and use treats.

Build physical confidence by letting the puppy explore smells and different types of footing, climbing over logs and being in and around water. Take him to pet stores and walk him around the neighborhood. Occasionally drive him

places. Many dogs develop stress and carsickness because the only time they go anywhere by car is to the vet. This is easily avoided if the puppy associates car trips with fun and the reward of being with you.

Talk to your vet about when your puppy will be protected by immunizations before taking your puppy to places such as pet stores and public parks. This age is usually around eighteen weeks old. By then he's ready for puppy kindergarten and training classes, which will provide structured socialization and learning.

Introduce Him to Activity

- Walk your dog through an outdoor strip mall or busy parking lot, encouraging him to keep his attention on you.

- Sit outside a coffee shop or on a park bench with him. Smile and say hello to people when appropriate.

Your dog will learn from your social cues. If you're relaxed and friendly, he will be, too.

- People are friendlier when you have a dog with you. Put a bandanna or backpack on him to make him more approachable.

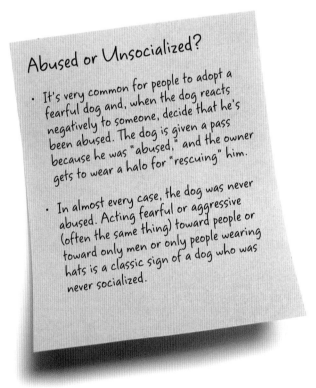

Abused or Unsocialized?

- It's very common for people to adopt a fearful dog and, when the dog reacts negatively to someone, decide that he's been abused. The dog is given a pass because he was "abused," and the owner gets to wear a halo for "rescuing" him.

- In almost every case, the dog was never abused. Acting fearful or aggressive (often the same thing) toward people or toward only men or only people wearing hats is a classic sign of a dog who was never socialized.

EXERCISE REQUIREMENTS
Make sure your dog gets her exercise needs fulfilled, and other behavior problems may disappear

There's an easy cure for many behavioral problems: exercise. Dogs are pack animals, like wolves who spend much of their time interacting and hunting. They have been bred for centuries to herd, hunt, and guard. Modern dogs don't work much and adapt to spending most of their time inside or in small yards, often alone. This is fine, but owners need to invest a little time in exercising Fido for both weight and behavioral management. Active breeds such as Labradors, goldens, collies, and many terriers are better behaved and easier trained when they get plenty of exercise, especially in their first few years of life. Activity level is not determined by size, although it's easier to exercise a little dog inside. Jack Russell terriers

Exercise

- Exuberant retrievers are easy to wear out with a tennis racquet or tennis-ball thrower.

- Few dogs get much exercise by merely being outside by themselves, even in a large yard. Like people, they benefit from aerobic and muscle-building activity.

- Friendly dogs benefit from having another dog to play with sometimes. Try play dates and daycare.

- Small dogs are easy to exercise indoors. Unlike bigger dogs, they can run full speed inside.

Treadmills

- Dogs can learn to use a treadmill, either one designed for dogs or the regular people kind.

- Start very slowly when introducing a dog to a treadmill. You might need to get on with him and use lots of treats or even start

- by feeding him there when it's turned off.

- Keep treadmill sessions short and don't let your dog run himself into exhaustion.

- This can "take the edge off" before practicing leash manners on a walk.

are small but have extremely high exercise requirements, whereas great Danes are laidback enough to be content with minimal daily exercise.

Exuberant dogs left to their own devices may bark, dig, be destructive, or develop anxiety or even aggressive behaviors. Exercising doesn't have to be a time-consuming chore. Play fetch in the back yard or even in the house. Put a backpack on the dog and take a short, brisk walk. Train him to run beside a bicycle or roller skates. Teach the dog tricks and do some obedience play-training. Arrange play dates with friends' dogs or look into doggie daycare. Sign up for classes in obedience or dog sports. Take your dog to a beach or a river. Find a petsitter or neighbor to take your dog for walks when you're at work. Look for interactive, problem-solving dog toys. Dogs can learn to enjoy running on a treadmill. Start a fitness walking routine for yourself and bring the dog along. Remember the saying: If you're overweight, your dog isn't getting enough exercise!

Jumping

- Controlled jumping is a fun game for dogs, but don't let them overdo it and avoid repeated jumping with a growing pup.

- Keeping jumps at elbow height or lower is generally safe.

- Toss toys and treats over for him to get.

- If he's unwilling to jump, start by having him jump over something flat on the ground or setting up a very low jump in a hallway so that he has no choice.

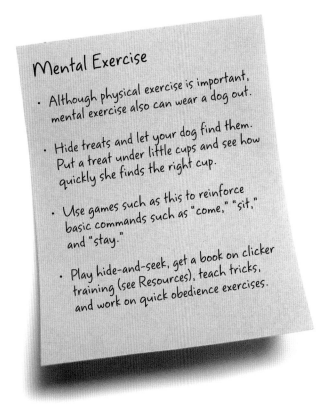

Mental Exercise

- Although physical exercise is important, mental exercise also can wear a dog out.

- Hide treats and let your dog find them. Put a treat under little cups and see how quickly she finds the right cup.

- Use games such as this to reinforce basic commands such as "come," "sit," and "stay."

- Play hide-and-seek, get a book on clicker training (see Resources), teach tricks, and work on quick obedience exercises.

OFF-LEASH GAMES

If you make yourself a valuable playmate, your dog looks to you for fun and guidance

Few dogs will run off and ignore their owners when off leash as long as there's a good bond, and the dogs have learned to be respectful and attentive to their owners. Some breeds—such as hounds and terriers, accustomed to following fascinating scents—will become very single-minded when on track. Dogs with high prey drive or a tendency toward dog

aggression will run after fast-moving things or may feel compelled to challenge every dog they see. These dogs shouldn't be off leash unless in securely fenced or controlled environments, and potentially aggressive dogs shouldn't ever go to dog parks.

Engaging with your dog and making it rewarding for him to

Alternate Play and Exercise

- If your dog regards you as the benevolent dictator—who provides all good things in his life from food to structure to fun—he really won't have any reason to take off the minute you unclip the leash.

- Your dog always wants to know what's in it for him.

- So, for keeping off-leash attention, arm yourself with his favorite things—usually food and toys!

- Play with him. Alternate control exercises (sit-stay) with attention ("watch me") and with play (tug or fetch).

Hide

- Hide periodically. Wait until Fido isn't watching and quickly step behind a tree. Say nothing.

- When he suddenly realizes that you're not around, he'll start racing back the way you just came. He might be rather worried that his benevolent dicta-

tor just disappeared!

- When he sees you (call him if you need to), make a huge fuss and remind him how valuable you are by rewarding him.

- Make a practice of this, and he'll learn to keep his eye on you.

stay with you are multifaceted. Staying with you means that he values you because you provide the good things in life and keep him safe. He respects you because you have clear rules and are fair to him. He also likes you because you're fun! So, go play. After he's trained to focus on you despite distractions, let him off leash, get a Frisbee or ball, and go play outside. Keep treats in your pocket for especially good displays of obedience. Call him to you randomly, give him a big reward, and send him off to resume walking or playing.

·············· GREEN ● LIGHT ··············

Always carry poop bags when you're on public property. Have your dog wear his backpack and carry extra bags there or get a baggie pouch that clips to his leash. Get in the habit of always keeping poop bags handy in purses, coat pockets, day packs, and your vehicle.

Be Mindful of Others

GET OUT & PLAY

Dog Parks

- For many dog owners, dog parks are the only places to let their dogs off leash to run and play. Be a watchful dog park patron.

- Pay attention and learn to recognize signs of escalating tension, dogs ganging up on another, or dominant displays.

- If you see any warning signs, get your dog and leave.

- Don't take a puppy to busy dog parks. One bad experience could affect him for life.

- Respect leash laws and let him go off leash only when it's legal.

- Be aware of wildlife. Walking off leash in the woods will be too tempting for some dogs because of deer and other animals. If you think he might chase or disturb other animals, keep him leashed.

- Make sure he always wears collar ID and have him microchipped as well, even if he never goes off leash. It's better to be safe than sorry.

FETCH & FRISBEE

It's not about just fetching a tennis ball: Learn some flashy tricks with a Frisbee

If you've ever watched a disc dog performance during a football game halftime show, you already know what amazing things can be done with one human, one disc, and one dog. If your dog likes fetching a tennis ball, she will really love catching a Frisbee. Frisbees are safer than tennis balls. A dog who spends many hours catching and mouthing a ball will wear her teeth down on the abrasive surface over time. Additionally, rare but tragic accidents have happened when dogs have caught high-velocity tennis balls in midair and choked. Frisbees (dedicated enthusiasts call them "discs") designed for dogs are a better choice. Canine Frisbees have ridges or soft designs, allowing them to be easily picked up or retrieved

Frisbee and Fetch

- The very fancy moves are developed on a solid foundation of training and learning techniques and safety for both dog and handler.

- Find a class or club to safely learn the more competitive moves. Improper technique can easily lead to orthopedic injury to your dog.

- Although any dog can play Frisbee, competitive disc dogs are usually 30–50 pounds and naturally athletic.

- Many competitors wear neoprene and padding under their clothing to protect them from a high-velocity dog's nails.

Next Steps

- Whether throwing a ball or a Frisbee, don't encourage a young dog to jump straight up for it until bone development is done —check with your vet.

- Until then, throw long and low. With practice, you can have a Frisbee fly a long way on a gentle curve.

- If you have a water-loving dog, have her retrieve from water. Swimming is wonderful exercise for dogs of any age.

150

from water. If your dog is not interested in a canine Frisbee at first, use it as his food bowl for several days. Play the "ready, ready" game and do short throws. Never throw it directly at him. Let him chase while you hold it just out of reach. Bring it out only for playtime, so that it's a special treat. Vary skimming it along the ground and throwing it up into the air. Be patient; it takes practice and maturity for a dog to be a great midair catcher.

MAKE IT EASY

Some dogs dislike the plastic discs but go wild for soft Frisbees. Terriers in particular seem to love these, as do any dogs who like to shake, tug, and "kill" their toys. Mix up throwing with brief tug games. Use the tug as the reward, not as the focus of the game.

Practice

- With practice, you can direct a Frisbee quite precisely. It starts with the proper grip for a basic throw.

- Use a wide, smooth arm movement and release the Frisbee just before your arm reaches full extension for longer throws.

- Try throwing it very close to the ground, so that it skips like a stone across water. Dogs love this one!

- Raise one leg in a stork position and throw the Frisbee backward through your leg.

Have Patience

- Soft dogs who get concerned about new things can use the Frisbee as a dinner plate for a few days.

- Start with short throws at or below your dog's eye level to catch his interest.

- Don't play until your dog is exhausted. For one thing, many dogs simply don't know when to quit. Also, it's always best to stop with your dog wanting a bit more. He'll be more eager for the next session.

TRACKING

Teach your dog some beginner tracking: It's not just for bloodhounds and beagles

Tracking, or following scent, is a natural behavior for dogs. Dogs are used to track game when hunting, to find missing persons, and to sniff out contraband and bombs—a dog's strong sense of smell has been used in many different jobs. Dogs are also taught to track for fun and competition, and it is a rewarding, low-cost activity for you and your dog. Although some breeds such as hounds are more natural trackers, every dog has the ability to follow scent.

Use a harness if possible because you don't want her to feel any "corrections" by being tugged by the collar. If you don't have a harness, use a regular buckle collar. Never use a choke, pinch, or any type of training collar for tracking.

Tracking Harness

- The tracking harness allows your dog to move freely with her head down yet still to be under control.

- You'll need a long line, 20 feet long at minimum. If you have a large or fast dog, you'll be moving quite quickly to keep up after she gets going.

- You'll also need articles such as old socks or cotton gloves. Use these to mark treats and turns and to help you remember where you laid the track.

Lay the Track

- It's OK if she sees you laying the track; she won't be trying to "cheat" by committing it to memory. When she starts sniffing, she'll be following her nose.

- After she's done a few little short tracks, lengthen the distance between treats and start introducing some 90-degree turns.

- You are guaranteed to forget where you made the turn. Cheap driveway marker flags make excellent indicators. Your dog will be too busy working to think about what those mean.

Start by teaching your dog to identify your scent and associate it with rewards by laying out a scent pad on grass. Trample a small area about 2 feet square with your feet. Not only will she track your scent, but she'll track the smell of crushed vegetation. Sprinkle some very small, extra good treats within the scent pad and, with your dog on leash, encourage her to nose around on the scent pad and find the treats. If she leaves the scent pad, gently guide her back.

Have someone hold her and put her on a stay or secure her while you lay a short, straight track. Make a scent pad and put a single treat in it. With little steps, walk out about 6 feet, make a small scent pad by stomping around, and lay another treat in it. Encourage your dog to find the first treat and follow the short track to the second treat. Praise lavishly when she finds it.

Increase distance and complexity over time, adding turns and taking your dog over variable surfaces.

Start Simple

- She'll probably overshoot the turns at first. Make it easy. Put a treat about 6 feet from the turn so that she gets rewarded.

- After she has the hang of it and you are laying longer and more complex tracks, minimize the number of treats and scent pads and have one big, extra special "jackpot" treat at the very end.

- Advanced dogs can follow a track on variable surfaces, in places with lots of conflicting scents, criss-crossing turns and aged tracks.

Do Not Distract

- With a bag of old socks and treats, you can lay tracks on walks for fun or try different locations.

- One important rule: Let her work and don't distract her with lots of babbling.

- Buy some cheap driveway marker flags to use as turn indicators, so that when you lay longer tracks you can remember just where the turn is if your dog misses it. (You are sure to forget!)

- She'll track much better if she's a little hungry for all those treats.

153

OTHER ACTIVITIES
Games for water dogs, digging dogs, herding dogs, sighthounds, lap dogs, and more

There is a plethora of dog activities and almost countless organizations. For many, you need neither a purebred dog nor an exquisitely trained one. Almost all the people involved in dog sports are just regular folks enjoying a hobby, making new friends, and playing with their dogs.

Some sports are open to particular breeds of dogs or groups

to give them an outlet for natural inclinations. Sighthounds chase mechanized lures over vast fields in lure coursing. Most terriers are eligible for earthdog, a sport in which the dogs burrow down twisty, human-made tunnels and "corner" their quarry—usually caged rats. (The rats are unharmed.) Herding dogs can herd, hounds and hunting dogs can hunt and

Training

- Some sports need little or no training if your dog is reasonably healthy and controlled. Weight pulling, earthdog, dock diving, and lure coursing are all pretty much just "jump in and play" activities.

- After you've picked a sport and perhaps practiced a bit, look online or call dog training facilities to locate clubs, events, and training.

- Spectators are always welcome at events, if you want to get a feel for it.

Instinct

- Sports that rely on a lot of instinct but also require a fair amount of training include hunting, field trials, tracking, and herding.

- Want to see how your dog would do as a herder or hunting dog? Find an organization and ask about instinct tests.

- Usually any dog of a suitable breed (depending on the organization—some welcome mixed-breed dogs) can be evaluated in a real-life test for a small fee.

compete in field trials, and dogs with carting heritage can win carting titles.

Most agility venues allow any dog regardless of pedigree to compete. Flyball competitions pit relay teams of fast dogs leaping over hurdles and retrieving a ball against each other for points. Dock dogs leap from docks into water after a thrown lure, competing for distance. Weight-pulling dogs, canine freestyle dogs, and disc dogs can be any breed, mix, or size. Additionally, 4-H and junior handling events are available in many venues for the under-eighteen crowd.

Obedience

Therapy Dogs

- Sports that require fairly extensive training and teamwork include obedience, agility, flyball, and disc dog. You'll need to take classes for any of these.

- Take classes just for fun but consider competing—that's great fun, too. Novice com-petition is fairly easy, and almost everyone and their dogs are making mistakes and enjoying themselves.

- Depending on the organization, mixed-breed dogs and purebreds alike can compete for titles in novice through elite trials.

- Do good. Therapy dogs visit hospitals, schools, and nursing homes. Some programs require merely your friendly dog to sit quietly while being read to by children who are improving their reading skills or to sit by a hospital bed while being petted.

- This is a really wonderful way to show off Fido and Fido's trick skills and costumes to an appreciative audience.

- Therapy dogs need to be nonaggressive and friendly and to have basic obedience skills. Breed and size are irrelevant.

THE BARKING DOG
Put barking under command, and guess what? You can train your dog to stop barking

Understanding why your dog barks excessively is the key to quieting him. We want our dogs to alert us, but we don't want them barking for hours at falling leaves. Boredom and breed tendency, or a combination of the two, are common reasons why dogs bark. Some herding and hunting dogs bark a lot because they were bred to. Bored dogs bark to amuse themselves. Hyper dogs start cussing at a squirrel, get wound up, and keep on barking. Nervous or territorial dogs bark to warn away Scary Things.

Don't yell when your dog is barking. That only reinforces the excitement level. Allow a few woofs, then calmly say, "Thank you" and call your dog. Reward and distract him when he

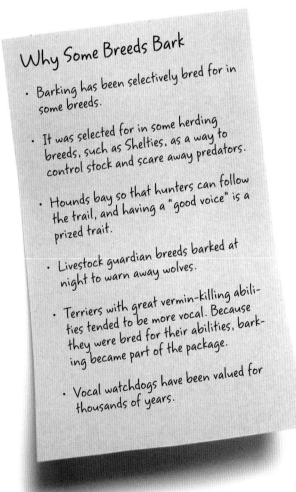

Why Some Breeds Bark

- Barking has been selectively bred for in some breeds.

- It was selected for in some herding breeds, such as Shelties, as a way to control stock and scare away predators.

- Hounds bay so that hunters can follow the trail, and having a "good voice" is a prized trait.

- Livestock guardian breeds barked at night to warn away wolves.

- Terriers with great vermin-killing abilities tended to be more vocal. Because they were bred for their abilities, barking became part of the package.

- Vocal watchdogs have been valued for thousands of years.

Teach Him to Bark

- Teaching a dog to bark on command can be a handy strategy because then it's easier to tell him to stop. Use a clicker and treats.

- Sometimes his barking is useful. Allow him to bark once or twice, then tell him, "That's enough. Come tell me about it," and call him to you.

- Give him a treat for coming right away and a stern "Ah! Ah!" if he continues barking.

comes to you. Done consistently, this can condition him into barking a couple of times, then looking to you for guidance. Make sure he gets sufficient exercise and training or schedule doggie daycare periodically—tired dogs don't bark.

If he barks when you're gone, try feeding him his meals in an interactive toy so that he has to work for his food. A run or playtime before work will help blow off energy. Excessive barking at visitors is often solved by giving him an alternate behavior, such as sitting for a treat, running for a toy, or showing off tricks. If he is fearful or acting aggressively (these look similar; if you're unsure, get a professional evaluation), you may have to separate and crate him until he has calmed down.

Barking can often be managed. If a dog barks when left alone outside, bring him in. If he barks at the front window, restrict window access. Antibark citronella collars can be used for some vocal dogs but not for dogs who bark because of separation anxiety or aggression—such collars can make their behavior worse.

Territorial Barks

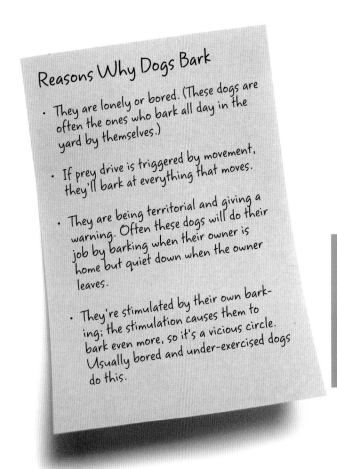

Reasons Why Dogs Bark

- They are lonely or bored. (These dogs are often the ones who bark all day in the yard by themselves.)

- If prey drive is triggered by movement, they'll bark at everything that moves.

- They are being territorial and giving a warning. Often these dogs will do their job by barking when their owner is home but quiet down when the owner leaves.

- They're stimulated by their own barking; the stimulation causes them to bark even more, so it's a vicious circle. Usually bored and under-exercised dogs do this.

- Barking at passersby is usually territorial. When you're home, call your dog after a couple of woofs and have him do something else, such as sit for a treat.

- Dogs who are triggered by visual stimuli such as watching people through a window will be quieter if they are simply not allowed access to the window. Use commonsense management solutions when possible.

- If he's social, consider taking him outside with a bag of treats to meet people he usually barks at.

GREETING SKILLS

Prevent boisterous jumping onto guests by teaching your dog cute greeting tricks instead

Dogs sniff muzzles (and butts) as part of their normal greeting rituals. Puppies and submissive dogs often lick the muzzles of older and more dominant dogs. So, when dogs jump up to greet us, they are engaging in very natural, albeit unwanted, greeting behavior. Picking up small dogs in response to jumping encourages more jumping. Negative attention

such as yelling or repeating "down" (which can confuse a dog taught that "down" is lying down) rarely works. What works is not letting the dog get a reward for the behavior and giving an alternate, acceptable greeting behavior instead.

When she tries jumping, avoid eye contact, cross your arms, remain silent, and quickly turn away. She wants contact and

Prep

- Have a bowl of treats by the front door. Make her sit and reward her repeatedly for doing so.

- Saying "No jump!" is a form of reinforcement for some dogs. The key is turning away silently and ignoring her for jumping and

rewarding her for anything that keeps all four on the floor.

- Keep greetings low key. Tell visitors to completely ignore your dog when they walk in and to pay attention only when she offers polite behavior.

Hold Her Paw

- Some dogs are not deterred by being ignored or have gotten away with jumping up for a long time.

- Try holding the dog's paws every time she jumps, without speaking or eye contact. Most dogs dislike

this. There is no need to squeeze or pinch her feet.

- Gently drop her after a few seconds and turn away. Praise her if she comes back to you and keeps all four feet on the floor.

affirmation by jumping, so don't give it to her. Commanding her to get off or pushing her affirms her jumping and is rarely effective. Most important, tell everyone she meets to do the same thing or keep her on leash so that she simply cannot jump onto strangers and thus reinforce the behavior. It is helpful to ignore her when you first walk in the door until she has settled down a bit, and avoid enthusiastic greetings.

As soon as she has "all four on the floor," praise her calmly. If she jumps up at the praise, turn away again. Start asking her for an alternate greeting behavior such as sitting and offering a paw. Some dogs like to go fetch a toy when someone walks in the door; others will sit up on their hind legs and look cute. Encourage any natural greeting behavior that doesn't involve jumping up onto people.

Don't allow your dog to jump up onto you or other people when they are sitting down; this gives her a confusing message. The key to curing jumping up is absolute consistency.

Avoid Play

- Some dogs like to greet newcomers with a toy in their mouths. Take advantage of this habit by praising it, as long as she's not jumping up.

- Avoid the temptation to respond by immediately playing with her because doing this can condition her to assume that all visitors will start playing the minute they walk in the door.

- Leash or crate your dog when people visit if the jumping could potentially cause harm or distress.

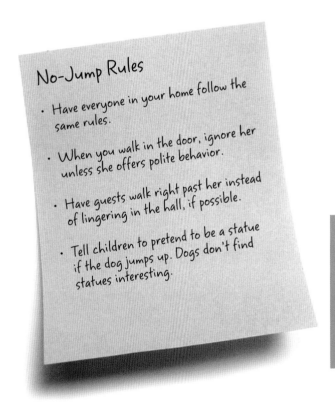

No-Jump Rules

- Have everyone in your home follow the same rules.

- When you walk in the door, ignore her unless she offers polite behavior.

- Have guests walk right past her instead of lingering in the hall, if possible.

- Tell children to pretend to be a statue if the dog jumps up. Dogs don't find statues interesting.

POTTYING IN PLACE

Impress your neighbors by having a dog who potties in place and on command

Entire books are dedicated to potty training, so we'll assume that you've already got that covered. Training your dog to potty on command is really a matter of understanding when he needs to go and providing some direction. Of course, if he doesn't need to go, all the commanding in the world won't make it happen! But it's very convenient when he uses just one part of the yard and is comfortable pottying on leash. Most dogs will pee when they need to, and many males, along with some females, will mark. Some dogs are shy about pooping, which can make them uncomfortable when kenneled or traveling.

The first step is knowing when he needs to go. Some dogs

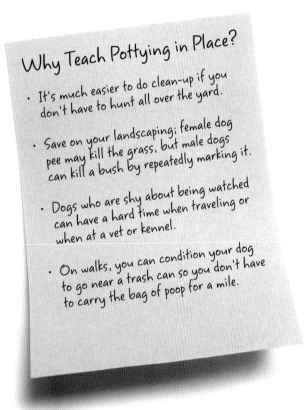

Why Teach Pottying in Place?

- It's much easier to do clean-up if you don't have to hunt all over the yard.

- Save on your landscaping; female dog pee may kill the grass, but male dogs can kill a bush by repeatedly marking it.

- Dogs who are shy about being watched can have a hard time when traveling or when at a vet or kennel.

- On walks, you can condition your dog to go near a trash can so you don't have to carry the bag of poop for a mile.

Find the Spot

- Use an out-of-the-way part of your yard or fence off an area and fill it with sand or fill dirt. If your dog likes to kick around a bit, make a little wall around it.

- Avoid using wood chips or mulch—these are hard to clean up properly. Never use cocoa mulch, which can be poisonous to dogs.

- A covered trash can and plastic sack are a perfect repository. Take the whole bag out on garbage day.

need to go right after waking up and eating breakfast. Others eat, then take a little postbreakfast nap, and then it's time to poop. Go outside with him. If he already has a spot, praise him when he goes there. If he's an all-over-the-yard kind of guy, put a long leash on him and stay out until he performs. It doesn't hurt to give him a treat afterward, either. If he's about to pee, that's easy to predict—say, "Go pee!" and pretend he's doing it on command.

Time Walks or Potty Trips

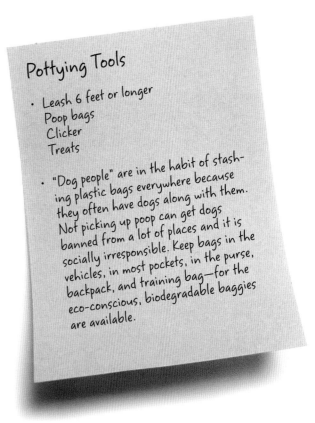

Pottying Tools

- Leash 6 feet or longer
  Poop bags
  Clicker
  Treats

- "Dog people" are in the habit of stashing plastic bags everywhere because they often have dogs along with them. Not picking up poop can get dogs banned from a lot of places and it is socially irresponsible. Keep bags in the vehicles, in most pockets, in the purse, backpack, and training bag—for the eco-conscious, biodegradable baggies are available.

- Try to time walks or potty trips when you know he needs to go. For adult dogs this is usually between one and two hours after a meal, but this time varies.

- Take him out on a long line, so that you're not hovering over him. This really inhibits some dogs.

- Don't get too enthusiastic or bossy when giving the "potty" command. Doing this can either distract or intimidate him.

- Give him a treat or even click-treat right after he's done with pooping.

DIGGING FOR TREASURE
Digging is in some dogs' genes, so teach them to dig for a purpose

Your dog might dig to make a little den or to regulate his temperature. Long-haired and northern breeds often do this. Terriers dig because they've been bred to burrow after vermin. What looks to you like a pristine lawn is a rich environment teeming with underground life that he smells and feels compelled to kill. Earthworms are no match for a determined terrier, and moles can drive her insane with longing. If your dog digs around the perimeter of your yard, she wants to take herself for a walk.

Providing a cool place for a hot dog will lessen her inclination to dig sleeping holes. Many people simply relinquish one corner of the yard so that the dog can turn it into a moonscape. A bored escape artist probably needs more stimulation, along with chicken wire or a concrete trench laid along the fence perimeter.

Why Dogs Dig

- Dogs dig for all sorts of reasons, but they never do anything on purpose to make us angry, including digging holes.

- Think management first. If she's supervised when outside, you can stop her from digging. If you leave her alone with access to your flower beds, there's nothing to stop her from digging, so why should she restrain herself?

- Setting aside her own digging area is one solution. Make it rewarding by burying treats and toys.

Invisible Fence Barrier

- If she has access to your whole yard but digs only in the flower or vegetable beds, consider an invisible fence barrier.

- Invisible fences can be set up within a fenced yard to keep dogs away from danger zones such as gardens and pools.

- Be prepared that she may simply redirect her digging to another part of the yard! If she does, a designated digging area might be the best solution.

For the dog who simply loves to dig, make it a game. Set aside a corner of the yard and fill it with sand or cheap fill dirt. A wading pool works brilliantly for this. Bury some favorite toys or rawhides in the sand and tell her to find that treasure. If she knows one of her toys by name, have her go digging for it.

················· GREEN ● LIGHT ··············

Give her the satisfaction of hunting for her food. Put several pieces of dry dog food in an empty plastic water bottle. Put a piece of masking tape over the top—she'll still smell the food. Bury it, along with some empty decoy bottles, and have her go to work.

Aversive Techniques

- Aversive techniques can be used, but they might not deter her, and she might simply start digging elsewhere.

- Try burying some of her poop in a favored digging spot.

- If that doesn't work, blow up a balloon and bury it. When she digs down to the balloon, and it bursts, she might be convinced to quit digging to avoid future unpleasant surprises. Be aware that this ploy works only if it really scares her.

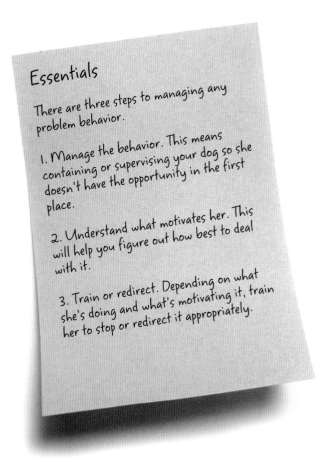

Essentials

There are three steps to managing any problem behavior.

1. Manage the behavior. This means containing or supervising your dog so she doesn't have the opportunity in the first place.

2. Understand what motivates her. This will help you figure out how best to deal with it.

3. Train or redirect. Depending on what she's doing and what's motivating it, train her to stop or redirect it appropriately.

FIXING BAD HABITS

INAPPROPRIATE CHEWING
First figure out why your dog chews things, then give him acceptable alternatives

Puppies bite as a way of interacting with their new world. Teething lasts roughly from four to eight months of age, during which time they are destructive, furry piranhas. Older puppies and dogs chew because they enjoy it or because they are stressed or bored.

For the first year of a pup's life, it's important to have plenty of appropriate chewies because the urge to chew is overwhelming, especially during teething. Gnawing loosens baby teeth and relieves painful gums as the adult teeth emerge. He's done with teething at seven or eight months old. For most puppies the destructive phase lasts for about the first year, as long as you have taught him what he's not allowed to

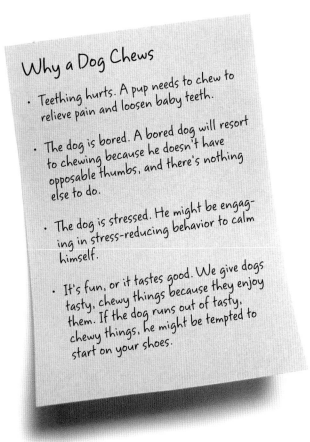

Why a Dog Chews

- Teething hurts. A pup needs to chew to relieve pain and loosen baby teeth.

- The dog is bored. A bored dog will resort to chewing because he doesn't have opposable thumbs, and there's nothing else to do.

- The dog is stressed. He might be engaging in stress-reducing behavior to calm himself.

- It's fun, or it tastes good. We give dogs tasty, chewy things because they enjoy them. If the dog runs out of tasty, chewy things, he might be tempted to start on your shoes.

Use Toys

- Look for toys that satisfy a dog's urge to chew and give him a problem to solve at the same time, such as requiring him to roll them in a certain direction to release treats.

- Make your own by tucking little pieces of food into the folds and seams of a cardboard box and let him shred the box to get the food.

- Mix water or unflavored gelatin with tiny treats and freeze in an ice cube tray or disposable cup.

chew and have given him appropriate alternatives.

Determine the motivation for destructive chewing in adult dogs. Often it's a simple matter of understimulation. High-energy dogs will find ways to amuse themselves if they're not played with and exercised daily. Walk or bike with your dog. If he plays well with others, arrange playdates with another dog. Look into doggie daycare—even one day a week will help. Teach him lots of tricks! Do short training sessions every day and involve the whole family. Work his body and mind, and many behavior problems will diminish.

········· YELLOW ●LIGHT ·········

Be careful with chew toys. Your dog may gnaw happily on what you give him, or he may be a power chewer who diligently destroys chewies and sometimes swallows bits. If he's the latter, make sure you give him only things that he can't destroy or that won't harm him if swallowed.

Signs of Loneliness

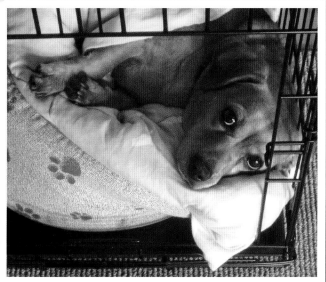

Focus

- If he destroys things only in your absence, he could be stressed about being alone. Consult a good behaviorist about separation anxiety if it's a real problem.

- Don't scold him for chewing things up after the fact. He won't understand, and it will make him more stressed.

- Problem chewing may require just simple management. Crate or contain him when you can't supervise and keep tempting items out of reach.

- Work on tricks that focus him on his toys, such as name that toy, putting toys away, and interactive toy games such as tug and retrieving.

- Practice control games such as leave it and drop.

- The value of exercise can't be stressed enough! A sleeping dog won't chew. Fetch and jumping games can be done indoors or out. A bike ride or jog in the morning helps him be calmer while everyone's away at work.

KIDS & DOGS
Make your dog child-safe by encouraging positive interactions and involving the kids

Children not only can help train the dog, but also they should, depending on their age. Too often, when a child gets bitten by the family dog, it's because the dog sees the child as a peer, not One Who Must Be Obeyed. Trick training is perfect because it's really all in fun. You might not want little Martha taking responsibility for potty training Fido, but she can surely teach him to shake hands or roll over. Always supervise kids and dogs, especially when there are visiting kids.

Interactive games engage both children and dogs. Test the skills of both by having a competition to see who can walk the longest around the house with the dog on leash in one hand and a potato balanced on a spoon in the other. Play

Kids and Dogs

- Show kids how to command Fido to do simple tricks and basic obedience exercises, such as shake paw, roll over, come when called, and sit.

- Teach them to give treats to dogs properly, without teasing.

- Kids learn empathy and self-control by interacting with a dog. The dog learns that being around a well-trained child can be rewarding and positive and that he needs to obey every family member, no matter how small.

Rules for the Family Dog

- The family dog should accept gentle petting and handling without discomfort or protest.

- A good daily exercise for everyone in the family is to stroke the dog from head to foot. This gets him used to being handled by everyone in his "pack."

- Puppies and children are naturally attracted to each other, but some children are unintentionally rough and need to be taught to gentle down. Both child and dog need training.

hide-and-seek, teaching the dog to go to each person in the family by name. Have your child hide a toy while Fido stays, then release him to find it. Round robin recalls are a great way to teach a puppy that it's fun to come to each family member, no matter how small. Depending on your pup's abilities, either have him just run to each person for a treat or come, then sit or do a trick for his reward.

Training Classes

- Look into 4-H or call training facilities and the local humane society about classes that your dog and child can take together.

- Children and their dogs can compete for titles in many venues, alongside adult competitors in the same ring.

- At most trials, there are separate ribbons for junior handlers, so that they rarely walk away empty-handed.

- Junior handlers are usually very warmly welcomed and encouraged because they're the future of the sport!

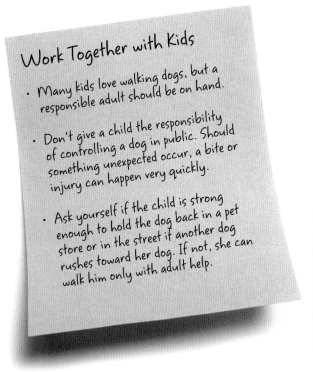

Work Together with Kids

- Many kids love walking dogs, but a responsible adult should be on hand.

- Don't give a child the responsibility of controlling a dog in public. Should something unexpected occur, a bite or injury can happen very quickly.

- Ask yourself if the child is strong enough to hold the dog back in a pet store or in the street if another dog rushes toward her dog. If not, she can walk him only with adult help.

MANAGING THE DOG PACK
Train multiple dogs individually at first for good manners and understand dog pack behavior

Dogs are pack animals, and dogs living with people regard people as part of the pack. Whether you have one dog or four, the key to having a stable pack is maintaining control.

Think of yourself as a benevolent dictator. Not only do you have to set fair boundaries and rules, but also you need to be aware of the dog pack dynamics and reinforce them. This

means acknowledging your top dog and not artificially elevating the status of the lower-ranking dogs. Feed and pay attention to your main dog first.

If she righteously snarks at a lower-ranking dog or puppy for being rude, don't comfort the other dog. This creates stress and confusion by upsetting the natural order. Be aware

Dog Social Behavior

- Most dogs in a household get along well, working out differences and status through a wide range of subtle signals and interactions.

- Unless you're skilled in the subtleties of canine body language, you'll miss

most of these interactions. If you learn them (see Resources), you will be a much better trainer!

- There are ebb and flow in status. Rarely is one dog always "dominant" and the other always "submissive."

Alpha Dogs

- A true "alpha" dog is rarely aggressive because she doesn't need to be. She successfully conveys through attitude and consistency that she's the boss, and the other dogs fall in line.

- A lower-status dog trying to challenge her is the most

likely to be aggressive and to start a fight.

- Remember this when you read about training methods that insist that you need to use force and punishment to be the "alpha" or pack leader!

of tensions and things that can lead to conflict, such as food and high-value toys left around.

The majority of dogs work out their status and get along beautifully for life, without any intervention from their owners. Dog pack status and behavior are largely geared toward avoiding conflict because cooperative living ensures pack well-being.

Not all dogs get along well, and some dogs are naturally more dominant and aggressive toward other dogs. This doesn't mean there's anything "wrong" with the dominant dog. It's natural dog behavior, especially in some of the feisty or independent breeds, such as terriers and some working dogs. Dogs bred to work in packs, such as many hunting dogs, tend to be more cooperative.

When considering a second dog, choose wisely. There is always less chance of conflict with opposite-sex dogs. Spend regular time playing and training each dog separately, even for just a few minutes a day. This maintains your bond and increases the chance that the dogs will be well behaved together.

Pack Mentality

* Doing things with your dogs in a group cements the pack mentality as long as you're in control and everyone is having fun.

* Look for a splitter leash for walks. This leash leashes the dogs together, eliminating tangling and confusion over which leash is attached to which dog.

* Walking together under control is an excellent way to introduce dogs. When they're moving forward, they're less inclined to worry about the other.

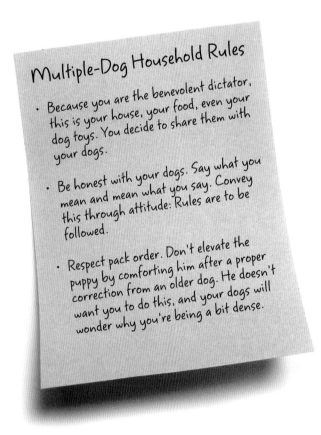

Multiple-Dog Household Rules

• Because you are the benevolent dictator, this is your house, your food, even your dog toys. You decide to share them with your dogs.

• Be honest with your dogs. Say what you mean and mean what you say. Convey this through attitude: Rules are to be followed.

• Respect pack order. Don't elevate the puppy by comforting him after a proper correction from an older dog. He doesn't want you to do this, and your dogs will wonder why you're being a bit dense.

UNDER & OVER

These easy tricks for your at-home dog team are guaranteed to impress your friends

Any impressive dog trick is three times more impressive with two dogs. A simple paw shake or rollover becomes quite a performance when two or more dogs are doing it at the same time or one after the other in quick succession. Two dogs spinning around for treats look really cute—extra points if you can get them to spin in opposite directions at the same time without getting dizzy! Try jumping tricks, with the dogs jumping in both the same and opposite directions at once.

Each dog must have individually learned the trick before working in a team. One problem you may have is both dogs complying with a command when you want only one to

Multiple Dogs and Tricks

- Your dogs probably perform at different speeds. This difference could be due to size, structure, or temperament.

- Don't worry if they're not synchronized—this would be difficult to achieve. Having two dogs perform the same trick still impresses the heck out of people.

- Look for ways to use the discrepancy. For instance, if one dog jumps fast and the other slow, have the fast one jump twice so that they both end up finishing at the same time.

Jump

- Teach one dog to jump over another. This is much harder for the dog who has to stay in place without wanting to get up and join in the fun or who has to worry about being landed on.

- At least one dog needs to have a very solid stay, and one needs to be a confident jumper.

- Have a partner hold and lavishly reward the staying "honor" dog, while you encourage the other to jump over.

perform. To solve this problem, add a cue before the command, such as a finger point or the dog's name. Or, if the dogs have a very solid "wait" or "stay" skill, tell one to wait, have the other perform, then tell the waiting dog, "OK, roll over!" If you have a partner, it helps to have another person steady one dog while the other performs.

It's essential that both dogs get along and won't squabble over rewards. It can help to train them far enough apart that they won't try to intercept treats at first.

Mind Your Praise

- Keep your excitement and enthusiasm level down when working with two dogs simultaneously; otherwise, you run the risk of them getting overstimulated and forgetting what they're supposed to do.

- This is a time to practice your calm, confident "alpha dog" pack leader skills so they stay focused on you and not on each other.

- When possible, practice exercises with dogs slightly apart from each other or on either side of you.

Why Train Separately First?

- It's a rare dog who can sit by without wanting to join in while you're interacting with the other. This takes a lot of self-control.

- Dogs often need different training—one may need encouragement to speed up, the other calmness to have self-control.

- It's confusing to them. Either correction or praise directed at one dog can make the other wonder what the first dog did to earn it.

171

SPEED SITTING COMPETITION
Make dog training a competitive game with multiple dogs, treats, and toys

We don't know if dogs are truly competitive, but we do know that they learn very quickly to do what works to get them rewards. A dog who is distracted or lagging during class often benefits by being put into her crate and being made to watch the other dogs having fun. It's even more effective if she sees her owner working with another dog. This is a

version of the restrained "ready, ready" game because it gets her frustrated and raring to go. After she is out of the crate, she will often perform with greater enthusiasm and focus.

Use this tendency to build drive and speed into any trick. Speed sitting is a fun game for multiple dogs. Arm yourself with a handful of excellent, small treats. Get your dogs'

Competitive Dogs

- Dogs get jealous, and if one dog gets all the rewards and the other none at all, the unrewarded one will either get sulky and stop working or might try to intercept the other's treat.

- Consider this if one dog stops sitting or just walks away. Call her over and

reward her for sitting anyway, so that she doesn't feel snubbed.

- Alternately, just reward them in the order they sit. Fastest dog first, slowest dog second.

Puppy Push-Ups

- Puppy push-ups are good practice for this game and can be played in much the same way.

- Got dog-savvy kids? Have one dog per child and make this a competition: The child with the most fast sits wins.

- Have them switch dogs to make it fair. Keep the game short—a minute or two—and make sure everyone gets rewarded at the end with treats, fetch, or running outside to the back yard to play.

attention and start walking through the house with them following you. Randomly say, "Sit!" while whirling around toward them. The fastest-sitting dog gets rewarded, while the other dog wonders where her treat is. Make this fast and fun, and it won't be long before the dogs figure it out. It can also work for a solo dog—reward only the very fast sits.

Sits are easy for most dogs, but this game can be used with any simple commands.

Speed and Compliance

- There are many ways you can play games involving speed and compliance. Have your dogs sit or down-stay and walk away.

- Turn, call them, and watch them scramble to get to the reward first.

- If you and your dogs are very proficient, have them stay, then call each by name. The rule is that the dog you called comes to you and that the others have to stay and wait their turn. A partner is useful for teaching this.

Sit at the Door Games

- Play sit at the door games. The fastest dog to sit gets to go through the door first for a reward.

- This also works for getting in and out of the vehicle, avoiding a logjam of dogs fighting to get in or out of one narrow car door.

- Vehicle manners are important. It's not safe for one dog, never mind several, to leap out whenever the door is opened, and it's better if they understand a release command for this.

GET YOUR TREAT
Teach your dog pack control, mealtime manners, and some useful tricks using dinner and treats

Owning multiple dogs means you have to be a bit of a control freak, especially if they are strong-minded dogs. Because food is a powerful motivator and a resource you control, it can be used to teach restraint and manners and, yes, to help establish you as top dog. The nice thing about using food as a control tool is that as long as the dog is being polite, she always gets rewarded. The underlying message is that your dogs don't own anything. You own the resources and choose to share in abundance, as any benevolent dictator would.

Your dogs should be polite about receiving meals. Sitting before release to the bowl is a good control exercise. Even the chummiest of canine housemates can be possessive

Don't Get Jealous

- Dogs get jealous. When you have more than one dog, each is very aware of what the other gets from you.

- Be fair to each but set rules. If one gets a treat for sitting, the other needs to sit nicely and control herself before she gets a treat, too.

- An older dog gets rewards before a pup. The pup will learn by watching, and your older dog has earned the right to come first.

Eating Habits

- Because eating is such a primitive and essential drive, it's natural for some dogs to want to guard their food from other dogs and for others to take it from an easily intimidated packmate.

- Managing this is easy. If you see any tension between your dogs around food, simply separate them for meals.

- You can spend lots of time correcting and trying to "fix" this, but some battles really aren't worth fighting.

about food with other dogs. If you notice one dog eating fast, then circling the slower dog or a dog bolting food with her ears back, make it more relaxing for everyone by feeding them in separate areas.

For a beginner exercise, have your dogs sit. Give them each a treat. The rules are simple: Stay seated, no grabbing, and you get rewarded. To get an idea of how literally dogs pattern and learn by repetition, sit on the floor, ask your dogs to sit, and give them a treat. For an interesting experiment, lie flat on the floor and try the same thing!

Try this more advanced exercise: Put some peanut butter on a spoon. With your dogs sitting, let one have a few licks. Say, "Leave it" and offer the spoon to the other dog for a taste. Repeat, moving back and forth until the spoon is clean. The dogs must remain seated and stop licking on your command. Practice this individually before putting it to the test with the whole crew.

Hunting Instincts

- If dogs are like a domesticated wolf pack, and packs work and hunt together to get food, it makes sense to have dogs "work" together for their meals.

- Unless you plan on releasing live rabbits and elk in your kitchen every few

days, satisfy their hunting instinct by asking for a basic sit or trick before the bowl goes down.

- It might not be the same as the thrill of a hunt, but it's a good exercise!

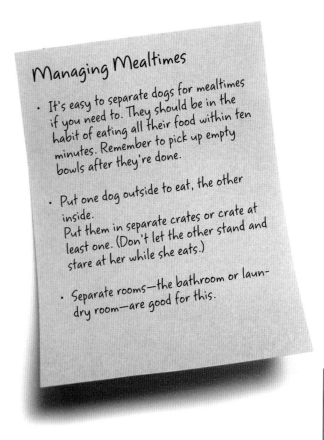

Managing Mealtimes

- It's easy to separate dogs for mealtimes if you need to. They should be in the habit of eating all their food within ten minutes. Remember to pick up empty bowls after they're done.

- Put one dog outside to eat, the other inside. Put them in separate crates or crate at least one. (Don't let the other stand and stare at her while she eats.)

- Separate rooms—the bathroom or laundry room—are good for this.

BIG DOG, LITTLE DOG
These tricks use the disparate sizes of two or more dogs for maximum cuteness

Capitalize on disparate sizes. It goes without saying that the dogs have to be friendly and gentle with each other. A goofball St. Bernard can seriously hurt a little Chihuahua in rough play. A big, calm dog and a willing, well-trained small one will make a great team.

If either dog will hold a leash in his mouth, and if at least one is well leash-trained, have one walk the other. Start by teaching the walker to hold a leash, using the same technique as teaching him to carry groceries. It's important to treat only if he drops the leash on your command. If he gets rewarded for just dropping it when he feels like it, then obviously he'll drop it more often to get rewarded. Some dogs

Big Dog, Little Dog

- Safety first. The dogs should know each other well and be very comfortable together.

- Before putting a little dog on top of a big dog, make absolutely sure that the big dog is OK with this!

- Dominant dogs place parts of their bodies, usually a head or paw, on another dog's shoulders in dominance displays. You need to know that your big dog won't resent the intrusion of a small dog on his back because the result can be tragic.

Dog Combinations

- The best combination is a smaller, agile dog and a large, calm dog. In most of these tricks, the big dog's job is to stay controlled and be a prop for the little dog.

- When training the little dog to stand on the big dog's back, reward or click-treat the little one for staying put while the big dog gets lots of reinforcement.

- It's easier to teach any of the "on the back" tricks with the bigger dog lying down at first.

will naturally hold and carry a leash without training. Now attach the leash to the walkee dog and practice short walks in a quiet area.

A burly dog can pull a smaller one in a cart or carry a tiny pooch in a backpack. The challenge here is to teach the little dog to stay put. Any time you teach a skill requiring calm, it's easiest to start with a well-exercised, somewhat worn-out dog. Giving a dog lots of treats—even a favorite chew toy—in the location you want him to stay in helps reinforce the idea that it's the best possible place to be.

A big dog who will stand in place provides a perfect structure for a little dog to weave through legs. Use a target stick to lure the little dog under and around the bigger dog and reward the big dog for standing still. This will be easiest with two people—one to reinforce the big dog and another to work with the smaller one.

Combination Tricks

- Combine tricks. For instance, have one dog go touch the other with a nose or paw. The small dog can be trained to put two feet up onto the big dog.

- Simultaneously have the other dog roll over or play dead. This is very cute when the big dog is the one who rolls over at the little dog's touch!

- Or teach the little dog to pull on the leash while the big dog either crawls or rolls over.

Embellishing the Trick

- The mighty mite can run under the big dog. If he is small enough, or not too long-bodied, you should be able to teach him to weave through the big dog's legs.

- A variation of this would be having your big guy lift a leg to allow the little one to pass under.

- These tricks depend on the sizes of both dogs and how tolerant your big one is! Simply running back and forth underneath a larger dog is a great trick, demonstrating both dogs' skills.

PERFORMING DOGS
Performing dogs have a long history, and there's still plenty of venues for talented canines

Some dogs are natural showoffs and love the attention they get from performing, whether it's doing tricks or strutting their stuff in the show ring. Others are a bit reticent and need to be given lots of praise and reinforcement in private before taking the show on the road.

Performing for others doesn't always mean being on stage or in a parade. Dogs are used for therapy work in hospitals and group homes. Even short weekly visits can ease loneliness and anxiety and speed healing. Programs letting children read aloud to dogs have been implemented in schools and libraries because this practice has been shown to improve reading skills. Several organizations certify dogs

Get Exposure

- Refine your routine and work through stage fright with easier venues.

- Ask your church about showing off at social events.

- Throw your own adult or children's parties or welcome invites.

- A therapy dog has lots of chances to perform.

- Approach schools and youth groups about staging a routine.

- Sign up for local parades.

- Attend animal shelter and rescue events.

Socialization

- This is where socialization becomes very important. If you want to perform outside of your home, your dogs need to be comfortable around strangers and in unfamiliar places.

- Practicing in the park, on walks, or in pet store aisles helps distraction-proof your dogs.

- Whether you have one dog or four, you'll need to know what will distract them. For some, it might be strange dogs; others may want to run over and meet every kid they see.

(just like yours, perhaps) as therapy dogs, and their volunteer owners take them to welcoming institutions. Having just one or two tricks to display to a hospital-bound senior or shy child is not only showing off but also therapeutic.

If you are involved with a training club or rescue organization, offer your tricky dogs for exhibitions and fundraisers. Find out how to participate in parades and fairs by contacting the organizers. Hone your dogs'—and your own—performance skills at home and in front of friends before trying small public venues. Work out a trick routine—consider including props,

costumes, and music—and videotape it. Send the video to local media outlets.

Do you think you and your dogs could do this professionally? After you've proofed your routine on the small stage, make a good video and compile several professional-quality photographs, put together a resume, and pitch reputable local talent agencies. You can do this with a single dog, too, of course. But agencies get many queries from people with talented dogs, and the competition is stiff. You'll have a definite edge with a multidog routine.

Props

- No matter how great you and your dog are as a team, you'll need props. If you use costumes, they should be a matching theme. Have a theme for your entire performance. Think of it as brand recognition!

- Work out routines that follow a simple story line

and incorporate audience participation—children especially love this.

- Have someone videotape your routine so you can see what needs polishing. Put it online and invite comments if you dare.

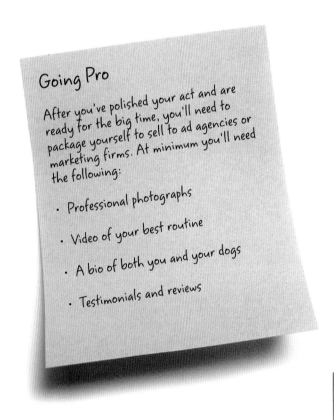

Going Pro

After you've polished your act and are ready for the big time, you'll need to package yourself to sell to ad agencies or marketing firms. At minimum you'll need the following:

- Professional photographs

- Video of your best routine

- A bio of both you and your dogs

- Testimonials and reviews

179

HIDE-N-SEEK

For one person or the whole family, this is a great indoor game to teach your dog

If there is a single game that teaches a dog to come when called, it's hide-and-seek. There is a lot you can do with this game. It's a fabulous tool for teaching a dog to come when called (also known as the "recall"). For more advanced dogs, use it to proof out-of-sight downs and stays. It can be played with multiple dogs and multiple people. And dogs

universally love it. If your pup doesn't have a solid recall, work on this first. Several times throughout the day, call him and make a big fuss when he gets to you. Call him for his meals, call him for treats, and sometimes just praise him without a treat. This should take very little time.

As with every trick, start easy. Go into another room and

Use a Partner

- If you don't have anyone to restrain Fido, just tiptoe out when he's not watching and call him. Of course, you won't be able to do this more than once in a row because he'll be on to your trick!

- If someone holds him for you, the person shouldn't

interact much with him unless the person is playing the "ready, ready" game.

- Staying put while you go out of sight is a good skill, leading to a more secure dog.

Round-Robin Recall Game

- Play this game with several people as a sort of round-robin recall game in which the dog has to find each person. Decide in advance what order everyone gets to be found.

- At first, arm everyone with a reward for the dog. When he finds someone else,

that person ignores him completely while the other keeps calling.

- When he willingly runs to find everyone when called, you can stop rewarding every time. When an activity is really fun, it becomes its own reward.

180

hide behind a door or large piece of furniture. Call your dog. Make a big fuss when he gets to you. The better he gets, the harder you can make the hiding places. At first you'll need someone else to hold him. Work on the "stay" command until he'll stay put when you're out of the room. Insecure dogs might have a hard time with this, so it's an especially important exercise for them. A dog who is comfortable when her owner leaves her alone is more secure, happier, and less likely to develop separation anxiety.

Incorporate challenges for the expert dog. Have him find you but put a really tempting treat nearby. His job is to have enough self-control to pass the treat by and stay focused on coming to you. If he carries things, have him bring you something. Put a jump in a doorway so that he has to jump to get to you. Make him work hard for those treats.

Games with Kids

- This is a great game to play with children. Anything that teaches Fido to be responsive and obedient to children is good for his overall manners. Tell the kids to pretend to be a statue if he finds them while someone else is calling him.

- He can also be taught to go find a particular person, following the canine courier rules in Chapter 9.

- Don't let him get bored with this game. The enthusiasm of most dogs will start waning by the tenth find.

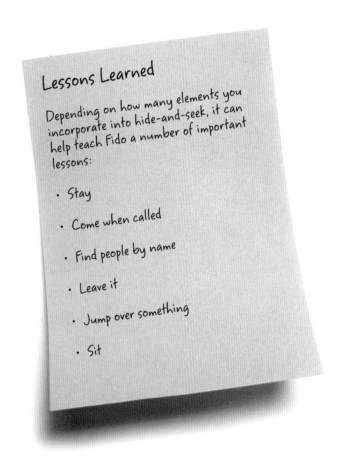

Lessons Learned

Depending on how many elements you incorporate into hide-and-seek, it can help teach Fido a number of important lessons:

- Stay
- Come when called
- Find people by name
- Leave it
- Jump over something
- Sit

INTELLIGENCE TESTS

Intelligence tests and tricks can involve figuring out where you hid the toy

Just like human IQ tests, canine intelligence tests will not necessarily say anything about your dog's intelligence. But they are fun to do, and if you have multiple dogs it is interesting to compare their problem-solving strategies. Because these are not diagnostic tests, you can customize them any way you want.

Put your dog on a stay or have someone hold her. Have three pillows, towels, or anything else soft and as similar as possible. Show her a treat and let her watch you put it under one of the pillows. Release her and see how quickly she goes to the right pillow. Does she use her paws or her nose to get to it? It's thought that a "smarter" dog will use her paws. Now

Beginner Tests

- A beginner test is to line up several upside-down cups with a treat under one of them. Let her watch you put the treat under and see if she goes directly to that cup or checks them all first.

- Now try it with her not watching and see if she's

any faster. Remember to change the cup location so she doesn't simply repeat what worked the last time.

- Try this with different objects, such as a cup, a bowl, and a baking pan. How does she do?

Use Toys

- Rub a piece of hot dog all over a toy and show it to her. Let her have a good sniff and get her excited about it.

- Now, without her watching, hide the toy somewhere out of sight but easily accessible.

- If she knows any of her toys by name, have her look for that particular toy.

- Escalate the difficulty level. Try putting the toy inside a cardboard box and seeing how she figures out that puzzle.

do the same thing, but before letting her go get the treat, walk her out of the room for a minute, then return and let her loose without saying anything. Does she go directly to the pillows and use her paws to get the treat again, or has she forgotten all about it? These tests may indicate nothing more than how treat-driven your dog is and whether she finds it more efficient to use her paws or her nose to get to it. A nose is more efficient because it's directly above her jaws.

Try putting a treat in the bottom of a disposable plastic cup. Now stuff a clean tea towel into the cup. Let her watch you do this. If she wants the treat, she has to figure out how to get past the towel. A smart dog should probably forget technicalities and simply use her teeth to rip the bottom of the cup apart, but most will spend considerable time nosing and rolling the cup around, and some just give up.

Use Creativity

- With a little creativity, you can think up all sorts of "find the stuffie" games. Hide things within things, on top of things, and under things.

- Don't let her get frustrated. She'll get demotivated quickly if she's unsuccessful. If it takes her more than sixty seconds or so to find the toy, help her out with a hint or two.

- Finding games can be played with two or more dogs, but make sure they all get rewarded one way or another at the end of each game.

Use Tracking Skills

- Incorporate tracking skills by laying out little treats or pieces of dry food for her to follow to a jackpot prize.

- You might have to do this with her on leash first, so she understands she's supposed to follow the treat trail to the end.

- The jackpot prize is important, so she understands there's a goal. It's even more fun if that's a puzzle, too— try a piece of hot dog in an old glove and see how she tackles it.

GROOMING
Have a home spa day for your dog and take care of several grooming tasks

With grooming, there's no real trick to be learned by your dog except patience. But grooming is important. When was the last time you checked Fido's ears, bathed, and brushed her? Even if you also take her to the groomer, ongoing maintenance keeps her looking good as well as makes the groomer's job easier.

Look inside your dog's ears. A little brown wax is normal; the skin should be pink; and there shouldn't be any odor. Routine ear cleaning keeps the ears healthy, especially in floppy-eared dogs. Pet stores carry ear cleaning solution, or make your own with a 50:50 mix of white vinegar and water.

Brushing needs to be done before a bath because brushing

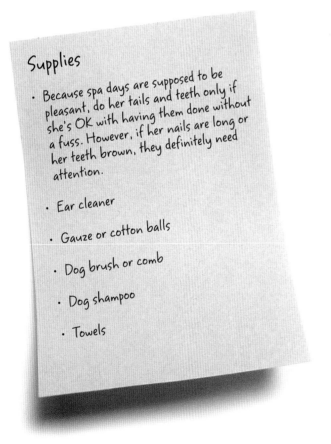

Supplies

- Because spa days are supposed to be pleasant, do her tails and teeth only if she's OK with having them done without a fuss. However, if her nails are long or her teeth brown, they definitely need attention.

- Ear cleaner

- Gauze or cotton balls

- Dog brush or comb

- Dog shampoo

- Towels

Cleaning the Ear

- Using a turkey baster, hold back the ear flap and gently pour a generous amount of ear cleaner down the canal. Massage the base of her ear until you hear a squishy sound, then let her shake.

- Do this outside or put a towel over her head to pre-

- vent ear cleaner gunk from flying everywhere.

- It is fine to use gauze wrapped around your finger to clean the visible parts of the outer ear but never poke anything down the ear canal.

helps loosen dead fur. While you brush, pay attention to her overall condition. Feel for skin lumps. Check her ears, teeth, eyes, and paws. Assess her weight, which can be hard to monitor in long-haired dogs. You should be able to feel all of her ribs—if you can't feel them, it's time for a diet! Her breath shouldn't smell terrible, and her gums should be pink. If there's redness along the gumline or brown tartar on her teeth, take her to the vet. Poor dental health isn't just a matter of stained teeth; it can lead to serious health problems.

Wet her down thoroughly and lather her up. It's easier to dilute the shampoo first so you don't get big blobs in one spot, which are harder to rinse out. Do her head last because she'll instinctively shake off when she gets water in her ears. You can put a cotton ball at the ear opening if she has droopy, furry ears. Rinse her completely and towel her dry or use a hair dryer at low setting, being careful not to get too close to her skin.

Brushing the Hair

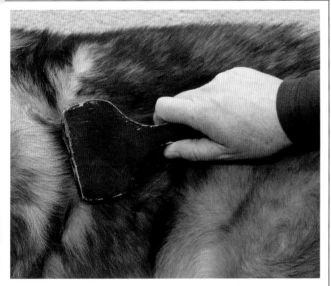

- A shedding blade works well to pull out undercoat on short-haired dogs. Use an undercoat rake for longer-haired dogs. After her bath, you can finish up with a softer brush to add shine.

- Dry winter air gives a dog dry skin and a dull coat.

Adding a little oil to her diet will help counteract this. Fish oil is a wonderful coat supplement, and the kind sold for people is fine.

- Always brush in the direction of hair growth.

Bathing

- Dogs don't need many baths. At maximum, once a month is sufficient. Any more than that can dry out her skin.

- Don't use people shampoo. Buy a good dog shampoo and use it sparingly.

- Small dogs can be bathed in the kitchen sink, which is especially handy if you have a faucet sprayer. Larger dogs can be bathed in the bathtub, and buying a spray attachment will make rinsing much easier. Use a drain screen to catch dog hair.

SPEED HEELING

You can play heeling games inside to sharpen your dog's obedience skills or leash manners

Heeling is pretty boring for dogs. They adjust their pace to ours, march along without being able to check pee mail, and, under the old rules of dog training, get jerked by the collar for every brief lapse of attention. Walking on leash will never be as much fun as being able to wander at her own pace, but because leash walking without pulling is such a challenge for many dogs and their owners, every little bit of practice helps, even if you do it inside. This is also a good way to work on off-leash heeling.

Grab a handful of treats, get her attention, and off you go heeling through the house. Make it fun and fast, up and down stairs, through rooms and around furniture. Incorporate

Walk Inside

- Walk inside when going outside isn't an option. Over the course of a long winter, you and Fido can log quite a few indoor miles.

- Practice heel sits along a wall, so she has no choice but to sit straight. This builds muscle memory, or the tendency for the body to fall into an often-repeated position naturally.

- It won't matter in real life, but in the obedience ring, the dog is penalized for sitting crooked.

Use a Leash

- Even if you never plan to set foot in the obedience ring, anything you do with your dog on a leash will reinforce the idea that paying attention to you can be rewarding.

- Use stairs for cardio work. Dogs benefit from cardiovascular exercise just as people do.

- Practice heeling in a figure-8 pattern around chairs.

- Play your favorite music and see how much you can get done in two- or three-minute bursts.

tricks. Have her do spins, have her walk forward and backward between your legs along a hallway, have her lie down, roll over, do a push-up or two, and jump over something. Put a plate with treats or a hot dog along your route and zip her past, with a reward for leaving it. It's a good strategy to do short training sessions and quit before your dog has a chance to get tired, so do this for just about three minutes at a time.

Go Beyond Heeling

- Don't stick to just plain old heeling. Set up some boards or poles on the ground and teach Fido to walk directly behind you.

- Keep her interest with a treat held behind your back or a target stick.

- Have her sit when you sit down, lie down when you do, or raise a paw when you raise your hand. Having your dog behind you mirroring what you do is an impressive trick!

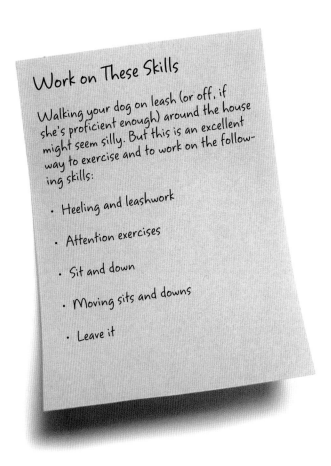

Work on These Skills

Walking your dog on leash (or off, if she's proficient enough) around the house might seem silly. But this is an excellent way to exercise and to work on the following skills:

- Heeling and leashwork

- Attention exercises

- Sit and down

- Moving sits and downs

- Leave it

FAMILY GAMES

Involve a group of people in these fast-paced games with one or more dogs

Some dogs become overexcited around a group of animated people. Set your dog up, then teach him that controlling himself gets him what he wants. Treats work better than toys to encourage stationary position. It depends partly on the individual dog's preferences, but generally, toys and games are used as a way to speed up performance or as a short, rewarding

play interlude, whereas treats are used to reward position.

Have everyone in the room run around, jump, and generally act crazy. One person calls, "Halt!" Everyone stops dead still. Whoever is closest to the dog—who is probably somewhat wound up—tells him to sit. He doesn't get his reward until he calms down and sits.

Relay Race

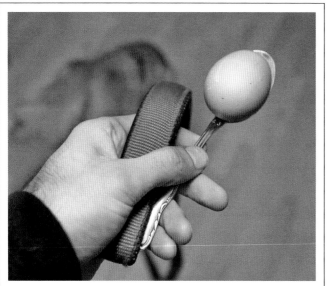

- Have a relay race. This can be done with multiple people and one dog or with multiple dogs.

- The person with the dog must cross the room, holding the dog's leash and a spoon in the same hand. The person balances a

potato or piece of fruit on the spoon.

- The goal is to see who can control the dog well enough to make it across the room without dropping the potato. You can also compete for speed as well as accuracy.

Round Robin

- To teach control to excitable dogs, play round robin.

- Everyone sits around the perimeter of the room. One by one, each person calls the dog, who must then sit or perform a trick on command for a treat.

- If doing this with a hyper dog, make sure that whatever he gets rewarded for is a controlled pause such as sit or down. This teaches him to gather himself and calm down before getting a reward.

Another version of this game has all players stop dead in their tracks, and a predesignated person calls the dog and has him sit. These are particularly good games for children because they teach children to manage the dog's behavior. They also teach the dog to regulate his own behavior and to be attentive to adults and children alike.

Play this game with multiple dogs and make it a contest—the first person to get his or her dog to sit is the winner. A harder version of this game has the dog lying down on command.

Hide 'N Seek

- Have one person hide, then lay a line of treats from one room to the other so the dog has to "track" the treats to get to the hidden person, who gives him a great reward.

- Set up a slalom course using plastic cones. Walk either backward or forward through the course, encouraging the dog to follow.

- The object of the game is to have the dog follow a person precisely without missing or knocking over the cones.

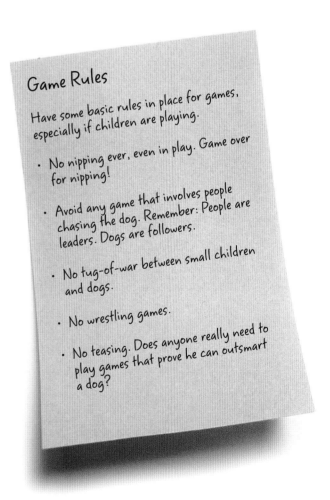

Game Rules

Have some basic rules in place for games, especially if children are playing.

- No nipping ever, even in play. Game over for nipping!

- Avoid any game that involves people chasing the dog. Remember: People are leaders. Dogs are followers.

- No tug-of-war between small children and dogs.

- No wrestling games.

- No teasing. Does anyone really need to play games that prove he can outsmart a dog?

189

BEDTIME GAMES
Teach your dog to roll up in a blankie and put herself to bed

The blanket trick is impressive and fairly simple if your dog understands "take it" and can hold something and roll over. You'll need a blanket large enough to wrap around your dog. If your dog has a hard time understanding how to hold onto something flimsy such as a blanket, attach one of her favorite toys to one corner with a large safety pin.

Spread the blanket on the floor and have her take a corner

of the blanket or the attached toy in her mouth. This might be tricky because she's probably not used to taking something in her mouth while lying down. (Remember how dogs learn by patterns.) You may need to spend some extra time and treats teaching her to grab and hold while lying down.

Now have her roll over onto her other side while holding the blanket. She'll probably pull it only over her shoulders, so

Say Goodnight

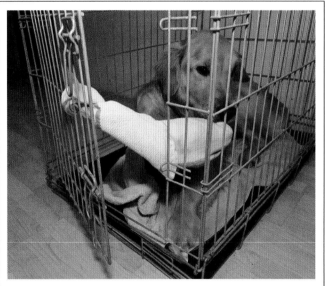

- Have Fido shut herself into her own crate. This is really cute! Get some stick-on magnets from a hardware store and fix them to the crate so that they keep the door closed.

- Tie a tab or toy to the inside of the door. (Your dog

needs to know "take it" for this.) Pull on it a bit to get her to tug.

- When the door shuts, the magnets will hold it. Click-treat through the door as soon as it's closed.

Get Tucked In

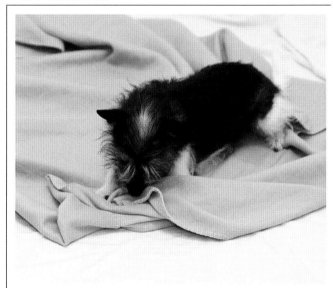

- Have your dog lie on the blanket, making sure there's enough excess that as she rolls, it will cover her. Praise her for staying on the blankie.

- Work on having her take the corner or the toy you

pinned to the corner. Click-treat for taking it.

- Spend time gently holding her mouth closed and praising her before asking her to roll over. She'll probably drop the toy as she rolls—this is the tricky part.

have her hold the position, ask if she wants to be tucked in, and cover her completely. If she releases the blanket while rolling, no reward. This part may need work—try holding her muzzle as she rolls and giving her a really excellent treat when she manages to hold onto it all the way over.

Next Steps

- It's important at this stage not to reward or treat for dropping midroll. She has to know that the only way she gets rewarded is by completing the exercise.

- Sit above her head and hold her muzzle as she rolls. If you're beside her, you'll be bending over and crossing your arm across her face.

- Have the biggest party ever when she completes the roll, then do it again.

- Repeat this three to five times and take a break.

Practice

- It will take some patience, but it's worth it. When she can do it without your help, sit about a foot away and practice that distance. Praise her for staying under the blankie for a minute or so before releasing her.

- Gradually work up to being across the room from her.

- With practice, you can call this "night, night" and send her across the room to her own bed, where she will wrap herself in the blankie.

FOOTWORK
Fast-paced footwork gets you and your dog primed for agility play

You can jump right into your first agility class without doing any foundation training beyond basic obedience. However, dogs learn faster when they've learned some foundation skills. Even if you never plan to do agility, these exercises teach Fido to stay with you and reinforce obedience training.

Agility dogs have to be used to working on both sides of their handlers instead of primarily on the left, as obedience

dogs do. Any dog working as a team member with her owner learns to stay attentive to signals, cues, and body language—and this goes for the nonsporting family dog, too.

Teach her to switch sides and to turn on a dime with this running game. Get her attention with a toy. It doesn't matter which side she's on. Run forward, keeping the toy just out of reach. Do an abrupt about-turn while simultaneously

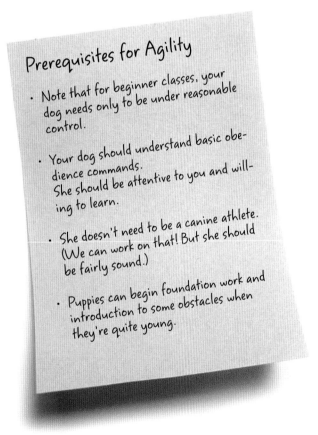

Prerequisites for Agility

- Note that for beginner classes, your dog needs only to be under reasonable control.

- Your dog should understand basic obedience commands. She should be attentive to you and willing to learn.

- She doesn't need to be a canine athlete. (We can work on that! But she should be fairly sound.)

- Puppies can begin foundation work and introduction to some obstacles when they're quite young.

Agility Courses

- Throughout an agility course, your dog has to both pay close attention to you and to be able to go out and do obstacles independently on command.

- Your job is just as important. You need to give her very clear directions.

- Try running and turning with your dog, without calling her or using your hands. Pay attention to your shoulders and how you move and how she follows you. You'll notice that if you commit to a direction, your dog will follow.

switching the toy to your other hand, so as she turns with you, she finds herself running on your other side. After a few turns, let her grab the toy. Vary the speed and distance between turns. You don't need much space—this can be done inside.

Practice short stays—a good starting-line stay is necessary for agility—by having her sit-stay. Get her excited about the toy and then throw it just as you give the release command. The trick here is to throw the toy in random directions. Doing this gets her attuned to your body language as she tries to anticipate your throw. Don't try to trick her by faking throws in different directions—that's not fair and defeats the purpose.

Get her out two or three times a week to run off leash if you can. There is nothing better for cardiovascular fitness and all-over body conditioning than a great off-leash romp.

Switch Sides

- Encourage her to switch sides and follow your turns using a toy.

- Dogs with a lot of formal obedience training are often at a disadvantage. They're used to working close to the handler, usually on the left, and following precise commands.

- Agility is much more fluid, although every bit as precise!

- Most mistakes made by the dog are actually handler mistakes—you gave her the wrong directions. Always remember this if you get frustrated with her!

Commands

- Hopefully, Fido has a reasonable stay command. Now you're going to spice it up. Tell her to stay and walk away about 10 feet.

- Turn and look at her. If she stays, go back, give her a tiny treat, and walk out again.

- Tell her, "Break!" and simultaneously throw a toy.

- Repeat this about five times but throw the toy in different directions. She'll learn to pay attention to your body language. No reward for breaking the stay!

REAR-FOOT AWARENESS

Tricks to make your dog surefooted and aware of what all four feet are doing

Dogs don't naturally think about how they are placing their rear legs, and in agility they learn not to hit jumps, to navigate narrow planks, and to maneuver through weave poles. These exercises increase surefootedness in any situation.

Randomly scatter about six poles or long sticks on the ground. Encourage her to walk over them, using a leash if you need to. Chances are that she'll avoid them with her front feet but will tend to step on them with her rear feet because she isn't as aware of her rear-foot placement. Make this a fun exercise with lots of encouragement, letting her work at her own pace. Eventually, she won't step on any poles. Praise and treat only for successfully clearing all of them. Keep this

Rear-Foot Awareness

- Rear-foot awareness is an important skill. Part of the reason for teaching it is safety. The more surefooted the dog, the less likely she'll be to slip and injure herself.

- These exercises are useful if you teach your dog to skateboard or push something with her front paws.

- Use a perch that is high enough to raise her front paws to about chest height. This makes it easy for her to maneuver around.

Target Stick

- A target stick will come in handy for little dogs.

- Don't nudge her feet in an effort to make her sidestep. Most dogs dislike this, and she'll probably step off. A little tap on her thigh will get her going sideways.

- At first she'll move just her front feet, leaving the rear ones behind. It doesn't take long for the light bulb to come on and have her sidestepping quite gracefully.

194

exercise short and fun, and as she gets more proficient you can work on adding poles and speed.

Another exercise is perch work. Use a weighted cooler, a large plastic container that won't slide, or anything else she can comfortably get her front feet onto. A clicker works well for this trick. Encourage her to put her front feet onto the perch. Immediately click-treat, putting the treat on the perch between her paws.

Stand next to her and gently nudge her hips sideways. If she steps off, just encourage her to get back into position.

Gently nudge again. The minute she moves laterally by side-stepping with her rear feet, click-treat. This feels awkward for many dogs at first, so be patient. Have her sidestep around the perch while keeping her front feet up and then reverse direction. Before long she'll be sidestepping around the perch without help. This is a very cute trick as well as great exercise. Add a ballerina skirt and some bling for maximum effect!

Poles

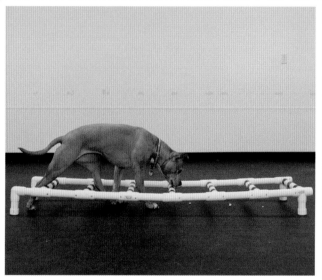

- At first, scatter the poles with plenty of room for her to step over them. Later you can jumble them a bit closer together.

- Don't say anything if she steps and slips a bit on a pole. This is valuable information for her—she's learning to be more nimble.

- A similar version of this uses a ladder laid on the ground and trains her to prance between the rungs. This is a bit harder, so it's best to start with the poles.

Improve Balance

- Improve balance by teaching her to walk along a board, at least 10 inches wide, laid flat along the ground. You'll probably have to lure her at first, using a leash.

- When she gets comfortable on it, put a small, soft object such as a rolled-up sock underneath so that it's a little wobbly and give her lots of praise for walking the plank.

- Exercises such as this help with dexterity and surefootedness on tippy surfaces.

PAUSE & TABLE GAMES

Practice turbocharged performance with the agility pause box and table

An agility table and pause box serve as safety and control stops on an agility course. The dog jumps either onto a sturdy table or into a PVC frame or "box" on the ground and holds a stay for five seconds before moving to the next obstacle. Teaching pause games helps with control and is a fun way to either send your dog to bed or have him get off furniture.

Depending on his size, tables are from 8 to 24 inches high. Although the table top dimensions are 3 feet square, your dog can successfully be taught using furniture, a storage container, or even large books for a tiny dog.

Encourage him to jump onto the "table" using treats, toys, or lots of praise. If using a clicker, click-treat for jumping up

Bench Command

- Choose a "table" with a nonskid surface. As your dog gains speed, you want him to have a sure foothold and not to slide right off the other side.

- Increase his drive to leap on. Hold his collar to restrain him while saying,

"Are you ready, ready, to go bench?"

- Keep the final objective in mind. The "bench" command means jump up and lie down in one fluid motion. Expect this and fade separate down commands quickly.

Stay

- He needs to stay for at least five seconds on pause obstacles. At first, just a second or two is fine.

- On release, don't encourage him to come to you (every once in a while is OK). On the course, he'll be going

from the table to the next obstacle, not to you.

- Increase drive and direction by throwing a toy on release. A treat is OK, but that makes him stop to eat it. A toy keeps him in motion.

and reward profusely for holding position. Initially, reward the dog for simply getting onto the table. Pair the action of jumping up onto the table with a command—"table," "bench," or whatever you choose.

Expect him to lie down after he is happily jumping up without giving a separate command. Give him treats in succession by placing them between his chest and between his legs to encourage him to hold the position. The faster he lies down, the more enthusiastic your reward should be.

Raise your criteria as he progresses. Stop rewarding for slow downs and request fast, fluid downs. At this point stop verbally telling him to lie down. You want him to start offering the behavior very quickly and automatically. Reward for only what you want.

Introduce a release word. After your dog is jumping up quickly and automatically lying down, ask him to hold the position and move off only on your word. Say "Break!" and enthusiastically release him.

Next Steps

- The 4-foot-square PVC pause box is used only in United Kennel Club (UKC) agility. UKC does not require an automatic down. At most levels, the judge will specify whether she wants a sit or down on pause obstacles.

- After Fido understands the concept, you can tell him "Box-sit" and "Box-down" for faster performance.

- Start increasing the distance for the box and table. Putting his meal on either will motivate him to go out!

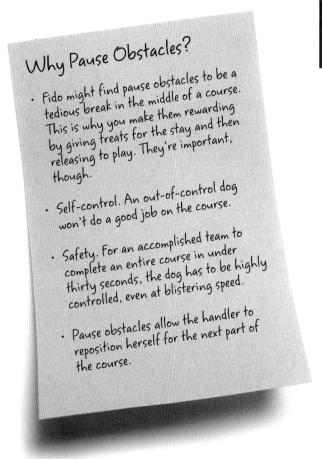

Why Pause Obstacles?

- Fido might find pause obstacles to be a tedious break in the middle of a course. This is why you make them rewarding by giving treats for the stay and then releasing to play. They're important, though.

- Self-control. An out-of-control dog won't do a good job on the course.

- Safety. For an accomplished team to complete an entire course in under thirty seconds, the dog has to be highly controlled, even at blistering speed.

- Pause obstacles allow the handler to reposition herself for the next part of the course.

WILD WEAVERS

Show your dog how to weave through poles like a seasoned agility pro

One of the most challenging agility skills is negotiating weave poles. Dogs have to bend their bodies in an unnatural way and be fast and accurate without missing poles. On top of all this, they must always enter the weave poles with their left shoulder to the first pole, no matter which direction they approach from. It is easiest to teach them by using two

poles and the correct weave entry to start with before adding poles.

Set two poles in place between 18 and 24 inches apart. (The space between the weave poles differs according to the organization.) Here's an easy way to make them. Buy driveway markers that are pushed into the ground. Get some

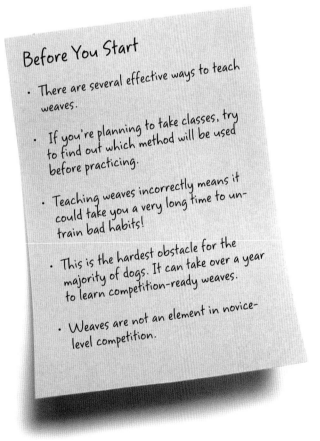

Before You Start

• There are several effective ways to teach weaves.

• If you're planning to take classes, try to find out which method will be used before practicing.

• Teaching weaves incorrectly means it could take you a very long time to untrain bad habits!

• This is the hardest obstacle for the majority of dogs. It can take over a year to learn competition-ready weaves.

• Weaves are not an element in novice-level competition.

Starting the Trick

• Starting with two weaves might seem elementary, but presenting an uninitiated dog with a set of six will utterly confuse him.

• Two poles give him lots of confidence and familiarity with little practice.

• If he is toy-driven, thrown toys work better than treats for weaves. The ultimate object is for him to drive forward through however many poles are before him. Treats make him pause to eat and keep him too focused on you.

1-inch PVC pipe cut into 3-foot lengths and slide them over the markers.

Start by encouraging him, but not luring him with food, to go between the poles. The moment his shoulders pass between the poles, click and throw a treat or toy ahead of him. Whatever you do, don't give the dog a treat from your hand—this is an independent exercise, and he shouldn't focus on you. No commands at this point.

After he's offering to go between the poles, you can name the exercise. (Warning: Calling it "weave" may result in your chanting "weeweeweewee" as he goes through a full set!)

Now make it more complex. Approach the poles from different angles and sides and send him from a distance. Increase the speed at which your dog goes through the poles. You can run with him at first, but also try working with a little distance and try to send him. Keep him focused on the exercise and the rewards, not on you. Now you can add poles, using both odd and even numbers so he doesn't get used to a pattern.

Next Steps

- The next step is usually where training methods diverge—there are several approaches to take.

- One is to put a second set of double poles several feet in front of the first and have him do both in a row.

The poles are slowly moved closer together.

- Other approaches are putting wires around a set of six so he stays in, using angled channel weaves, or simply adding more poles one or two at a time.

Maintain Focus

- Stick a little piece of masking tape on his shoulder if you keep forgetting which side is his left (that can get confusing because you approach weaves from different directions).

- Don't be tempted to use food in your hand to lure Fido through the poles.

- If you get him reliant on focusing on you instead of on the poles ahead, he'll constantly miss poles, and you'll have a terrible time fixing this. Use toys, thrown treats, or a target stick.

CRATE GAMES

Games make crates fun places and hone agility skills at the same time

Crate games are a foundation for agility training. You can also use crate games to strengthen your dog's overall training and teach her to love the crate.

Add value to being in the crate by rewarding her for being in there and for not rushing the door when you open it. Feed her in the crate. When you open the door, reach in and toss a treat toward the back of the crate while praising her for not rushing out. Have a release word such as "break" for her coming out of the crate.

Play the "crate up" game with a clicker. Give her the "crate" command and the moment all four feet are in the crate, click-treat. If she sits or lies down without being asked, click and

The Crate

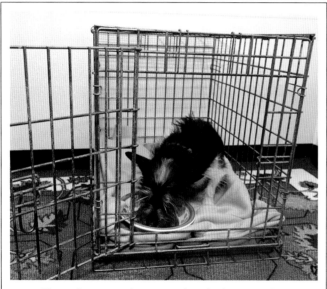

- Feed her in her crate. There is no better way to create a positive association.

- Don't let your dog spend too much time locked in a crate. She should be out and being active and learning as much as possible. Crates are wonderful tools,

  but she learns nothing by staying locked in her crate except . . . how to stay in her crate.

- Many people have a sturdy "at home" crate and a fold-able, soft crate for traveling, classes, and trials.

A Happy Place

- Make the crate a happy place to go to, using food, play, and encouragement.

- Don't use the crate as pun-ishment, ever! It's fine to use it as a timeout for a wild pup, but never crate her up in anger.

- When she's going to take a nap, periodically close her in the crate even if you're home. She shouldn't associ-ate being locked in the crate only with your leaving the house.

jackpot several treats while telling her how wonderful she is. Make it easy for her by throwing the treats in instead of making her reach out of the crate to take them. You want her to understand that being fully inside the crate is the very best place she can be.

Use the crate when playing with toys, too. If she likes fetch, throw the toy into the crate for her to retrieve. If she likes to play tug, wait until all four feet are inside the crate and enthusiastically tug with her. The moment a foot leaves the crate, stop playing. Resume when she backs up into the crate

again. Give her the idea that she gets rewarded only for being fully inside her crate.

Place a treat inside the crate but don't let her go get it. Hold her collar and play the "ready, ready" game. Let go, say, "Crate up!" and watch her fly into the crate. Gradually increase distance so she will run in from across the room.

Cozy Crate

- Also make the crate a happy place to stay in.

- Reinforce her for keeping all four feet in the crate using whatever reinforcement works best for her. When leaving her there with the door open, don't expect her to stay without having a release command.

- Get one of the dog toys that is stuffed with food and frozen or an excellent chewie and reserve it for crate time only when she has to spend time locked in.

Use the Crate in Practice

- Pretend that the crate is an agility obstacle and practice having her race in on your "crate up!" command, no matter what angle she approaches from.

- Put something great inside the crate and play the "ready, ready" game to build a little frustration so that on release, she races in.

- Make sure you feed a little less at mealtime to make up for the treats your dog gets during training.

GO AROUND
Teach your dog to move away from you in any direction you direct him

The object of the go around game is to send your dog away from you in a certain direction. Many agility maneuvers involve directing the dog out to perform an obstacle from a distance. This basic exercise teaches your dog to move away from you and to go left or right and can be customized for various tricks.

Start easy with something he can go around in one simple move, such as a pole in the ground or dining room chair. This is similar to spin, except he's running around something. Lure him with the target stick or a swung toy instead of a treat in your hand. This is an independent exercise, and he should focus on the task, not on you. Tell him, "Go around" and lure

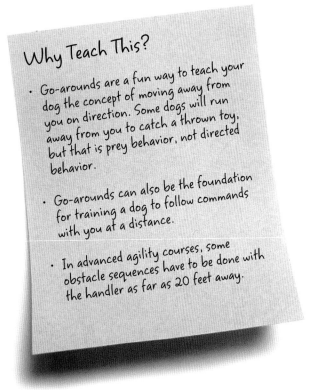

Why Teach This?

• Go-arounds are a fun way to teach your dog the concept of moving away from you on direction. Some dogs will run away from you to catch a thrown toy, but that is prey behavior, not directed behavior.

• Go-arounds can also be the foundation for training a dog to follow commands with you at a distance.

• In advanced agility courses, some obstacle sequences have to be done with the handler as far as 20 feet away.

Single Weave Pole

• Start with something easy, such as a single weave pole.

• At first, you'll probably have to use a target stick or a dangled toy. Fade this out as soon as possible. Try flinging a toy or treat around the obstacle if you can manage to bring it into a circle.

• Vary the obstacle, sometimes using something bulky and lower to the ground, such as a bucket, sometimes something taller and narrower, such as the pole.

him around the object in a fluid circle, rewarding him when he completes it.

Because you don't want him to pattern this action with you standing close by, start increasing the distance from which you direct him as soon as he gets the concept. When he hesitates, take quick steps toward the object while telling him to go around. Start doing this with different objects. He'll need some help when you have him go around things where he loses sight of you, so give lots of encouragement.

Increase the Obstacles

Embellishing the Trick

- Teach him to go around a standing person, the cat, even another sitting dog. These have no applications for agility, but they'll expand his repertoire and make for cute tricks!

- Work up to obstacles that make him lose sight of you momentarily. You might find that he resists this at first. Use lots of encouragement to give him confidence.

- When you get to really big obstacles such as your car, you may need a partner to help call him around.

- Another trick to teach confidence with distance is layering. This means putting an obstacle between the two of you and having him perform something— for example, a jump.

- Set up your jump and have him do it a few times.

- Now put a chair in to one side of the jump. Position him, then direct him to jump with the chair between you and the jump. In agility, you may have to direct him around one obstacle to take another.

CANINE FREESTYLE

Dance with your dog to compete, to impress others, or just to have fun

Canine freestyle, or heelwork to music, is a creative dance routine set to music. It showcases the dog's obedience skills, tricks, and ability to work closely with her handler. At beginner levels, it's a wonderful way to blend standard obedience moves such as heeling with tricks. Advanced freestyle teams exhibit some truly stunning moves and a high degree of

training and teamwork. Look online for freestyle videos to get an idea of what a polished routine looks like.

Part of the fun is coming up with a routine tailored to your dog's style and abilities. It's just as possible to create an impressive routine for an older or low-speed dog as it is for a turbo-charged young obedience champion. Think *Swan*

Prerequisites

- Freestyle is open to any willing person and dog. No special skills are required, and you don't have to know how to dance!

- Dogs of any size, breed, or breed mix can compete.

- Your dog should have basic obedience skills, including heeling.

- Your dog needs to be confident and controllable around other people, dogs, and people in funny costumes. She should be reasonably sound.

- If she can do basic obedience and manage to walk a few blocks, she's fit enough.

Freestyle

- Go online to look at video-sharing and freestyle sites for videos of routines. Look for amateur videos as well as examples of world-class competitors so you don't get intimidated!

- Find out if there are any performances at events near you and go watch.

- Get a feel for this in the comfort of your home first by doing some free-form dancing with your dog. No rules, just fun. Do it alone or have someone help you come up with ideas.

Lake instead of *Flight of the Bumblebee.* Choose music that moves you both. Costumes are also an important element. Both handler and dog dress up, although a costume should be minimal for the dog and never impede movement.

The requirements are simple. Both you and your dog should enjoy working as a team, and your dog should have some basic obedience skills and a willingness to learn new tricks. You don't have to be a good dancer, and your dog doesn't have to be an athlete.

ZOOM

Freestyle evolved in several countries during the late 1980s and early 1990s. Possibly as an outgrowth of equine dressage and agility training, it was used as a way to enliven traditional obedience. It's developed into an international canine sport in its own right under the umbrella of several worldwide organizations.

Experiment with Music

- Experiment with different styles of music. Bear in mind your dog's personality and background (as well as your own).

- Your dog might get overexcited and jump around if you start dancing wildly right away. Start with some slower movements. Encour-

age Fido to stay with you as you move.

- Don't give him any commands and pay attention to his responses. Think about routines you've watched and how you can use his style to come up with your own routine.

Add Commands

- Start adding some commands. Stick with basic ones at first, such as heeling to the beat or having him sit-stay while you walk around him (try backward!).

- Alternate control positions, such as stay and down, with movements such as heeling, spinning, or jumping.

Remember that you can use some simple props in freestyle, such as a cane.

- You can certainly put together routines yourself, but a freestyle class or workshop will speed learning and enrich your repertoire of moves.

THE WEAVE & WALK

This basic freestyle move is easy to teach, fun to do, and impressive as heck

Unless your dog is a giant breed, teach her to weave in and out through your legs as you walk. If you've watched any freestyle videos, you already know how impressive this looks! The basic move is not so difficult. It will take practice before the two of you are moving smoothly, but a few minutes a day will get you there.

Start with your dog off leash standing beside you. Have a treat in hand. A target stick (or one target stick in each hand) makes this much easier because you'll start by luring. Take an exaggerated, big step with the leg farthest from her. As you do so, lure her under that leg. Encourage her to turn as she comes through your leg so that she's positioned to step

First Steps

- In this first step (so to speak), make sure you practice with both legs and with Fido starting on either side of you.

- If you notice she has a harder time with one side or direction than the other, do that one a little more often and reward it frequently.

- Practice about three times with each leg per session. Don't do more than two steps at a time for now.

Envision the Final Effect

- Envision the final effect. It is a smooth, flowing movement, with Fido doing a serpentine move, instead of a zigzag.

- So what you want her to do is actually walk in as straight a line as possible while you continuously step over her.

- Very smooth weave walking is harder with a tall dog because you have to step higher. Modify the walk into a prance or march if you need to.

forward through the other leg. Make the same step with your other leg, luring her through and curling her body around.

Work on the first two steps until you are both fairly fluid. This is similar to teaching agility weave poles. Now add a third step and continue working until she's stepping easily back and forth under your legs as you walk forward. Increase speed as she gets better at this until you are both walking smoothly in unison.

Practice

- It will take practice to build speed, and this can be as challenging for you as for your dog.

- Unless you have your heart set on a fast routine, there's no need to make this really fast. With larger dogs,

going too fast can look a bit choppy.

- Aim for walking at a natural walking pace and vary your speed as you practice. It's OK to have a touch signal for your dog to slow her down or speed her up.

Use Costumes

- Keep moves such as this in mind when thinking up costumes. Obviously a ball gown isn't going to work well!

- Dogs don't wear elaborate costumes in freestyle because nothing should impede their movement. Often the dogs wear no

costume besides some discreet neckwear.

- You don't want anything dangling, swinging, or getting in your dog's way.

- Practice in costume as well. Believe it or not, something as simple as a change of shoes can put your dog off.

WALKING SIDEWAYS & BACKWARD
Heel backward, sideways, or on either side: Much more fun than basic obedience

Freestyle involves not only basic heeling but also heeling on both sides, backward, and at higher levels, even sideways. An accomplished dog can walk backward or sideways away from the handler for 20 feet or more. This takes a lot of training, but it starts with teaching your dog on leash and next to you.

Arm yourself with treats, put a leash on your dog, and position him so he's between you and a wall or straight barrier. If he's small, use a target stick. Dogs will naturally swing their rear to the side when walking backward, so you need to help him build muscle memory by keeping him going straight back. Step back, giving him treats just above his nose level,

Flashy Moves

- In some of the flashiest moves, the dog walks sideways and backward or incorporates a spin into her heeling.

- To get an idea of how hard it is for a dog, have someone put a leash on you and walk you around the room, randomly asking you to walk sideways, backward, and spin in different directions while walking.

- You probably find this harder than it looks—and you know all the rules! Now imagine how this is for your dog.

Next Steps

- Use a dowel or something different from the target stick (unless you're not using a target stick) to guide your dog into stepping sideways. He's used to following the target stick with his nose, and you don't want him getting confused here.

- Don't put any food on the dowel for the same reason.

- You want your dog paying attention to you and not thinking about you tapping his knee with something that might have peanut butter on the end.

KNACK DOG TRICKS

208

keeping his head up. Practice this daily for a few minutes on each side.

Sidestepping is a bit harder, and broad-chested dogs find it quite an unnatural move. Again, it's normal for a dog's rear to get left behind when he has to walk sideways. Use a light stick. Show it to him, stroking his flank and back with it. Have him on leash and step sideways into him while at the same time gently nudging his rear knee with the stick so his front and rear feet move in parallel.

Reward

Embellishing the Trick

- With your dog at heel beside you, take a small step sideways into him while giving his left knee a nudge.

- One step is all—reward! Repeat as necessary and remember to work him on both sides.

- To teach him to heel backward, work along a wall so that he can't swing to the side. Keep him on a short leash to keep him right by you and give him lots of tiny treats as you say, "Heel back."

- Another impressive freestyle move is the dog walking backward from the owner in a straight line.

- Again, his natural tendency is to swing out his rear so that he walks in a curve. Practice this between two boards, again keeping the

treats at nose level so he doesn't have to reach up.

- Start with walking with him, then direct him back while staying put. Reward for every step at first; this isn't easy for him.

DANCING IN PLACE
Have your dog dance in place to the beat as you move around her

If Fido can offer a paw, she can do this move. She doesn't have to lift her feet high for this to be effective, but she does need to understand how to lift her paws while standing up instead of from the usual sit. Work on this the same way you taught the basic paw shake but have her standing up. To Fido, this will be a wholly different move, so have a separate command such as "step" and a hand cue. Work on "step" and "other step" using your left-hand and right- hand cues to indicate which paw to raise. At first, stand right in front of her so she can't move forward.

It may be easier to use a clicker for this trick. Click-treat for every paw raise. Decide on the final effect. A slight paw raise will result in a little bobbing move, which is cute, but as you speed her up, she'll start merely shuffling back and forth. A

Starting the Trick

- Initially train this move with some boards on either side of Fido, so she doesn't end up stepping sideways. If she tends to move forward and back, box her in with low boards.

- Make sure she has enough wiggle room to lift and lower her feet and move her back feet without worrying about stepping on a board.

- Pay attention to her natural stance and don't force her to tuck her feet in unnaturally.

Next Steps

- You can use the dowel to tickle the backs of her ankles to get her to raise her feet. She may or may not move her back feet—let her do what comes naturally as long as she stays in one spot.

- She might feel a little unsteady at first, so don't rush her. Reward for every paw raise.

- If she tries to sniff or play with the dowel, get her attention —if she knows the "watch me" command, use that.

much flashier move is a prance in place. Initially, click-treat for any paw raise and gradually increase your requirement for a high raised paw, clicking only for what you want. Don't expect more than a bent foreleg at elbow height—any higher than that is probably uncomfortable for her.

MAKE IT EASY

Use your left and right hands to give her clear hand signals for which paw to raise. This can be incorporated into a dance routine and used to speed her up or slow her down in time to the music tempo, so she isn't jitterbugging quickly to a slow tune.

- Practice with the boards for a week or more to help her build muscle memory. Take them away one at a time.

- Get her excited when she sees you put the boards down. Ask her if she's "ready, ready to go step?"

- Never approach training sessions as work. Think of training as a way to relax and play with your dog. She'll pick up her cues from you and will be ready to play.

Mirror Actions

- Play with having her mirror your actions. You raise one foot, she raises the corresponding paw. You raise your hand, she waves bye-bye.

- Bend at the waist and tell her "down." If she's done puppy push-ups, have her go up and down on your physical cue.

- If she'll roll over on command, put her through a little routine, then ask if she's tired and have her roll over and "take a nap."

211

BOWING TO THE CROWD
Have her take a bow and add a flourish for the adoring crowd

Having your dog bow to her adoring crowd after a stellar performance is practically mandatory and can be used as a finale for any trick. It's also a very nonthreatening way for your dog to introduce herself to children, especially if she's large. It's an easy trick for most dogs to learn.

Have her stand at your side. She may be used to lying down on command with you standing in front of her, so changing the parameters will make this a separate move for her. Because "bow" and "down" sound similar, change it a bit to make it clear. Try "play-bow," putting the emphasis on "play," or "curtsey." Vary whatever physical cue you may be using as well.

Give your command while lowering the treat down between her knees so she has to tuck her head a little.

Bowing

- A bow is a friendly invitation to play in canine body language.

- This is a handy trick for a friendly dog, especially if she's large. Instruct her to bow when meeting other dogs or children. Her intent might not be there, but it is a very nonthreatening posture.

- Because a play-bow means "let's play," a toy reward upon release is very appropriate! Don't condition her to a vigorous game after every bow, though, or she'll expect this.

Next Steps

- Holding your dog with the leash running from her collar, under her belly, and up the other side is a nonforceful way to keep her from dropping her rear end.

- This can be a little easier to coordinate. Don't pull up on the leash; exert just enough pressure to keep her butt in the air.

- This is also a good trick when you are teaching her to stand in place or when you want her to stand for a vet's examination or to be weighed.

Chances are that she'll try lowering her butt as well as her head because this is going to feel like "down" to her at first. Put your hand on her belly to keep her rump in the air, and as soon as her elbows are down, treat (or click-treat). Start having her hold the position for several seconds by giving her multiple tiny treats as long as she's holding the bow.

Rewards

- After she understands the bow position, you can give her tiny treats both to encourage her to hold it and to let her keep her head in a natural, comfortable position.

- Always reward low so she doesn't need to crane upward to stare at you.

- Watch for signs of discomfort —in the real world, dogs don't hold this position for very long. Don't make her hold it for more than twenty seconds maximum.

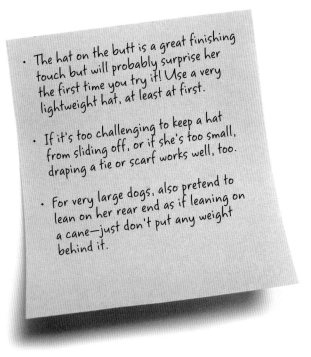

- The hat on the butt is a great finishing touch but will probably surprise her the first time you try it! Use a very lightweight hat, at least at first.

- If it's too challenging to keep a hat from sliding off, or if she's too small, draping a tie or scarf works well, too.

- For very large dogs, also pretend to lean on her rear end as if leaning on a cane—just don't put any weight behind it.

COMBINING MOVES
Put moves together for a fun routine for the living room or a wider audience

The speed heeling exercise can be useful in coming up with a routine. First, you need to find your dog's rhythm and experiment with combinations of tricks and heeling. Consider all sorts of music. If your dog will be a quick and flashy performer, choose something up-tempo; for more slow and deliberate hounds, a ballad might work better. Does your dog have an ethnicity you can use as inspiration? A bagpipe jig for a Scottish terrier, mariachi music for your Chihuahua. Pick a piece of music you like because you'll be listening to it a lot! It might be a while before you start donning costumes and performing in public, but keep costumes in mind as well.

Freestyle

- You can do a lot with freestyle without ever taking a class, but at some point joining a club and taking classes will make you and your dog a much better team.

- Practice in front of a mirror at home. Like videotaping, this allows you to see how you and your dog look to others. If you're a little shy, this helps you work on your moves before taking a class or going public.

- You'll be able to catch repeated mistakes and identify things that need a little more work that you'll never notice otherwise.

- Dancers, gymnasts, and weightlifters all use mirrors to check their form.

Performances

- Even the simplest routine will impress the heck out of people. Show off to family and friends.

- Offer to put on a performance at churches, schools, or nursing homes. If you and your dog work together as a therapy team, demonstrate wherever you volunteer.

- If you have a local club and you have children, consider freestyle as a family activity or something for your child to be involved in.

214

Spend some time trying different music and just goofing around with your dog. Even doing basic obedience routines to music can help relax you, making your dog perform differently. Play with various combinations of moves. Stagger fast action with more controlled exercises and build in some pauses and positions. This is also more visually interesting to watch because it builds tension and also helps your dog stay controlled. A typical beginner routine is two to four minutes long and is long enough to create an interesting routine but short enough to keep your dog's interest.

Canine freestyle is both a sport incorporating tricks and obedience and a dance. The handler does not need to be athletic or a great dancer. Although the handler's moves are part of the routine and judged in competition, her purpose is primarily to highlight and show off her dog's skill.

Competition

- Competition rules vary by organization. Within the routine, certain elements usually need to be included, such as heeling. Judging is based on handler control and the dog's skill in executing each element.

- Some novice competitions allow you to use a leash in portions of your routine.

- There are separate classes for juniors under age eighteen and for people with disabilities.

- Correction collars and harsh techniques are usually grounds for disqualification from the ring.

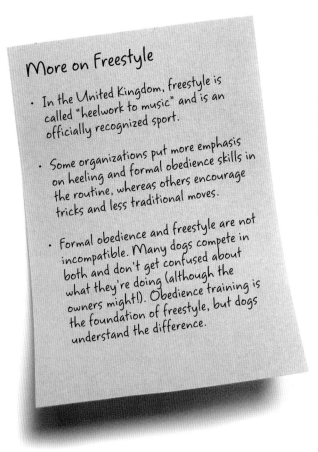

More on Freestyle

- In the United Kingdom, freestyle is called "heelwork to music" and is an officially recognized sport.

- Some organizations put more emphasis on heeling and formal obedience skills in the routine, whereas others encourage tricks and less traditional moves.

- Formal obedience and freestyle are not incompatible. Many dogs compete in both and don't get confused about what they're doing (although the owners might!). Obedience training is the foundation of freestyle, but dogs understand the difference.

PUT IT TOGETHER

The most complex tricks are really a series of basic actions strung together

Nobody is going to tell you that putting together a complex trick is simple—it's not. The dogs you see in the obedience and agility ring have trained for hundreds, sometimes thousands, of hours. Even dogs doing more naturally instinctive work, such as hunting, herding, and tracking, have many hours of training. Those who do it for sport find the journey just as much fun as the destination. Learning to work as a team with a different species is like learning a foreign language and bonding with an alien. Use not only the tricks you've taught your dog but also the teaching methods.

A few great trainers are born that way, but for most of us it's a learned skill. Part of it is understanding your dog. What

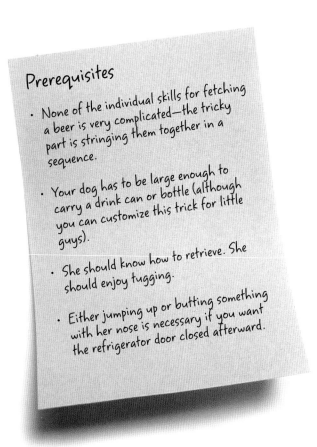

Prerequisites

• None of the individual skills for fetching a beer is very complicated—the tricky part is stringing them together in a sequence.

• Your dog has to be large enough to carry a drink can or bottle (although you can customize this trick for little guys).

• She should know how to retrieve. She should enjoy tugging.

• Either jumping up or butting something with her nose is necessary if you want the refrigerator door closed afterward.

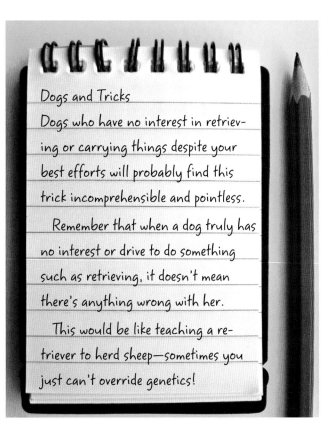

Dogs and Tricks

Dogs who have no interest in retrieving or carrying things despite your best efforts will probably find this trick incomprehensible and pointless.

Remember that when a dog truly has no interest or drive to do something such as retrieving, it doesn't mean there's anything wrong with her.

This would be like teaching a retriever to herd sheep—sometimes you just can't override genetics!

motivates her best, and what demotivates her. Does she learn quickly and then get bored with repeating the same actions, or does she take a while to get there but remains as steady as a rock? Does she get annoyed with you when your timing is off or your instructions unclear, or does she uncomplainingly do her best to comply with your fumbled attempts at communication?

When you get frustrated, remind yourself that you learn more from the challenging dogs than the easy ones!

ZOOM

Don't overtrain: The theory of latent learning holds that skills that are learned but not practiced routinely can still be fully remembered at a later date when the need arises. Some trainers notice that despite a long interval between training sessions, their dog not only recalls earlier training but also performs impeccably.

Practice

For Faster Success

You won't train this in a day, but these tips will make it go faster:

- Train a portion of the trick every day for about three minutes.

- Use all your tricks: Play the "ready, ready" game, train him before a meal, make it fun.

- No matter what, end each session on a successful note.

- Expect to take at least several weeks of short daily sessions to teach this trick. Sequencing requires patience and some trial and error.

- Look at it this way: You can decide not to train this at all, and in six months you'll still have a dog who can't get you a beer.

- Or you can start now, and in six months your willing dog will get you a cold one on command.

GET A DRINK

GET A DRINK

Basic retriever skills: Just make sure he doesn't drink it on the way back

You need a special beer can (or plastic water bottle—just use the same item throughout the training phase). If your dog is unwilling to hold a cold metal can in his mouth—not surprising—put a foam insulating sleeve over it. If you've taught "take it," "find it," or finding toys by name, he's going to learn this quite quickly. Name your beer can. Let's call it "Stan." Fido is going to spend some time taking Stan from you, releasing Stan to your hand, and going across the room to pick up Stan. As soon as Stan becomes a favorite toy, Fido is going to learn to take it from the refrigerator shelf.

Pattern this behavior by putting the beer can near the refrigerator and telling Fido to go fetch. Make it an integral

Retrieving the Beer

- Few dogs are willing to take a full can of cold beer in their mouths, so wrap it in an insulating sleeve first.

- Obviously, don't use glass bottles for this. Mistakes will be made.

- Spend time playing with the can. Toss it, roll it, hide it for him. Because the final objective is for him to relinquish the can into your hand, remember to back-chain and encourage him to give it to you nicely.

Practice

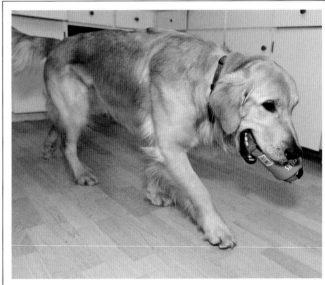

- If he is funny about the can but will fetch other things, try getting him to touch it and click treat for each nose-touch.

- Then toss it a foot or two and click-treat him for touching it on the ground.

- Eventually he'll pick it up. Then make a big fuss when he relinquishes it to you.

- Try practicing it with an empty can first. It could be that the feeling of the liquid shifting is off-putting to him.

part of the game that the beer gets fetched in and from the kitchen. He already knows that if he brings the beer to you, he gets rewarded big time. Get him excited about the beer and let him see you put it into the refrigerator. Standing right next to him, tell him to get it. Gradually increase distance, leaving the refrigerator door open. give him treats only for bringing the can all the way to you.

······· YELLOW ● LIGHT ·······

If Fido likes to crush his toys, work on him taking and holding the can gently. The insulator sleeve will help. To avoid accidents, practice with an empty can at first or fill it with a little sand and duct tape the opening so he gets used to the weight.

Next Steps

- Your dog might be used to dropping balls or stuffed toys at your feet, but this isn't going to work with a carbonated beverage if you want to drink it afterward.

- Play the trading game by giving him an excellent treat in return for the can but only if he puts it into your hand or lap.

- If he drops it, don't say anything but don't reward him either. Just pick it up and try again.

Getting the Beer from the Fridge

- There are several ways you can break down actually getting the beer from the fridge.

- First, try simply opening the door, getting him excited about the beer can, putting it into the fridge, and telling him to get it. If you're lucky, that's all it will take.

- If not, have him fetch it from the floor in front of the fridge for a while, with the door open or closed. Then ask him to try from the fridge again.

GET A DRINK

219

GO OPEN THE FRIDGE
Tie a rope to your fridge handle and watch your dog master this easy trick

There are components of this trick that very small dogs simply won't be able to manage. A 4-pound Yorkie can't be expected to pull open a refrigerator door and carry a can of beer in his tiny jaws. Modify the trick for toy dogs. He can open a cupboard and fetch your toothbrush—trick training always requires some creativity and flexibility!

Tie a rope, towel, or a tug toy to the refrigerator door. Tell him to take it. If he doesn't understand, restrain him briefly with one hand and flap the rope with your other. Play the "ready, ready" game and get him wanting it. You might need to play enthusiastically with it first before tying it to the door.

Encourage him to pull it. It's easier if it is long enough for

Starting the Trick

- Choose a towel or piece of knotted rope that Fido really enjoys playing tug with. It needs to be something that can be tied and untied from the fridge door handle with ease.

- A heavy piece of nylon rope, knotted up for good grabbing action, will work well for most dogs.

- Play! Play tug with him but only for a few minutes at a time. Then put the tug away.

Next Steps

- Tie the rope to the door handle. If he's excited about his new toy, he'll be eager to play some more.

- Get him excited and encourage him to pull on it. Be really excited when he does.

- Steady the door so it doesn't fly open and whack him in the face if he's a power puller. He'll need to get used to the door flying open and learn to regulate his tugging.

220

you to grasp the end by the handle and pull back. Let the game be the reward for now. Let him get used to the door opening, then quickly direct him into the fridge and have him at least touch the bottle for a treat. You're going to set him up from the start to open the door and move toward the next part of the trick. Name this part of the trick "Where's the Beer?"

More Next Steps

- If he already knows how to get the beer from the fridge, tell him to get it. As soon as he gives it to you, give him a treat or click-treat.

- If he doesn't get the beer from the shelf first, have him at least touch it with his nose for a treat.

- It will be easier if he already understands how to get the beer from the shelf because he'll know what to do next when the door opens.

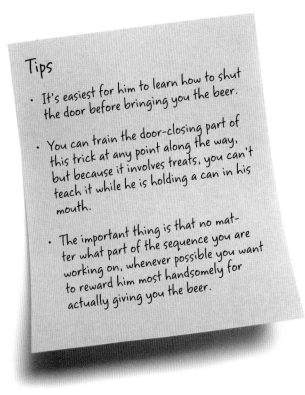

Tips

- It's easiest for him to learn how to shut the door before bringing you the beer.

- You can train the door-closing part of this trick at any point along the way, but because it involves treats, you can't teach it while he is holding a can in his mouth.

- The important thing is that no matter what part of the sequence you are working on, whenever possible you want to reward him most handsomely for actually giving you the beer.

GET A DRINK

221

GET BEER, CLOSE FRIDGE
Two more easy tricks for your dog to learn with your help and a beer

Fido already knows that if he brings you the beer, he gets rewarded big time. Get him excited about the beer and let him see you put it into the refrigerator. Standing right next to him, tell him to get it. Gradually increase distance.

The hardest part of this entire performance is going to be teaching Fido to close the refrigerator door. Any dog large enough to carry a beer can in his mouth is large enough to jump up onto the door with enough weight behind his forepaws to close it. He'll need to feel comfortable with the sensation of the door swinging closed as he jumps up on it. This can be reinforced by dabbing something edible high enough on the door that he has to jump up to get. Do this with the door closed, then gradually open the door so he gets used to it closing.

Starting the Trick

- For most dogs, jumping up onto the refrigerator door will be the easiest way to close it. If you have a giant breed such as a Great Dane, teach a nose-touch to get the door closed instead.

- Dab some squeezy food up on the door and ask Fido to jump for it.

- Steady the door at first so it doesn't close too abruptly. Practice this until he's jumping up onto the clean door, then turning to you for his reward.

Next Steps

- Stand by the door and have Fido take the can from the fridge.

- Quickly have him jump onto the door, turn to you, and give you the beer.

- This might take a few tries if he's used to bringing the beer directly to you, and he might drop it before he jumps onto the door. Be patient. Say nothing if he drops the can; just have him retake it and try again.

Add the beer can because he can't lick peanut butter off the door with a can in his mouth. Have him jump up, turn around, and give you the can and then immediately give him a big reward. Practice this step often enough that he sees closing the door and relinquishing the can as a single act that gets him rewarded.

Use Praise and Treats

- If you're still giving him treats for the can, don't let him see it before asking him to jump onto the door because that may distract him.

- Try using the target stick to encourage him to close the door.

- Very enthusiastic praise while he's in the process of shutting the door might make him think he's done. Wait until he's completed everything before giving verbal praise. Too much talking can be distracting.

Practice

- At first, you'll have to walk Fido through this routine, encouraging him along the way.

- Try sitting in the living room and having someone else walk him through it as well.

- Whenever possible, physically hang back and let him go ahead to do any of these tasks, encouraging only when you need to. Keep the end goal in mind, which is him going into the kitchen alone and bringing you back a beer.

TROUBLESHOOTING THE BEER RUN

Use these troubleshooting techniques for any hitch in the learning process

Realize that for Fido, getting you a beer is not a single exercise. For him, it is a big set of small tricks that needs to be done in a particular order. Therefore, every time he's having a problem with something, the first thing to try is breaking the behavior down into even smaller steps and reinforcing successful execution with tons of praise and reward.

For example, he is unwilling to tug the rope to open the fridge door. First, spend lots of time letting him play with the rope before tying it to the door. Get a clicker, bring him over to the rope, and waggle it. Click-treat for the slightest movement toward it. After he's learned to pay attention to the rope, raise the criteria.

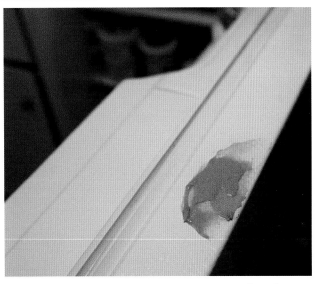

First Steps

- The first key step to figuring out why he is getting stuck on any part of this is understanding why.

- If he seems distracted or slow, play the "ready, ready" game, train in shorter increments, and train before mealtime so he works harder for treats.

- An overeager dog who drops the can to get the treat early needs more control. Have him sit for five seconds holding the can before his reward. Tone down your enthusiasm if he's picking up on that.

Fade Rewards Over Time

- Spend enough time working on each separate component until he's about 80 percent reliable on compliance before linking it to another component.

- Fade reward from every time to intermittent. If he expects a treat for each action, he'll be unwilling to go to the next step without one.

- If you haven't been using a clicker, try it. This can help Fido have an "aha!" moment and get unstuck.

Now he has to touch the rope to get his click-treat. Then he has to grab it. Then he has to pull on it. Sound slow? It may be, but there isn't any hurry.

Fido might not feel comfortable doing this whole chain of behaviors unless you're by his side. After all, if you've trained him with treats, how can you reward him from across the room? Remember to phase out treats early, giving them intermittently and reserving the jackpot treat for last.

MAKE IT EASY

If he seems to be having difficulty with any part of this, spend some time training just that sequence for a while, without the other parts. Remember latent learning from earlier in this chapter? Make it very special and rewarding, help him succeed frequently, then try the whole sequence again.

Troubleshooting

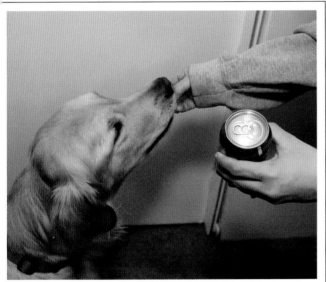

- Fido frequently drops the can: Spend several sessions rewarding heavily for releasing the can to you. See if he'll drop it into your lap more readily instead.

- He won't do anything unless you're next to him: Use a target stick to send him ahead. Then find a longer stick and use that.

- He forgets to close the fridge: Work on the "get beer-close fridge-relinquish beer" sequence for a while and reward only when he gives you the beer.

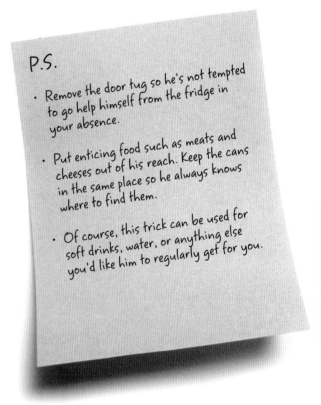

P.S.

- Remove the door tug so he's not tempted to go help himself from the fridge in your absence.

- Put enticing food such as meats and cheeses out of his reach. Keep the cans in the same place so he always knows where to find them.

- Of course, this trick can be used for soft drinks, water, or anything else you'd like him to regularly get for you.

ALWAYS THANK YOUR DOG

Give your dog great care and thank her often for being so entertaining

Write a list of everything your dog has learned. Include things that we take for granted that no animal would do without human intervention, such as training for potty, coming when called, accepting a leash and crate, retrieving toys, and not biting us when we screw up. Include every word and gesture she knows. Of course, include all her tricks. Don't forget to break the tricks down into components, just as she had to do when she learned them. It's a pretty long list, isn't it? Just for fun, now write a list of everything you've learned from your dog. If you're like most of us, it's a much shorter list.

Thank your dog. Even when she makes mistakes—as do we all—she is trying her best. Dogs don't intentionally try

Keep the Dog Lean

- Your dog won't be the best she can be unless she's healthy and well cared for. She needs good nutrition, routine grooming, and preventative veterinary care.

- One of the most important—and easiest—things you can do for her is keep her lean. Excess fat causes numerous health problems and will shorten her life. Overfeeding her isn't fair.

- Establish a relationship with a good veterinarian. Bring her in at least once a year for a wellness check.

Pay Attention to Dental Health

- Pay attention to her dental health. Give her teeth-cleaning chews and get into the habit of brushing her teeth.

- Keep nails clipped short. If she's really challenging, it won't cost much to drop by your vet or groomer every four to six weeks for nail clipping.

- Brush her regularly. It's good bonding for both of you and keeps her fur shiny.

- Check her ears and do routine cleaning, especially if she's a droopy-eared dog.

to make us mad or frustrated. They're animals, with animal drives and instincts. Their natural inclination is to avoid conflict, get what they want out of life, and generally have fun. That they don't run away or bite us more often for thwarting their desires and making them do all sorts of silly things is, quite frankly, astonishing.

Your dog works hard to understand you. She doesn't judge but rather accepts you at face value. She's patient when you don't get what she's telling you, and she never lies. Dogs have no guile and are very honest creatures.

Never lie to your dog. Say what you mean and mean what you say. Set rules clearly and fairly. Don't give her any commands that she can't obey and that you cannot enforce. Lavish her with praise and affection whenever you think she deserves it and sometimes just because you feel like it.

Train your dog because it's fulfilling for her and makes her a better canine citizen and hug her frequently.

Exercise

- Play with her often, even a few minutes a day and even if she has another dog to play with.

- Make sure she gets enough exercise. Dogs don't automatically exercise by themselves, even if they have a large yard.

- Both physical and mental exercise will keep a dog calmer and better behaved. Play-training, tricks, dog sports, and walking or biking with her provide both. As an added benefit, your health and fitness will improve.

Socialize

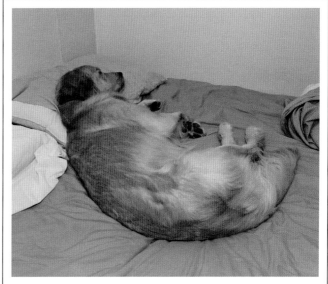

- Socialize her so she is friendly and confident around new people and in different situations. Isolated dogs are more likely to have behavior problems, including biting.

- Be firm, fair, and consistent in training. Dogs don't love us because we cuddle them. They love us because they trust and respect us. Without training, you don't get the trust and respect.

- Of course, you should also cuddle your dog when she deserves it.

RESOURCE DIRECTORY

Now that you've gotten hooked on the fun and rewards of dog training, here are some great books, Web sites for gear, and organizations that will help you hone your skills and explore further.

Books

Aloff, Brenda, *Canine Body Language: A Photographic Guide Interpreting the Native Language of the Domestic Dog*, Dogwise Publishing, 2005

Ammen, Amy, and Kitty Foth-Regner, *Hip Ideas for Hyper Dogs*, Howell Book House, 2007

Bloeme, Peter, *Frisbee Dogs, How to Raise, Train and Compete*, Sky Houndz, 1991, 1994

Donaldson, Jean, *The Culture Clash*, James & Kenneth Publishers, 1996

Kramer, Charles, *Rally-O - The Style of Rally Obedience, 3rd Edition*, Fancee Publications, 2005

Miller, Pat, *The Power of Positive Dog Training*, Howell Book House, 2008

Pryor, Karen, *Don't Shoot the Dog*, Bantam Books, 1999

Rugaas, Turid, *On Talking Terms with Dogs: Calming Signals*, Dogwise Publishing , 2005

Simmons-Moake, Jane, *Agility Training: The Fun Sport for All Dogs.* Howell Book House, 1991

Miscellaneous

Agility supplies and magazine:
www.cleanrun.com

Dog goggles:
www.Doggles.com

General dog supplies:
www.jefferspet.com

Sporting Organizations and Kennel Clubs

American Kennel Club:
www.akc.org/events

Canadian Kennel Club:
www.ckc.ca

Canine freestyle:
www.canine-freestyle.org

Therapy Dog Organizations

The following are national organizations, many can help you find local chapters which offer training and certification.

Alpha Affiliates, Inc.
PO Box 176
Mendham, NJ 07945 0176
Telephone (973) 539-2770
Fax (973) 644-0610
E-mail: AlphaAffiliates@webtv.net

The Bright & Beautiful Therapy Dogs, Inc.
80 Powder Mill Road
Morris Plains, New Jersey
(888) 738-5770
E-mail: info@golden-dogs.org

Put your training skills to work with Canine Companions for Independence, an organization that raises assistance dogs for the disabled: www.cci.org

Canine freestyle:
www.worldcaninefreestyle.org

CPE agility:
www.k9cpe.com

Disc dogs:
www.iddha.com

Kennel Club (United Kingdom):
www.thekennelclub.org.uk

International Weight Pulling Association
www.iwpa.net

United Kennel Club:
www.ukcdogs.com/WebSite.nsf/
WebPages/DogWhatKindsOfShows

USDAA agility:
www.usdaa.com

Delta Society
289 Perimeter Rd. East
Renton, WA 98055
(425) 679-5500
www.deltasociety.org

The Foundation for Pet Provided Therapy, Inc.
(AKA Love on a Leash)
PO Box 6308
Oceanside, CA 92058
(760) 740-2326
E-mail: info@loveonaleash.org

Paws For Friendship, Inc.
P O Box 341378
Tampa, FL 33694
(813) 961-2822
(402) 850-7476
Jan Schmidt, President
E-mail: jenniesmom@pawsforfriendshipinc.org

Therapy Dogs International
88 Bartley Rd.
Flanders NJ 07836
(973) 252-9800
www.tdi-dog.org

Training Resources

Certification Council for Professional Dog Trainers:
www.ccpdt.org

Clicker Training:
www.clickerlessons.com

Clicker Training (Karen Pryor):
www.clickertraining.com

Training Books, DVDs and Gear:
Dogwise
P. O. Box 2778
Wenatchee, WA 98807

(800) 776-2665
E-mail to: mail@dogwise.com
www.dogwise.com

General Dog Sports:
www.dogpatch.org

General Dog Sports:
www.dogplay.com

General Dog Sports:
www.workingdogweb.com

Rally-O:
www.rally.canissapiens.com

GEAR

Active Gear
Bicycle trailers for dogs:
www.bicycletrailers.com
www.justpetstrollers.com

Biking, swimming and hiking gear for dogs:
www.hunterk9.com

Video how-to of skateboarding dogs and suggested
skateboards:
www.squidoo.com/skateboarding-dogs

Weight pulling competition harness:
www.harnessesbycarol.com
www.weightpullharness.com

Backpacks
Web sites with a variety of packs in a range of prices:
www.hunterk9.com
www.petmountain.com
www.REI.com
www.ruffwear.com
www.sitstay.com

Dogwear
Boots, slickers, coats:
www.ruffwear.com
www.sitstay.com

Dresses and costumes:
www.doggievogue.com
www.glamourdog.com

Dresses, outfits and real gear:
www.petmountain.com

Eco-friendly Gear
Web sites with organic, all-natural, or recycled dog gear, food,
or supplies:
A Natural Home
www.anaturalhome.com

Belladog
www.belladog.com

Branch
www.branchhome.com

Earth Dog
www.earthdog.com

www.dog.com
www.dogwise.com
www.drsfostersmith.com
www.jbpet.com

Eco dog toys:
www.earthdoggy.com

Earth Doggy
www.earthdoggy.com

EcoAnimal
www.ecoanimal.com

Great Green Pet
www.greatgreenpet.com

Green Dog Pet Supply
www.greendogpetsupply.com

Natural Pet Market
www.naturalpetmarket.com

Planet Dog
www.planetdog.com

Toys
Web sites with an assortment of toys for your dog:

Trick Gear
Web sites with agility equipment, toys, treats, books, and videos for training your dog:
www.clickertraining.com

www.dogwise.com

www.mightymitedoggear.com

www.sitstay.com

EXERCISE & HEALTH

Food (Diets)

Natural or raw food diets:
www.aplaceforpaws.com
www.barfworld.com
www.globaldognaturalpetproducts.com
www.olivegreendog.com

Commercial dog food manufacturers:
www.hillspet.com
www.iams.com
www.pedigree.com
www.purina.com

General Information

About.com "Ask the vet":
http://vetmedicine.about.com/

Health care articles from Drs Foster and Smith pet supply company:
www.peteducation.com

Humane Society of the United States site with tips about pet care, choosing a vet, adoption, etc:
www.hsus.org/pets

Library of health care articles written by veterinarians:
www.petplace.com

Training videos, pet care info, dog breed selector quiz:
http://animal.discovery.com/pet-planet/

Grooming Needs

Grooming supply companies:
www.cherrybrook.com

www.drsfostersmith.com
www.groomers.com
www.showdogstore.com

Bonham, Margaret, *Dog Grooming for Dummies,* 2006

Gleeson, Eileen, *Ultimate Dog Grooming,* Firefly, 2007

Treats

All kind of treats:
www.dog.com
www.drsfostersmith.com

Training treats:
www.dogsupplies.com
www.sitstay.com
www.zukes.com

BREEDS

Dog Breed Web Sites

American Kennel Club guides to dog breeds, breeders, clubs and rescue groups:
www.akc.org

Breed info and links to breed clubs:
www.westminsterkennelclub.org

Directories of breed clubs, dog related groups:
www.netpets.com

Directories of breed specific rescue groups:
www.allaboutdogsandcats.com/Dogs/BreedRescue.html
www.loveofbreeds.com/Rescue.html

Directory of dog breeders:
www.breeders.net

General Breed Information

Dog Breed Info Center
www.dogbreedinfo.com

Just Dog Breeds
www.justdogbreeds.com

Mixed-breed Organizations

American Mixed Breed Obedience Registration
www.ambor.us

Crossbreed & Mongrel Club
www.crossbreed-and-mongrel-club.org.uk

Mixed Breed Dog Clubs of America
www.mbdca.org

Puppies

Books

Dunbar, Ian, *Before and After Getting Your Puppy: The Positive Approach to Raising a Happy, Healthy, and Well-behaved Dog,* New World Library, 2004

Kern, Nancy, *The Whole Dog Journal Handbook of Dog and Puppy Care and Training,* The Lyons Press, 2007

Monks of New Skete, *The Art of Raising a Puppy,* Little, Brown and Company, 1991

Web Site

Breeding Better Dogs
www.breedingbetterdogs.com

Theory and Breeds

Books

Budiansky, Stephen, *The Truth about Dogs,* Viking Penguin, 2000

Coppinger, Raymond, and Lorna Coppinger, *Dogs: A Startling New Understanding of Canine Origin, Behavior and Evolution,* Scribner, 2001

Coren, Stanley, *Why We Love the Dogs We Do,* Simon & Schuster, 1998

GLOSSARY

Agility: Dog sport in which handler and dog navigate an obstacle course, being judged on technique and speed.

Back-chaining: Teaching the last behavior in a chain of behaviors first. This provides confidence and speeds learning.

Break: An alternate to the word "OK" for releasing a dog from a stay position. Some people prefer this word because, unlike "OK," it's not a word the dog will hear frequently.

Break down: Breaking a behavior into smaller components and teaching each component separately at first, so the dog understands the whole behavior more easily.

Carting, dog carting: An activity in which one or two dogs pull a cart, either to haul a load for work or to pull people or weights for fun.

Clicker, clicker training: A clicker is a small handheld device that makes a distinctive "click" sound as a marker when the dog has performed the correct action. Clicking is paired with a treat reward to reinforce behaviors.

Conformation, dog show: A competition in which pure-bred dogs compete in the show ring for the distinction of which conforms most closely to the ideal breed standard.

Correction: Anything that lets the dog know she has done something undesirable. Corrections range from a sharp word to aversives such as collar jerks.

Dock diving: A relatively new sport in which dogs run and leap from the end of a dock into deep water after a thrown toy, competing for distance.

Drive: A dog's urge to fulfill a working or instinctual need, such as herding, chasing, or defending territory. In general terms, a high-drive dog is less suitable for a family pet because of high exercise and training needs. Lower-drive dogs are more laidback and often easier to live with.

Earthdog: A terrier sport in which dogs are dispatched down a narrow human-made hole to find a caged animal, usually a rat. The rat is unharmed.

Freestyle, canine freestyle: A sport in which the dog and handler perform a dance routine to music. It often includes some very complex moves and elements of formal obedience training, such as precise heeling.

Handler: Any person who trains or shows a dog. A handler can be a paid professional at a dog show or an owner training or showing her dog.

Harness: Gear going around the dog's chest and ribs, allowing the dog to pull a cart, sled, weight, or track without pressure being applied to a collar.

Head harness: Wraps around the dog's head and muzzle, used instead of a collar for leash control. When the dog attempts to pull, her head is automatically pulled around back toward her handler so she can't move forward.

Lure coursing: A sport, primarily for sighthounds, that allows them to chase a lure via mechanized trolleys over a large field.

Mixed breed: A dog with two or more breeds in his lineage.

Muscle memory: The tendency to move or position yourself in the same way after enough repetition. For a dog, this would include eventually sitting straight or learning to weave through agility poles.

Obedience trial: A sanctioned event in which dogs compete for points toward obedience titles or championships.

Pack: The family, human or canine, with whom the dog lives. Three or more dogs are a canine pack and may exhibit different behaviors as a group than singly.

Patterning, patterned behavior: Any behavior or action that becomes habitual. Most animals, including dogs, learn quickly through reinforcement and repetition.

Positive reinforcement: Any training technique that involves rewarding a dog for correct behavior with praise, treats, or play.

Punishment: Unlike a correction, which is given before or during an undesirable action, punishment is given after the action. Typically, punishment is ineffective and not recommended.

Purebred: Any dog with parents and ancestors of a single recognized breed, registered or not.

"Ready, ready" game: Holding the dog, either physically or under a controlled stay, to build a little frustration so that on release she'll be fast and enthusiastic to perform a subsequent action.

Release: A signal, usually a verbal command such as "OK" or "Break," that lets the dog know the exercise is finished or he is released from a stay.

Resource guarding: Aggressive defense of anything a dog holds valuable. This is usually food and toys, but a dog can resource guard anything, including locations such as the bed and even people.

Schutzhund: A dog sport originating in Germany for working and police dogs. It emphasizes equal importance being given to obedience, tracking, and protection.

Sequencing: Linking a series of learned skills together into a routine.

Sighthounds: Dogs in the hound group who hunt primarily by sight, such as greyhounds and whippets.

Target stick: A stick used to guide dogs. It can be used to direct a dog away, out of the handler's reach, or to guide small dogs to prevent constant bending over.

Therapy dog: A dog who provides comfort to others, usually in assisted living homes, hospitals, and schools.

Tracking: A directed activity in which the dog's natural scenting ability is used to follow a predetermined, set track.

Training collar: Any collar that is uncomfortable when the dog pulls on leash or that can be used to give corrections. These include prong and chain collars. Also refers to electronic shock fence collars, types of bark collars, and electronic collars used for distance control and problem solving.

United Kennel Club: An American registry for both purebred and mixed-breed dogs. Although the club sanctions and holds dog shows, its emphasis is on working and sporting events.

Weight pulling: A sport in which harnessed dogs compete to pull the most weight on a wheeled wagon or snow sled.

INDEX

abused *vs.* unsocialized, 145
aggression
    antibark collars and, 157
    dominance displays, 2, 33
    group classes addressing, 22
    guardian dogs, 96
    pack status and, 168
    play-growling *vs.*, 56
    resource guarding, 33, 78, 79, 174
    socialization affecting, 145
agility training
    complex tricks, techniques for, 26
    contact zones, 26
    footwork, 192–93
    jumping, 91
    pause obstacles, 196–97
    pedigree and breeds for, 155
    prerequisites for, 192
    rear-foot awareness, 194–95
    rewards during, 14
    treats for, 15
    weaving, 198–99
alpha dogs, 168
anticipating commands, 51
anxiety
    development and reinforcement of, 11, 30, 147
    separation, 157, 165, 181
arthritis, 4, 51
article scent discrimination, 116–17
associate clues, 45
attention, importance of, 72
attention exercises, 108–9

back-chaining, 27, 34
backpacks, 134–35
bang, you're dead, 86–87
barking
    bad behavior reinforcement, 28
    breeds prone to, 7, 98, 156
    as communication, 32, 33
    for counting, 98–99
    as drug- and cadaver-sniffing dog communication, 121

    training for, 98, 156–57
bathing, 185
bedtime games, 190–91
beer retrieval, 218–25
behavior management, 19, 28–29, 163. *See also specific behaviors*
bell ringing, 128–29
bicycling with dogs, 140–41
biting
    bad behavior reinforcement, 28
    isolation and, 227
    nipping or play-, 2, 25, 189
    resource guarding and, 79
blanket tricks, 190–91
Bloodhounds, 97
board walking, 195
body language, 59
bonding, 10, 101
boogie board surfing, 139
boots, protective, 141
boredom
    behaviors indicating, 156, 157, 163, 164
    and losing focus, 31
    rewards for activities inducing, 24
bowing, 212–13
breaking down, 26–27
breeds
    exercise requirements and, 146–47
    intelligence and, 96–97
    prone to barking, 7, 98
    training abilities and, 6–7
bribing, 40–41
brushing, 185, 226

cadaver-sniffing dogs, 121
canine freestyle, 204–5, 214–15
cart pulling, 136–37
catch toys, 16
cats, 122–23
chasing, 16, 25, 189
chewing, 164–65
Chihuahuas, 5
children

bowing to, 212
family games with, 188–89
heeling exercises with, 187
hide-n-seek games with, 181
roll over and, 65
safety with dogs and, 166–67
supervision of, 81
tug games with, 57
chows, 7
classes, group training, 22–23, 81, 167
clicker training
on-leash, 46–47
overview, 18–19, 36–39
puppy push-ups using, 50
turn your head, 44–45
click-treat, 36, 37, 45
clothing for dogs, 5, 132–33, 141, 205, 207
coats, reflective or cooling, 132–33
collars, 12–13, 34
collies, 146
coming when called, 11, 27, 48–49, 82
communication
body language, 59
of dog, 32–33, 35
honesty, 169, 227
with puppies, 10–11
troubleshooting problems with, 35
vocabulary building, 100
competitions, 22, 172–73, 215
confidence
dog, 32
trainer, 33
confusion, 32, 33
contact zones, 26
control, 72–73, 75
cookie on the nose, 88–89
corrections
appropriate use of, 100
consequences of, 2, 19, 25, 101
encouragement alternatives to, 1
timing of, 29
costumes, 133, 205, 207
counting, 98–99
crate games, 200–201
crawling, 71
cues, verbal, 45, 47

dancing in place, 210–11

deliveries, 104–5
dental health, 226
development, 4, 141, 143
diarrhea, 15
digging, 8, 162–63
disobedience, 42
distractions, 35, 53, 178
dog parks, 149
dominance and dominant dogs, 2, 31, 33, 168–69, 176
down, 50–51, 114–15
drives
food, 8–9, 25, 35
pack, 9, 96
play, 2
prey, 8, 62–63, 96, 157
drop, 57, 130–31
drop it, 78–79
drug-sniffing dogs, 121

ear care, 184, 226
emotional displays, 102–3
encouragement, 1, 42, 81, 104
exercise requirements, 4, 146–47, 227

family games, 188–89
fencing, invisible, 162
fetch
basic training, 62–63
with Frisbees, 150–51
toy clean up, 130–31
toys for, 16
finish, 112–13
flip finish, 112, 113
focus, 23, 30, 31, 165, 199
food
as motivation, 8–9, 25, 35
multiple dogs and manners with, 174–75
teaching control with, 74
as training lure, 21, 71
as treats, 8, 9, 14–15
footwork, 192–93
4-H groups, 167
freestyle, 204–5, 214–15
Frisbee fetch, 150–51
front & finish, 112–13

gear, doggie, 132–33
go-arounds, 202–3

goodbye wave, 84–85
grabbing behaviors, 51, 80–81
Great Danes, 5, 147
greetings, 158–59, 212
grocery carry, 126–27
grooming, 184–85, 226
growling, 56, 79
guardian dogs, 96
gun dogs, 6

halters, 13, 55
hard (dominant) dogs, 31, 176
harnesses, 12, 136, 152
health issues
    dental, 226
    diarrhea, 15
    joint problems, 4, 5
    jump safety, 67
    slipped knee caps, 5
    weight control, 5, 226
heeling, 110–11, 186–87, 204–5
heelwork to music (freestyle), 204–5, 214–15
herding dogs, 7, 97
hide-n-seek, 180–81, 189
hiding games, 148
high five, 84–85
honesty, 169, 227
honor dogs, 23, 170, 171
hunting dogs, 6, 97, 98
hunting instincts, 175
hyperactive dogs, 30, 156, 188

innate abilities, 96
intelligence, canine, 96–97
intelligence tests, 182–83

Jack Russell terriers, 147
joint problems, 4, 5
jumping
    basic training for, 66–67
    to close refrigerators, 222–23
    controlled, 90–91
    for exercise, 147
    multiple dog training, 170
    onto people, 72, 158–59
    retrieve &, 118–19

kisses, giving, 102

knee caps, slipping, 5

Labradors, 6, 146
layering, 203
leadership, 31, 33, 56–57, 189
leashes, 12–13, 58–59
leash training
    clickers with, 46–47
    heeling, 110–11, 186
    no-pull, 54–55, 73
leave it, 76–77
left- *vs.* right-handed, 61
liver-flavored treats, 15
loneliness, 157, 165
long-distance learning, 58–59
luring, 40–41, 93, 94
luxating patellas, 5

mealtime manners, 174–75
mental exercise, 147
modified abilities, 97
motivation. *See also* rewards; treats
    drive as, 8–9, 96
    giving encouragement as, 1, 42
    identifying, 32
    praise, 9, 36, 79
    trick training and, 1
moving sits & downs, 114–15
multiple dogs. *See also* pack drive and behaviors
    clicker training with, 18, 39
    combinations for disparate sizes, 176–77
    easy tricks for, 170–71
    general "come" commands for, 49
    grabby behavior, 81
    household rules for, 169
    mealtime manners, 174–75
    retrieving items, 125
    separate training for, 171
    speed sitting competitions, 172–73
muscle building, 93
music routines, 204–5

Newfoundlands, 5
newspaper retrieval, 124–25

obedience training
    article scent discrimination, 116–17
    with freestyle competition, 215

front & finish, 112–13
group classes, 23
heeling, 110–11
moving sits and downs, 114–15
as process, 23
puppies and, 10–11
sit commands, 27
treat techniques, 15
off-leash games, 148–49
older dogs, 51, 61
overheating, 141
overtraining, 217

pack dogs, 96
pack drive and behaviors, 9, 25, 96, 168–69
parks, dog, 149
pause obstacles, 196–97
people find, 104–5
people food, as treats, 15
perch work, 194, 195
performance opportunities, 178–79, 214
personality and temperament. *See also aggression*
 breeds and, 6–7
 independence *vs.* dependence, 9
 soft *vs.* hard dogs, 30, 31, 43, 151, 176
 training styles and, 3, 30–31
play
 benefits of, 24–25, 227
 greet training and, 149
 predatory, 8
 purpose of, 3
 rules for, 25
 structured, 2, 22
play dead, 86–87, 100
pole walking, 195
Pomeranians, 5
poop pick up, 149, 161
potty in place, 160–61
praise, 9, 36, 79
prey drive, 8, 62–63, 96, 157
proofing, 53
punishment, 2, 11, 23, 200. *See also* corrections
puppies
 agility training prerequisites, 192
 chewing behaviors, 164–65
 children and, 166
 dog parks and, 149
 early foundation training for, 10–11

 in group training classes, 22, 23
 leash training and, 55
 location acclimation, 11
 play training for isolated, 56
 reward timing and, 29
 socialization and, 144, 145
 weight pulling and, 143
puppy push-ups, 50–51, 172

Rally-O obedience ring, 114
reactions of dogs, 2
ready, ready game, 49, 82–83
rear-foot awareness, 194–95, 209
refrigerator opening and closing, 220–25
relay races, 188
release, 57, 74–75, 79, 87
remote controls, 120–21
resource guarding, 33, 78, 79, 174
restrained recall, 82
retrievers, 6, 96, 146
retrieving
 basic training for, 63
 drinks from refrigerator, 218–25
 item deliveries, 104–7
 and jumping, 118–19
 searching for items and, 120–25
rewards. *See also* clicker training; treats
 during competitions, 14
 fading out, 41, 94
 multiple dogs and, 174
 overview and definitions, 24, 36, 40, 41
 timing and, 28–29
 troubleshooting using, 35
 using toys as, 9, 16–17
right- *vs.* left-handed, 61
roll over, 64–65
round robin, 188
round-robin recall games, 180
routines, 214–15

salute, patriotic, 85
scent discrimination, 116–17
search and rescue dogs, 155
search and retrieve items, 120–25
self-control, 72–73, 82–83
separation anxiety, 157, 165
sequencing, 94–95, 216–17
shake hands, 60–61, 85

INDEX

Shelties, 98
shut down, 32
sighthounds, 7
sit
   at door games, 173
   on haunches, 92–93
   moving, 114–15
   positioning in obedience training, 27
   puppy push-ups with, 50–51
   puppy training and, 29
sit pretty, 92–93
size considerations, 4–5, 92–93, 176–77
skateboarding, 138–39
sled pulling, 136–37
sneezing, 65
socialization, 144–45, 178, 227
soft dogs, 30, 31, 43, 151
speed and compliance, 51, 172–73
spin around, 68–69
sporting dogs, 6, 97, 98
sports, miscellaneous, 154–55
stand, 50–51
standard poodles, 7
stay, 74–75, 193, 196
stay & wait, 52–53
sticks, target, 20–21, 70, 71, 91
strengthening exercises, 93
stress, 32, 33, 164
stroller pushing, 139
structured play, 2
submissive (soft) dogs, 30, 31, 43, 151

table games, 196–97
take it, 57
take it nice, 80–81
television remotes, 120–21
temperament. *See* personality and temperament
terriers, 6, 7, 142, 146, 147, 151
thanking dogs, 226–27
therapy dogs, 155
timing, 28–29, 38, 42–43
toy breeds, 7, 12
toys
   clean up, 130–31
   fetching specific, 106–7
   intelligence tests using, 182
   as motivation, 9
   overview, 16–17

tracking, 8, 152–53, 183
trading, 78
treadmills, 146
treats
   breeds disinterested in, 30
   as bribes, lures or rewards, 40–41
   fading out, 41, 94
   food as, 8, 9, 14, 15
   grabbing behaviors, 80–81
   overview, 14–15
   small dogs and, 7
   timing of, 18
   toys as, 9, 16–17
   weight control tips for, 5
trick training, overview, xii, 1–3. *See also related topics*
troubleshooting tips, 34–35, 43
tug games, 16, 56–57
tug toys, 16
turn your head, 44–45

uncontrolled dogs, 73
urination, 160–61

verbal cues, 45, 47
vests, safety, 141

wait, 52–53
wait & release, 74
walking. ***See also*** heeling
   between/through legs, 70–71
   on boards, 195
   on hind legs, 92
   over poles, 195
   sideways and backward, 208–9
   weave and, 206–7
watch me, 108–9
waving goodbye, 84–85
weave & walk, 206–7
weaving, 198–99
weight control, 5, 226
weight pulling, 14, 142–43

Yorkies, 5